MznLnx

Missing Links Exam Preps

Exam Prep for

Managerial Economics

Samuelson & Marks, 5th Edition

The MznLnx Exam Prep is your link from the texbook and lecture to your exams.
The MznLnx Exam Preps are unauthorized and comprehensive reviews of your textbooks.

All material provided by MznLnx and Rico Publications (c) 2010
Textbook publishers and textbook authors do not particpate in or contribute to these reviews.

MznLnx

Rico
Publications

Exam Prep for Managerial Economics
5th Edition
Samuelson & Marks

Publisher: Raymond Houge
Assistant Editor: Michael Rouger
Text and Cover Designer: Lisa Buckner
Marketing Manager: Sara Swagger
Project Manager, Editorial Production: Jerry Emerson
Art Director: Vernon Lowerui

Product Manager: Dave Mason
Editorial Assitant: Rachel Guzmanji
Pedagogy: Debra Long
Cover Image: Jim Reed/Getty Images
Text and Cover Printer: City Printing, Inc.
Compositor: Media Mix, Inc.

(c) 2010 Rico Publications

ALL RIGHTS RESERVED. No part of this work covered by the copyright may be reproduced or used in any form or by an means--graphic, electronic, or mechanical, including photocopying, recording, taping, Web distribution, information storage, and retrieval systems, or in any other manner--without the written permission of the publisher.

Printed in the United States
ISBN:

For more information about our products, contact us at:
Dave.Mason@RicoPublications.com

For permission to use material from this text or product, submit a request online to:
Dave.Mason@RicoPublications.com

Contents

CHAPTER 1
Introduction to Economic Decision Making — 1

CHAPTER 2
Optimal Decisions Using Marginal Analysis — 12

CHAPTER 3
Demand Analysis and Optimal Pricing — 19

CHAPTER 4
Estimating Demand — 31

CHAPTER 5
Forecasting — 40

CHAPTER 6
Production — 53

CHAPTER 7
Cost Analysis — 62

CHAPTER 8
Decision Making under Uncertainty — 77

CHAPTER 9
The Value of Information — 84

CHAPTER 10
Perfect Competition — 91

CHAPTER 11
Monopoly — 102

CHAPTER 12
Oligopoly — 113

CHAPTER 13
Game Theory and Competitive Strategy — 124

CHAPTER 14
Regulation, Public Goods, and Benefit—Cost Analysis — 133

CHAPTER 15
Asymmetric Information and Organizational Design — 153

CHAPTER 16
Baraainina and Neaotiation — 163

CHAPTER 17
Auctions and Competitive Bidding — 168

CHAPTER 18
Linear Programming — 174

CHAPTER 19
Capital Budgeting — 177

ANSWER KEY — 187

TO THE STUDENT

COMPREHENSIVE

The *MznLnx* Exam Prep series is designed to help you pass your exams. Editors at MznLnx review your textbooks and then prepare these practice exams to help you master the textbook material. Unlike study guides, workbooks, and practice tests provided by the texbook publisher and textbook authors, *MznLnx* gives you **all** of the material in each chapter in exam form, not just samples, so you can be sure to nail your exam.

MECHANICAL

The MznLnx Exam Prep series creates exams that will help you learn the subject matter as well as test you on your understanding. Each question is designed to help you master the concept. Just working through the exams, you gain an understanding of the subject--its a simple mechanical process that produces success.

INTEGRATED STUDY GUIDE AND REVIEW

MznLnx is not just a set of exams designed to test you, its also a comprehensive review of the subject content. Each exam question is also a review of the concept, making sure that you will get the answer correct without having to go to other sources of material. You learn as you go! Its the easiest way to pass an exam.

HUMOR

Studying can be tedious and dry. MznLnx's instructional design includes moderate humor within the exam questions on occassion, to break the tedium and revitalize the brain

Chapter 1. Introduction to Economic Decision Making

1. Economics:

    - _____, the desire to own something and the ability to pay for it
    - _____ curve, a graphic representation of a _____ schedule
    - _____ deposit, the money in checking accounts
    - _____ pull theory, the theory that inflation occurs when _____ for goods and services exceeds existing supplies
    - _____ schedule, a table that lists the quantity of a good a person will buy it each different price
    - _____ side economics, the school of economics at believes government spending and tax cuts open economy by raising _____

    a. Variability
    b. Production
    c. McKesson ' Robbins scandal
    d. Demand

2. _____s is the social science that studies the production, distribution, and consumption of goods and services. The term _____s comes from the Ancient Greek oá¼°κονομῖα from oá¼¶κος (oikos, 'house') + vÏŒμος (nomos, 'custom' or 'law'), hence 'rules of the house(hold)'. Current _____ models developed out of the broader field of political economy in the late 19th century, owing to a desire to use an empirical approach more akin to the physical sciences.

    a. Economic
    b. Inflation
    c. Energy economics
    d. Opportunity cost

3. _____, is a branch of economics that applies microeconomic analysis to decision methods of businesses or other management units. As such, it bridges economic theory and economics in practice. It draws heavily from quantitative techniques such as regression analysis and correlation, Lagrangian calculus (linear.)

    a. Managerial economics
    b. Forward exchange market
    c. Black-Litterman model
    d. Club goods

4. In economics, a _____ exists when a specific individual or enterprise has sufficient control over a particular product or service to determine significantly the terms on which other individuals shall have access to it. Monopolies are thus characterized by a lack of economic competition for the good or service that they provide and a lack of viable substitute goods. The verb 'monopolize' refers to the process by which a firm gains persistently greater market share than what is expected under perfect competition.

    a. 130-30 fund
    b. 1921 recession
    c. 100-year flood
    d. Monopoly

5. The phrase _____, according to the Organization for Economic Co-operation and Development, refers to 'creative work undertaken on a systematic basis in order to increase the stock of knowledge, including knowledge of man, culture and society, and the use of this stock of knowledge to devise new applications [sic]'

New product design and development is more than often a crucial factor in the survival of a company. In an industry that is fast changing, firms must continually revise their design and range of products. This is necessary due to continuous technology change and development as well as other competitors and the changing preference of customers.

Chapter 1. Introduction to Economic Decision Making

    a. 1921 recession   b. Research and development
    c. 100-year flood   d. 130-30 fund

6. _____ is used to assign the available resources in an economic way. It is part of resource management.

In strategic planning, is a plan for using available resources, for example human resources, especially in the near term, to achieve goals for the future.

    a. Resource allocation   b. 100-year flood
    c. 1921 recession   d. 130-30 fund

7. A _____ is a situation that involves losing one quality or aspect of something in return for gaining another quality or aspect. It implies a decision to be made with full comprehension of both the upside and downside of a particular choice.

In economics the term is expressed as opportunity cost, referring the most preferred alternative given up.

    a. Friedman-Savage utility function   b. Nonmarket
    c. Whitemail   d. Trade-off

8. _____ is the acquisition of goods and/or services at the best possible total cost of ownership, in the right quantity and quality, at the right time, in the right place and from the right source for the direct benefit or use of corporations or individuals, generally via a contract. Simple _____ may involve nothing more than repeat purchasing. Complex _____ could involve finding long term partners - or even 'co-destiny' suppliers that might fundamentally commit one organization to another.

    a. Sole proprietorship   b. Pre-emerging markets
    c. Golden umbrella   d. Procurement

9. The _____ consists of a number of economic theories which describe the nature of the firm, company including its existence, its behaviour, and its relationship with the market.

In simplified terms, the _____ aims to answer these questions:

1. Existence - why do firms emerge, why are not all transactions in the economy mediated over the market?
2. Boundaries - why the boundary between firms and the market is located exactly there? Which transactions are performed internally and which are negotiated on the market?
3. Organization - why are firms structured in such specific way? What is the interplay of formal and informal relationships?

Despite looking simple, these questions are not answered by the established economic theory, which usually views firms as given, and treats them as black boxes without any internal structure.

Chapter 1. Introduction to Economic Decision Making

The First World War period saw a change of emphasis in economic theory away from industry-level analysis which mainly included analysing markets to analysis at the level of the firm, as it became increasingly clear that perfect competition was no longer an adequate model of how firms behaved. Economic theory till then had focussed on trying to understand markets alone and there had been little study on understanding why firms or organisations exist.

a. Technology gap
b. Khazzoom-Brookes postulate
c. Policy Ineffectiveness Proposition
d. Theory of the firm

10. A _____ refers to any type debt instrument, such as a loan, bond, mortgage that does not have a fixed rate of interest over the life of the instrument. Such debt typically uses an index or other base rate for establishing the interest rate for each relevant period. One of the most common rates to use as the basis for applying interest rates is the London Inter-bank Offered Rate, or LIBOR

a. Moneylender
b. Money market
c. Disposal tax effect
d. Floating interest rate

11. _____ is the process of estimation in unknown situations. Prediction is a similar, but more general term. Both can refer to estimation of time series, cross-sectional or longitudinal data.

a. 100-year flood
b. 130-30 fund
c. 1921 recession
d. Forecasting

12. _____, in strategic management and marketing is, according to Carlton O'Neal, the percentage or proportion of the total available market or market segment that is being serviced by a company. It can be expressed as a company's sales revenue (from that market) divided by the total sales revenue available in that market. It can also be expressed as a company's unit sales volume (in a market) divided by the total volume of units sold in that market.

a. Pricing science
b. Customer to customer
c. Product differentiation
d. Market share

13. In economics, _____ is the process by which a firm determines the price and output level that returns the greatest profit. There are several approaches to this problem. The total revenue--total cost method relies on the fact that profit equals revenue minus cost, and the marginal revenue--marginal cost method is based on the fact that total profit in a perfectly competitive market reaches its maximum point where marginal revenue equals marginal cost.

a. Profit margin
b. Normal profit
c. 100-year flood
d. Profit maximization

14. _____ is an offer (often competitive) of setting a price one is willing to pay for something. A price offer is called a bid. The term may be used in context of auctions, stock exchange, card games, or real estate transactions.

a. Normal good
b. Bord halfpenny
c. Bidding
d. Central limit order book

15. _____ is one of the four Ps of the marketing mix. The other three aspects are product, promotion, and place. It is also a key variable in microeconomic price allocation theory.

a. Point of total assumption
b. Pricing
c. Guaranteed Maximum Price
d. Premium pricing

16. The _____ is the official currency of 16 of the 27 member states of the European Union (EU.) The states, known collectively as the Eurozone, are Austria, Belgium, Cyprus, Finland, France, Germany, Greece, Ireland, Italy, Luxembourg, Malta, the Netherlands, Portugal, Slovakia, Slovenia, and Spain. The currency is also used in a further five European countries, with and without formal agreements and is consequently used daily by some 327 million Europeans.
   a. Import and Export Price Indices
   b. Euro
   c. IRS Code 3401
   d. Equity capital market

17. _____ is a branch of applied mathematics that is used in the social sciences (most notably economics), biology, engineering, political science, international relations, computer science, and philosophy. _____ attempts to mathematically capture behavior in strategic situations, in which an individual's success in making choices depends on the choices of others. While initially developed to analyze competitions in which one individual does better at another's expense (zero sum games), it has been expanded to treat a wide class of interactions, which are classified according to several criteria.
   a. Discriminatory price auction
   b. Proper equilibrium
   c. Dollar auction
   d. Game theory

18. In economics, a model is a theoretical construct that represents economic processes by a set of variables and a set of logical and/or quantitative relationships between them. The _____ is a simplified framework designed to illustrate complex processes, often but not always using mathematical techniques. Frequently, _____s use structural parameters.
   a. AD-IA Model
   b. Economic model
   c. ACCRA Cost of Living Index
   d. ACEA agreement

19. A _____ strategy is the planned method of delivering goods or services to a target market and distributing them there. When importing or exporting services, it refers to establishing and managing contracts in a foreign country.

Many companies successfully operate in a niche market without ever expanding into new markets.

   a. Customer centricity
   b. Market entry
   c. Deep discount broker
   d. Forfaiting

20. In microeconomics, _____ is quite simply the conversion of inputs into outputs. It is an economic process that uses resources to create a good or service that is suitable for exchange. This can include manufacturing, storing, shipping, and packaging.
   a. MET
   b. Production
   c. Solved
   d. Red Guards

21. In economics, _____ and economies of scale are related terms that describe what happens as the scale of production increases. They are different terms and should not be used interchangeably.

_____ refers to a technical property of production that examines changes in output subsequent to a proportional change in all inputs (where all inputs increase by a constant factor.)

   a. Customer equity
   b. Returns to scale
   c. Constant returns to scale
   d. Necessity good

Chapter 1. Introduction to Economic Decision Making 5

22. A _____ is:

   - Rewrite _____, in generative grammar and computer science
   - Standardization, a formal and widely-accepted statement, fact, definition, or qualification
   - Operation, a determinate _____ for performing a mathematical operation and obtaining a certain result (Mathematics, Logic)
     - Unary operation
     - Binary operation
   - _____ of inference, a function from sets of formulae to formulae (Mathematics, Logic)
   - _____ of thumb, principle with broad application that is not intended to be strictly accurate or reliable for every situation. Also often simply referred to as a _____
   - Moral, an atomic element of a moral code for guiding choices in human behavior
   - Heuristic, a quantized '_____' which shows a tendency or probability for successful function
   - A regulation, as in sports
   - A Production _____, as in computer science
   - Procedural law, a _____ set governing the application of laws to cases
     - A law, which may informally be called a '_____'
     - A court ruling, a decision by a court
   - In the U.S. Government, a regulation mandated by Congress, but written or expanded upon by the Executive Branch.
   - Norm (sociology), an informal but widely accepted _____, concept, truth, definition, or qualification (social norms, legal norms, coding norms)
   - Norm (philosophy), a kind of sentence or a reason to act, feel or believe
   - 'Rulership' is the concept of governance by a government:
     - Military _____, governance by a military body
     - Monastic _____, a collection of precepts that guides the life of monks or nuns in a religious order where the superior holds the place of Christ
   - Slide _____

   - '_____,' a song by Ayumi Hamasaki
   - '_____,' a song by rapper Nas
   - '_____s,' an album by the band The Whitest Boy Alive
   - _____s: Pyaar Ka Superhit Formula, a 2003 Bollywood film
   - ruler, an instrument for measuring lengths
   - _____, a component of an astrolabe, circumferator or similar instrument
   - The _____s, a bestselling self-help book
   - _____ Project (Run Up-to-date Linux Everywhere), a project that aims to use up-to-date Linux software on old PCs
   - _____ engine, a software system that helps managing business _____s
   - Ja _____, a hip hop artist
     - R.U.L.E., a 2005 greatest hits album by rapper Ja _____
   - '_____s,' a KMFDM song

a. Demand
c. Rule
b. Technocracy
d. Procter ' Gamble

Chapter 1. Introduction to Economic Decision Making

23. _____ measures the nominal future sum of money that a given sum of money is 'worth' at a specified time in the future assuming a certain interest rate rate of return; it is the present value multiplied by the accumulation function.

The value does not include corrections for inflation or other factors that affect the true value of money in the future. This is used in time value of money calculations.

- a. Future-oriented
- b. Negative gearing
- c. Present value
- d. Future value

24. _____ is the value on a given date of a future payment or series of future payments, discounted to reflect the time value of money and other factors such as investment risk. _____ calculations are widely used in business and economics to provide a means to compare cash flows at different times on a meaningful 'like to like' basis.

Money value fluctuates over time: $100 today are not worth $100 in five years.

- a. Future value
- b. Present value of costs
- c. Tax shield
- d. Present value

25. _____ is the a method of technical and economic research of the systems for purpose to optimize a parity between system's consumer functions or properties and expenses to achieve those functions or properties.

This methodology for continuous perfection of production, industrial technologies, organizational structures was developed by Juryj Sobolev in 1948 at the 'Perm telephone factory'

- 1948 Juryj Sobolev - the first success in application of a method analysis at the 'Perm telephone factory' .
- 1949 - the first application for the invention as result of use of the new method.

Today in economically developed countries practically each enterprise or the company use methodology of the kind of functional-cost analysis as a practice of the quality management, most full satisfying to principles of standards of series ISO 9000.

- Interest of consumer not in products itself, but the advantage which it will receive from its usage.
- The consumer aspires to reduce his expenses
- Functions needed by consumer can be executed in the various ways, and, hence, with various efficiency and expenses. Among possible alternatives of realization of functions exist such in which the parity of quality and the price is the optimal for the consumer.

The goal of _____ is achievement of the highest consumer satisfaction of production at simultaneous decrease in all kinds of industrial expenses Classical _____ has three English synonyms - Value Engineering, Value Management, Value Analysis.

- a. Willingness to pay
- b. Function cost analysis
- c. Staple financing
- d. Monopoly wage

26. _____, or a _____ is the concept of a resulting effect (cf. cause and effect, arising from another action. In general terms, it is used to indicate that all human actions, particularly crime and sin, have profound effects.
   a. Variability
   b. Solved
   c. Rule
   d. Consequence

27. _____, in microeconomics, are the cost advantages that a business obtains due to expansion. They are factors that cause a producere;s average cost per unit to fall as scale is increased. _____ is a long run concept and refers to reductions in unit cost as the size of a facility, or scale, increases.
   a. Isoquant
   b. Economic production quantity
   c. Economies of scale
   d. Underinvestment employment relationship

28. In economics, the _____ can be defined as the graph depicting the relationship between the price of a certain commodity, and the amount of it that consumers are willing and able to purchase at that given price. It is a graphic representation of a demand schedule. The _____ for all consumers together follows from the _____ of every individual consumer: the individual demands at each price are added together.
   a. Cost curve
   b. Demand curve
   c. Wage curve
   d. Kuznets curve

29. An _____ is a market form in which a market or industry is dominated by a small number of sellers (oligopolists.) Because there are few participants in this type of market, each oligopolist is aware of the actions of the others. The decisions of one firm influence, and are influenced by, the decisions of other firms.
   a. ACCRA Cost of Living Index
   b. ACEA agreement
   c. Oligopsony
   d. Oligopoly

30. In mathematics, a _____ of a function of several variables is its derivative with respect to one of those variables with the others held constant (as opposed to the total derivative, in which all variables are allowed to vary.) _____s are useful in vector calculus and differential geometry.

The _____ of a function f with respect to the variable x is written as f'_x, $\partial_x f$, or $\partial f/\partial x$.

   a. 130-30 fund
   b. Partial derivative
   c. 1921 recession
   d. 100-year flood

31. A _____ is a set of exclusive rights granted by a state to an inventor or his assignee for a limited period of time in exchange for a disclosure of an invention.

The procedure for granting _____s, the requirements placed on the _____ee and the extent of the exclusive rights vary widely between countries according to national laws and international agreements. Typically, however, a _____ application must include one or more claims defining the invention which must be new, inventive, and useful or industrially applicable.

   a. Bank regulation
   b. Patent
   c. Bona fide occupational qualification
   d. Long service leave

Chapter 1. Introduction to Economic Decision Making

32. A _____ is a set of mathematical equations which describe the behavior of an object of study in terms of random variables and their associated probability distributions. If the model has only one equation it is called a single-equation model, whereas if it has more than one equation, it is known as a multiple-equation model.

In mathematical terms, a _____ is frequently thought of as a pair (Y,P) where Y is the set of possible observations and P the set of possible probability distributions on Y.

   a. Statistical model
   b. Population modeling
   c. Window function
   d. 100-year flood

33. _____s are financial contracts whose values are derived from the value of something else (known as the underlying.) The underlying value on which a _____ is based can be an asset (e.g., commodities, equities (stocks), residential mortgages, commercial real estate, loans, bonds), an index (e.g., interest rates, exchange rates, stock market indices, consumer price index (CPI) -- see inflation _____s), weather conditions bonds or other forms of credit.
   a. 130-30 fund
   b. 100-year flood
   c. Derivative
   d. Second derivative

34. _____ is an online peer-reviewed magazine published by the Agricultural ' Applied Economics Association (AAEA) for readers interested in the policy and management of agriculture, the food industry, natural resources, rural communities, and the environment. _____ is published quarterly and is available free online. It is currently one of three outreach products offered by AAEA, along with the more timely Policy Issues and the forthcoming Shared Materials section of the AAEA Web site.
   a. 130-30 fund
   b. 1921 recession
   c. 100-year flood
   d. Choices

35. The terms '_____' and 'independent variable' are used in similar but subtly different ways in mathematics and statistics as part of the standard terminology in those subjects. They are used to distinguish between two types of quantities being considered, separating them into those available at the start of a process and those being created by it, where the latter (_____s) are dependent on the former (independent variables.)

In traditional calculus, a function is defined as a relation between two terms called variables because their values vary.

   a. 130-30 fund
   b. 100-year flood
   c. 1921 recession
   d. Dependent variable

36. The terms 'dependent variable' and '_____' are used in similar but subtly different ways in mathematics and statistics as part of the standard terminology in those subjects. They are used to distinguish between two types of quantities being considered, separating them into those available at the start of a process and those being created by it, where the latter (dependent variables) are dependent on the former (_____s.)

The _____ is typically the variable being manipulated or changed and the dependent variable is the observed result of the _____ being manipulated.

Chapter 1. Introduction to Economic Decision Making

a. ACEA agreement
b. Independent variable
c. AD-IA Model
d. ACCRA Cost of Living Index

37. In economics and sociology, an _____ is any factor (financial or non-financial) that enables or motivates a particular course of action, or counts as a reason for preferring one choice to the alternatives. It is an expectation that encourages people to behave in a certain way. Since human beings are purposeful creatures, the study of _____ structures is central to the study of all economic activity (both in terms of individual decision-making and in terms of co-operation and competition within a larger institutional structure.)
   a. Isocost
   b. Economic reform
   c. Incentive
   d. Epstein-Zin preferences

38. _____ is an economic system in which wealth, and the means of producing wealth, are privately owned. Through _____, the land, labor, and capital are owned, operated, and traded for the purpose of generating profits, without force or fraud, by private individuals either singly or jointly, and investments, distribution, income, production, pricing and supply of goods, commodities and services are determined by voluntary private decision in a market economy. A distinguishing feature of _____ is that each person owns his or her own labor and therefore is allowed to sell the use of it to employers.
   a. Socialism for the rich and capitalism for the poor
   b. Creative capitalism
   c. Late capitalism
   d. Capitalism

39. _____ is the increase in the amount of the goods and services produced by an economy over time. It is conventionally measured as the percent rate of increase in real gross domestic product, or real GDP. Growth is usually calculated in real terms, i.e. inflation-adjusted terms, in order to net out the effect of inflation on the price of the goods and services produced.
   a. ACCRA Cost of Living Index
   b. AD-IA Model
   c. ACEA agreement
   d. Economic growth

40. In economics, _____ is the difference between a company's total revenue and its opportunity costs. It is the increase in wealth that an investor has from making an investment, taking into consideration all costs associated with that investment including the opportunity cost of capital.

Profit is the factor income of the entrepreneur.

   a. Operating profit
   b. ACCRA Cost of Living Index
   c. Economic profit
   d. Accounting profit

41. A _____ provision refers to any program which seeks to provide a minimum level of income, service or other support for many marginalized groups such as the poor, elderly, and disabled people. _____ programs are undertaken by governments as well as non-governmental organizations (NGOs.) _____ payments and services are typically provided at the expense of taxpayers generally, funded by benefactors, or by compulsory enrollment of the poor themselves.
   a. 1921 recession
   b. Social welfare
   c. 100-year flood
   d. 130-30 fund

42. _____ is generally measured by standards such as real (i.e. inflation adjusted) income per person and poverty rate. Other measures such as access and quality of health care, income growth inequality and educational standards are also used. Examples are access to certain goods (such as number of refrigerators per 1000 people), or measures of health such as life expectancy.

a. 100-year flood
c. Remuneration
b. Standard of living
d. 130-30 fund

43. _____ in economics and business is the result of an exchange and from that trade we assign a numerical monetary value to a good, service or asset. If Alice trades Bob 4 apples for an orange, the _____ of an orange is 4 apples. Inversely, the _____ of an apple is 1/4 oranges.
   a. Premium pricing
   b. Price war
   c. Price book
   d. Price

44. The _____ is an important selective, mainly private, international organization designed by its founders to supervise and liberalize international trade. The organization officially commenced on 1 January 1995, under the Marrakesh Agreement, succeeding the 1947 General Agreement on Tariffs and Trade (GATT.)

The _____ deals with regulation of trade between participating countries; it provides a framework for negotiating and formalising trade agreements, and a dispute resolution process aimed at enforcing participants' adherence to _____ agreements which are signed by representatives of member governments and ratified by their parliaments.

   a. 2009 G-20 London summit protests
   b. Backus-Kehoe-Kydland consumption correlation puzzle
   c. World Trade Organization
   d. Bio-energy village

45. In economics and finance, _____ is the change in total cost that arises when the quantity produced changes by one unit. It is the cost of producing one more unit of a good. Mathematically, the _____ function is expressed as the first derivative of the total cost (TC) function with respect to quantity (Q.)
   a. Quality costs
   b. Khozraschyot
   c. Variable cost
   d. Marginal cost

46. In economics, _____ describes the state of a market with respect to competition.

   - Perfect competition, in which the market consists of a very large number of firms producing a homogeneous product.
   - Monopolistic competition where there are a large number of independent firms which have a very small proportion of the market share.
   - Oligopoly, in which a market is dominated by a small number of firms which own more than 40% of the market share.
   - Oligopsony, a market dominated by many sellers and a few buyers.
   - Monopoly, where there is only one provider of a product or service.
   - Natural monopoly, a monopoly in which economies of scale cause efficiency to increase continuously with the size of the firm. A firm is a natural monopoly if it is able to serve the entire market demand at a lower cost than any combination of two or more smaller, more specialized firms.
   - Monopsony, when there is only one buyer in a market.

The imperfectly competitive structure is quite identical to the realistic market conditions where some monopolistic competitors, monopolists, oligopolists, and duopolists exist and dominate the market conditions. The elements of _____ include the number and size distribution of firms, entry conditions, and the extent of differentiation.

Chapter 1. Introduction to Economic Decision Making 11

These somewhat abstract concerns tend to determine some but not all details of a specific concrete market system where buyers and sellers actually meet and commit to trade.

a. Monopolistic competition
b. Human capital
c. Labour economics
d. Market structure

47. _____s are expenses that change in proportion to the activity of a business. In other words, _____ is the sum of marginal costs. It can also be considered normal costs.

a. Quality costs
b. Variable cost
c. Cost allocation
d. Cost-Volume-Profit Analysis

48. In economic models, the _____ time frame assumes no fixed factors of production. Firms can enter or leave the marketplace, and the cost (and availability) of land, labor, raw materials, and capital goods can be assumed to vary. In contrast, in the short-run time frame, certain factors are assumed to be fixed, because there is not sufficient time for them to change.

a. Long-run
b. Diseconomies of scale
c. Price/performance ratio
d. Productivity world

49. _____s is concerned with the tasks of developing and applying quantitative or statistical methods to the study and elucidation of economic principles. _____s combines economic theory with statistics to analyze and test economic relationships. Theoretical _____s considers questions about the statistical properties of estimators and tests, while applied _____s is concerned with the application of _____ methods to assess economic theories.

a. Econometric
b. Evolutionary economics
c. Experimental economics
d. Economic

50. A _____ is a group of people or organizations sharing one or more characteristics that cause them to have similar product and/or service needs. A true _____ meets all of the following criteria: it is distinct from other segments (different segments have different needs), it is homogeneous within the segment (exhibits common needs); it responds similarly to a market stimulus, and it can be reached by a market intervention. The term is also used when consumers with identical product and/or service needs are divided up into groups so they can be charged different amounts.

a. Pricing science
b. Market Segmentation Index
c. Customer to customer
d. Market segment

51. _____ or net present worth (NPW) is defined as the total present value (PV) of a time series of cash flows. It is a standard method for using the time value of money to appraise long-term projects. Used for capital budgeting, and widely throughout economics, it measures the excess or shortfall of cash flows, in present value terms, once financing charges are met.

a. Maturity
b. Net present value
c. Refinancing risk
d. Future value

Chapter 2. Optimal Decisions Using Marginal Analysis

1. _____s is the social science that studies the production, distribution, and consumption of goods and services. The term _____s comes from the Ancient Greek oá¼°κονομῖα from oá¼¶κος (oikos, 'house') + vΐŒμος (nomos, 'custom' or 'law'), hence 'rules of the house(hold)'. Current _____ models developed out of the broader field of political economy in the late 19th century, owing to a desire to use an empirical approach more akin to the physical sciences.
   a. Energy economics
   b. Economic
   c. Inflation
   d. Opportunity cost

2. In economics, _____ is the difference between a company's total revenue and its opportunity costs. It is the increase in wealth that an investor has from making an investment, taking into consideration all costs associated with that investment including the opportunity cost of capital.

   Profit is the factor income of the entrepreneur.

   a. ACCRA Cost of Living Index
   b. Accounting profit
   c. Operating profit
   d. Economic profit

3. _____ is one of the four Ps of the marketing mix. The other three aspects are product, promotion, and place. It is also a key variable in microeconomic price allocation theory.
   a. Point of total assumption
   b. Premium pricing
   c. Guaranteed Maximum Price
   d. Pricing

4. Economics:

   - _____, the desire to own something and the ability to pay for it
   - _____ curve, a graphic representation of a _____ schedule
   - _____ deposit, the money in checking accounts
   - _____ pull theory, the theory that inflation occurs when _____ for goods and services exceeds existing supplies
   - _____ schedule, a table that lists the quantity of a good a person will buy it each different price
   - _____ side economics, the school of economics at believes government spending and tax cuts open economy by raising _____

   a. Production
   b. McKesson ' Robbins scandal
   c. Variability
   d. Demand

5. In economics, the _____ is an economic law that states that consumers buy more of a good when its price decreases and less when its price increases.

   There are certain goods which do not follow this law. These include Veblen and Giffen goods

   a. Law of demand
   b. Financial crisis
   c. Market failure
   d. Georgism

Chapter 2. Optimal Decisions Using Marginal Analysis

6. In economics, _____ is the process by which a firm determines the price and output level that returns the greatest profit. There are several approaches to this problem. The total revenue--total cost method relies on the fact that profit equals revenue minus cost, and the marginal revenue--marginal cost method is based on the fact that total profit in a perfectly competitive market reaches its maximum point where marginal revenue equals marginal cost.
   a. Profit margin
   b. Normal profit
   c. 100-year flood
   d. Profit maximization

7. A _____ or labor union is an organization of workers who have banded together to achieve common goals in key areas and working conditions. The _____, through its leadership, bargains with the employer on behalf of union members (rank and file members) and negotiates labor contracts (Collective bargaining) with employers. This may include the negotiation of wages, work rules, complaint procedures, rules governing hiring, firing and promotion of workers, benefits, workplace safety and policies.
   a. Consumer goods
   b. Trade union
   c. Case-Shiller Home Price Indices
   d. Guaranteed investment contracts

8. In economics, _____ refers to the ability of a person or a country to produce a particular good at a lower marginal cost and opportunity cost than another person or country. It is the ability to produce a product most efficiently given all the other products that could be produced. It can be contrasted with absolute advantage which refers to the ability of a person or a country to produce a particular good at a lower absolute cost than another.
   a. Hot money
   b. Comparative advantage
   c. Triffin dilemma
   d. Gravity model of trade

9. In economics, the _____ can be defined as the graph depicting the relationship between the price of a certain commodity, and the amount of it that consumers are willing and able to purchase at that given price. It is a graphic representation of a demand schedule. The _____ for all consumers together follows from the _____ of every individual consumer: the individual demands at each price are added together.
   a. Kuznets curve
   b. Cost curve
   c. Wage curve
   d. Demand curve

10. The _____ is the official currency of 16 of the 27 member states of the European Union (EU.) The states, known collectively as the Eurozone, are Austria, Belgium, Cyprus, Finland, France, Germany, Greece, Ireland, Italy, Luxembourg, Malta, the Netherlands, Portugal, Slovakia, Slovenia, and Spain. The currency is also used in a further five European countries, with and without formal agreements and is consequently used daily by some 327 million Europeans.
    a. Euro
    b. IRS Code 3401
    c. Equity capital market
    d. Import and Export Price Indices

11. In neoclassical economics and microeconomics, _____ describes the perfect being a market in which there are many small firms, all producing homogeneous goods. In the short term, such markets are productively inefficient as output will not occur where mc is equal to ac, but allocatively efficient, as output under _____ will always occur where mc is equal to mr, and therefore where mc equals ar. However, in the long term, such markets are both allocatively and productively efficient.
    a. Law of supply
    b. Co-operative economics
    c. General equilibrium
    d. Perfect competition

Chapter 2. Optimal Decisions Using Marginal Analysis

12. In microeconomics, _____ is the term used to refer to total when marginal cost is subtracted from marginal revenue. Under the marginal approach to profit maximization, to maximize profits, a firm should continue to produce a good until _____ is zero. Profit Maximization - The Marginal Approach.
   a. Holding period return
   b. Marginal profit
   c. Corporate synergy
   d. Lehman scale

13. In microeconomics, _____ is the extra revenue that an additional unit of product will bring. It is the additional income from selling one more unit of a good; sometimes equal to price. It can also be described as the change in total revenue/change in number of units sold.
   a. Reservation price
   b. Market demand schedule
   c. Long term
   d. Marginal revenue

14. In economics and finance, _____ is the change in total cost that arises when the quantity produced changes by one unit. It is the cost of producing one more unit of a good. Mathematically, the _____ function is expressed as the first derivative of the total cost (TC) function with respect to quantity (Q.)
   a. Quality costs
   b. Khozraschyot
   c. Variable cost
   d. Marginal cost

15. In economics, _____ are business expenses that are not dependent on the activities of the business They tend to be time-related, such as salaries or rents being paid per month. This is in contrast to variable costs, which are volume-related (and are paid per quantity.)

In management accounting, _____ are defined as expenses that do not change in proportion to the activity of a business, within the relevant period or scale of production.

   a. Quality costs
   b. Fixed costs
   c. Cost of poor quality
   d. Cost-Volume-Profit Analysis

16. In business, _____, Overhead cost or _____ expense refers to an ongoing expense of operating a business. The term _____ is usually used to group expenses that are necessary to the continued functioning of the business, but do not directly generate profits.

_____ expenses are all costs on the income statement except for direct labor and direct materials.

   a. ACEA agreement
   b. AD-IA Model
   c. Overhead
   d. ACCRA Cost of Living Index

17. In finance, the _____s between two currencies specifies how much one currency is worth in terms of the other. It is the value of a foreign natione;s currency in terms of the home natione;s currency. For example an _____ of 102 Japanese yen to the United States dollar means that JPY 102 is worth the same as USD 1.
   a. ACEA agreement
   b. Interbank market
   c. ACCRA Cost of Living Index
   d. Exchange rate

Chapter 2. Optimal Decisions Using Marginal Analysis

18. _____ is a financial mechanism in which a debtor obtains the right to delay payments to a creditor, for a defined period of time, in exchange for a charge or fee. Essentially, the party that owes money in the present purchases the right to delay the payment until some future date. The discount, or charge, is simply the difference between the original amount owed in the present and the amount that has to be paid in the future to settle the debt.
    a. Maximum life span
    b. Generalized linear model
    c. Discounting
    d. Certified Risk Manager

19. _____, in strategic management and marketing is, according to Carlton O'Neal, the percentage or proportion of the total available market or market segment that is being serviced by a company. It can be expressed as a company's sales revenue (from that market) divided by the total sales revenue available in that market. It can also be expressed as a company's unit sales volume (in a market) divided by the total volume of units sold in that market.
    a. Customer to customer
    b. Market share
    c. Product differentiation
    d. Pricing science

20. _____ is the a method of technical and economic research of the systems for purpose to optimize a parity between system's consumer functions or properties and expenses to achieve those functions or properties.

This methodology for continuous perfection of production, industrial technologies, organizational structures was developed by Juryj Sobolev in 1948 at the 'Perm telephone factory'

- 1948 Juryj Sobolev - the first success in application of a method analysis at the 'Perm telephone factory' .
- 1949 - the first application for the invention as result of use of the new method.

Today in economically developed countries practically each enterprise or the company use methodology of the kind of functional-cost analysis as a practice of the quality management, most full satisfying to principles of standards of series ISO 9000.

- Interest of consumer not in products itself, but the advantage which it will receive from its usage.
- The consumer aspires to reduce his expenses
- Functions needed by consumer can be executed in the various ways, and, hence, with various efficiency and expenses. Among possible alternatives of realization of functions exist such in which the parity of quality and the price is the optimal for the consumer.

The goal of _____ is achievement of the highest consumer satisfaction of production at simultaneous decrease in all kinds of industrial expenses Classical _____ has three English synonyms - Value Engineering, Value Management, Value Analysis.

    a. Staple financing
    b. Monopoly wage
    c. Willingness to pay
    d. Function cost analysis

21. _____ is the term denoting either an entrance or changes which are inserted into a system and which activate/modify a process. It is an abstract concept, used in the modeling, system(s) design and system(s) exploitation. It is usually connected with other terms, e.g., _____ field, _____ variable, _____ parameter, _____ value, _____ signal, _____ device and _____ file.

a. AD-IA Model
b. ACCRA Cost of Living Index
c. ACEA agreement
d. Input

22. _____, is a branch of economics that applies microeconomic analysis to decision methods of businesses or other management units. As such, it bridges economic theory and economics in practice. It draws heavily from quantitative techniques such as regression analysis and correlation, Lagrangian calculus (linear.)

a. Managerial economics
b. Club goods
c. Black-Litterman model
d. Forward exchange market

23. The terms '_____' and 'independent variable' are used in similar but subtly different ways in mathematics and statistics as part of the standard terminology in those subjects. They are used to distinguish between two types of quantities being considered, separating them into those available at the start of a process and those being created by it, where the latter (_____s) are dependent on the former (independent variables.)

In traditional calculus, a function is defined as a relation between two terms called variables because their values vary.

a. 130-30 fund
b. Dependent variable
c. 1921 recession
d. 100-year flood

24. The terms 'dependent variable' and '_____' are used in similar but subtly different ways in mathematics and statistics as part of the standard terminology in those subjects. They are used to distinguish between two types of quantities being considered, separating them into those available at the start of a process and those being created by it, where the latter (dependent variables) are dependent on the former (_____s.)

The _____ is typically the variable being manipulated or changed and the dependent variable is the observed result of the _____ being manipulated.

a. AD-IA Model
b. ACEA agreement
c. ACCRA Cost of Living Index
d. Independent variable

25. _____ is an offer (often competitive) of setting a price one is willing to pay for something. A price offer is called a bid. The term may be used in context of auctions, stock exchange, card games, or real estate transactions.

a. Central limit order book
b. Bord halfpenny
c. Bidding
d. Normal good

26. _____ is the acquisition of goods and/or services at the best possible total cost of ownership, in the right quantity and quality, at the right time, in the right place and from the right source for the direct benefit or use of corporations or individuals, generally via a contract. Simple _____ may involve nothing more than repeat purchasing. Complex _____ could involve finding long term partners - or even 'co-destiny' suppliers that might fundamentally commit one organization to another.

a. Golden umbrella
b. Sole proprietorship
c. Pre-emerging markets
d. Procurement

Chapter 2. Optimal Decisions Using Marginal Analysis

27. Let f be a differentiable function, and let f'(x) be its derivative. The derivative of f'(x) (if it has one) is written f''(x) and is called the _____ of f. Similarly, the derivative of a _____, if it exists, is written f'''(x) and is called the third derivative of f.
   - a. Weighted
   - b. 100-year flood
   - c. Second derivative
   - d. 130-30 fund

28. _____s are financial contracts whose values are derived from the value of something else (known as the underlying.) The underlying value on which a _____ is based can be an asset (e.g., commodities, equities (stocks), residential mortgages, commercial real estate, loans, bonds), an index (e.g., interest rates, exchange rates, stock market indices, consumer price index (CPI) -- see inflation _____s), weather conditions bonds or other forms of credit.
   - a. 130-30 fund
   - b. 100-year flood
   - c. Second derivative
   - d. Derivative

29. In economic models, the _____ time frame assumes no fixed factors of production. Firms can enter or leave the marketplace, and the cost (and availability) of land, labor, raw materials, and capital goods can be assumed to vary. In contrast, in the short-run time frame, certain factors are assumed to be fixed, because there is not sufficient time for them to change.
   - a. Productivity world
   - b. Price/performance ratio
   - c. Long-run
   - d. Diseconomies of scale

30. _____ in economics and business is the result of an exchange and from that trade we assign a numerical monetary value to a good, service or asset. If Alice trades Bob 4 apples for an orange, the _____ of an orange is 4 apples. Inversely, the _____ of an apple is 1/4 oranges.
   - a. Premium pricing
   - b. Price book
   - c. Price war
   - d. Price

31. In economics, the concept of the _____ refers to the decision-making time frame of a firm in which at least one factor of production is fixed. Costs which are fixed in the _____ have no impact on a firms decisions. For example a firm can raise output by increasing the amount of labour through overtime.
   - a. Product Pipeline
   - b. Hicks-neutral technical change
   - c. Short-run
   - d. Productivity model

32. In mathematical optimization, the method of _____s provides a strategy for finding the maximum/minimum of a function subject to constraints.

For example, consider the optimization problem

$$\text{maximize } f(x, y)$$
$$\text{subject to } g(x, y) = c.$$

We introduce a new variable (λ) called a _____, and study the Lagrange function defined by

$$\Lambda(x, y, \lambda) = f(x, y) + \lambda\Big(g(x, y) - c\Big).$$

(λ may be either added or subtracted.) If (x,y)‰ is a maximum for the original constrained problem, then there exists a λ such that (x,y,λ)‰ is a stationary point for the Lagrange function (stationary points are those points where the partial derivatives of Λ are zero.)

a. Radfar ratio
b. 130-30 fund
c. 100-year flood
d. Lagrange multiplier

33. To _____ is to impose a financial charge or other levy upon a taxpayer by a state or the functional equivalent of a state.

_____es are also imposed by many subnational entities. _____es consist of direct _____ or indirect _____, and may be paid in money or as its labour equivalent (often but not always unpaid.)

a. 1921 recession
b. 100-year flood
c. Tax
d. 130-30 fund

Chapter 3. Demand Analysis and Optimal Pricing

1. Economics:

    - _____, the desire to own something and the ability to pay for it
    - _____ curve, a graphic representation of a _____ schedule
    - _____ deposit, the money in checking accounts
    - _____ pull theory, the theory that inflation occurs when _____ for goods and services exceeds existing supplies
    - _____ schedule, a table that lists the quantity of a good a person will buy it each different price
    - _____ side economics, the school of economics at believes government spending and tax cuts open economy by raising _____

    a. Variability
    c. McKesson ' Robbins scandal
    b. Demand
    d. Production

2. _____ is the process of understanding, anticipating and influencing consumer behavior in order to maximize revenue or profits from a fixed, perishable resource This process was first discovered by Dr. Matt H. Keller. The challenge is to sell the right resources to the right customer at the right time for the right price.

    a. Yield management
    c. Coopetition
    b. Subscription
    d. Freebie marketing

3. In economics, _____ is the ratio of the percent change in one variable to the percent change in another variable. It is a tool for measuring the responsiveness of a function to changes in parameters in a relative way. Commonly analyzed are _____ of substitution, price and wealth.

    a. Elasticity of demand
    c. ACEA agreement
    b. ACCRA Cost of Living Index
    d. Elasticity

4. A _____ is a group of people or organizations sharing one or more characteristics that cause them to have similar product and/or service needs. A true _____ meets all of the following criteria: it is distinct from other segments (different segments have different needs), it is homogeneous within the segment (exhibits common needs); it responds similarly to a market stimulus, and it can be reached by a market intervention. The term is also used when consumers with identical product and/or service needs are divided up into groups so they can be charged different amounts.

    a. Market Segmentation Index
    c. Pricing science
    b. Market segment
    d. Customer to customer

5. In algebra, a _____ is a function depending on n that associates a scalar, det(A), to an n×n square matrix A. The fundamental geometric meaning of a _____ is a scale factor for measure when A is regarded as a linear transformation. _____ s are important both in calculus, where they enter the substitution rule for several variables, and in multilinear algebra.

For a fixed nonnegative integer n, there is a unique _____ function for the n×n matrices over any commutative ring R. In particular, this function exists when R is the field of real or complex numbers.

a. 1921 recession
c. 100-year flood
b. Determinant
d. 130-30 fund

6. _____ is the acquisition of goods and/or services at the best possible total cost of ownership, in the right quantity and quality, at the right time, in the right place and from the right source for the direct benefit or use of corporations or individuals, generally via a contract. Simple _____ may involve nothing more than repeat purchasing. Complex _____ could involve finding long term partners - or even 'co-destiny' suppliers that might fundamentally commit one organization to another.
  a. Pre-emerging markets
  b. Sole proprietorship
  c. Procurement
  d. Golden umbrella

7. _____ is an offer (often competitive) of setting a price one is willing to pay for something. A price offer is called a bid. The term may be used in context of auctions, stock exchange, card games, or real estate transactions.
  a. Bord halfpenny
  b. Normal good
  c. Central limit order book
  d. Bidding

8. In economics, the _____ can be defined as the graph depicting the relationship between the price of a certain commodity, and the amount of it that consumers are willing and able to purchase at that given price. It is a graphic representation of a demand schedule. The _____ for all consumers together follows from the _____ of every individual consumer: the individual demands at each price are added together.
  a. Kuznets curve
  b. Demand curve
  c. Wage curve
  d. Cost curve

9. _____ in economics and business is the result of an exchange and from that trade we assign a numerical monetary value to a good, service or asset. If Alice trades Bob 4 apples for an orange, the _____ of an orange is 4 apples. Inversely, the _____ of an apple is 1/4 oranges.
  a. Price
  b. Price war
  c. Premium pricing
  d. Price book

10. A _____ is a counterfeit agreement among industries. It is an informal organization of producers that agree to coordinate prices and production. _____s usually occur in an oligopolistic industry, where there is a small number of sellers and usually involve homogeneous products.
  a. 100-year flood
  b. Shill
  c. Shanzhai
  d. Cartel

11. _____ is the transition of a national economy from monopoly control by groups of large businesses to a free market economy. This change rarely arises naturally, and is generally the result of regulation by a governing body.

A modern example of _____ is the economic restructuring of Germany after the fall of the Third Reich in 1945.

  a. Decartelization
  b. Monopolization
  c. Complementary monopoly
  d. Market power

12. In economics and sociology, an _____ is any factor (financial or non-financial) that enables or motivates a particular course of action, or counts as a reason for preferring one choice to the alternatives. It is an expectation that encourages people to behave in a certain way. Since human beings are purposeful creatures, the study of _____ structures is central to the study of all economic activity (both in terms of individual decision-making and in terms of co-operation and competition within a larger institutional structure.)

a. Incentive
b. Epstein-Zin preferences
c. Isocost
d. Economic reform

13. In consumer theory, an _____ is a good that decreases in demand when consumer income rises, unlike normal goods, for which the opposite is observed. It is a good that consumers demand increases when their income increases. Inferiority, in this sense, is an observable fact relating to affordability rather than a statement about the quality of the good.
    a. Export-oriented
    b. Information good
    c. Independent goods
    d. Inferior good

14. In economics, _____s are any goods for which demand increases when income increases and falls when income decreases but price remains constant, i.e. with a positive income elasticity of demand. The term does not necessarily refer to the quality of the good.

Depending on the indifference curves, the amount of a good bought can either increase, decrease, or stay the same when income increases.

   a. Bord halfpenny
   b. Financial contagion
   c. Normative economics
   d. Normal good

15. A _____ is an object whose consumption increases the utility of the consumer, for which the quantity demanded exceeds the quantity supplied at zero price. _____s are usually modeled as having diminishing marginal utility. The first individual purchase has high utility; the second has less.
    a. Pie method
    b. Merit good
    c. Good
    d. Composite good

16. _____ is a broad label that refers to any individuals or households that use goods and services generated within the economy. The concept of a _____ is used in different contexts, so that the usage and significance of the term may vary.

Typically when business people and economists talk of _____s they are talking about person as _____, an aggregated commodity item with little individuality other than that expressed in the buy/not-buy decision.

   a. 100-year flood
   b. 130-30 fund
   c. 1921 recession
   d. Consumer

17. _____ is a branch of applied mathematics that is used in the social sciences (most notably economics), biology, engineering, political science, international relations, computer science, and philosophy. _____ attempts to mathematically capture behavior in strategic situations, in which an individual's success in making choices depends on the choices of others. While initially developed to analyze competitions in which one individual does better at another's expense (zero sum games), it has been expanded to treat a wide class of interactions, which are classified according to several criteria.
    a. Dollar auction
    b. Discriminatory price auction
    c. Proper equilibrium
    d. Game theory

Chapter 3. Demand Analysis and Optimal Pricing

18. _____ is the change in population over time, and can be quantified as the change in the number of individuals in a population using 'per unit time' for measurement. The term _____ can technically refer to any species, but almost always refers to humans, and it is often used informally for the more specific demographic term _____ rate, and is often used to refer specifically to the growth of the population of the world.

Simple models of _____ include the Malthusian Growth Model and the logistic model.

    a. 100-year flood   b. Population dynamics
    c. 130-30 fund   d. Population growth

19. A _____ represents the combinations of goods and services that a consumer can purchase given current prices and his income. Consumer theory uses the concepts of a _____ and a preference map to analyze consumer choices. Both concepts have a ready graphical representation in the two-good case.

    a. Budget constraint   b. Quality bias
    c. Joint demand   d. Revealed preference

20. _____ exists when sales of identical goods or services are transacted at different prices from the same provider. In a theoretical market with perfect information, no transaction costs or prohibition on secondary exchange (or re-selling) to prevent arbitrage, _____ can only be a feature of monopoly and oligopoly markets, where market power can be exercised. Otherwise, the moment the seller tries to sell the same good at different prices, the buyer at the lower price can arbitrage by selling to the consumer buying at the higher price but with a tiny discount.

    a. Loss leader   b. Lerner Index
    c. Transfer pricing   d. Price discrimination

21. A _____ or complement good in economics is a good which is consumed with another good; its cross elasticity of demand is negative. - It is two goods that are bought and used together. This means that, if goods A and B were complements, more of good A being bought would result in more of good B also being bought.

    a. Manufactured goods   b. Final good
    c. Free good   d. Complementary good

22. Price _____ is defined as the measure of responsiveness in the quantity demanded for a commodity as a result of change in price of the same commodity. It is a measure of how consumers react to a change in price. In other words, it is percentage change in quantity demanded by the percentage change in price of the same commodity.

    a. Elasticity   b. ACCRA Cost of Living Index
    c. ACEA agreement   d. Elasticity of Demand

23. _____ is a common market structure where many competing producers sell products that are differentiated from one another (ie. the products are substitutes, but are not exactly alike.) Many markets are monopolistically competitive, common examples include the markets for restaurants, cereal, clothing, shoes and service industries in large cities.

    a. Financial crisis   b. Mathematical economics
    c. Perfect competition   d. Monopolistic competition

24. _____ is defined as the measure of responsiveness in the quantity demanded for a commodity as a result of change in price of the same commodity. It is a measure of how consumers react to a change in price. In other words, it is percentage change in quantity demanded as per the percentage change in price of the same commodity.

Chapter 3. Demand Analysis and Optimal Pricing 23

a. Price elasticity of Demand
b. 100-year flood
c. 1921 recession
d. 130-30 fund

25. _____ is one of the four Ps of the marketing mix. The other three aspects are product, promotion, and place. It is also a key variable in microeconomic price allocation theory.

a. Premium pricing
b. Guaranteed Maximum Price
c. Point of total assumption
d. Pricing

26. _____ is the elasticity of one variable with respect to another between two given points.

The y _____ of x is defined as:

$$E_{x,y} = \frac{\% \text{ change in } x}{\% \text{ change in } y}$$

where the percentage change is calculated relative to the midpoint

$$\% \text{ change in } x = \frac{x_2 - x_1}{(x_2 + x_1)/2}$$

$$\% \text{ change in } y = \frac{y_2 - y_1}{(y_2 + y_1)/2}$$

The midpoint _____ formula was advocated by R. G. D. Allen due to the following properties: (1) symmetric with respect to the two prices and two quantities, (2) independent of the units of measurement, and (3) yield a value of unity if the total revenues at two points are equal.

a. ACCRA Cost of Living Index
b. Arc elasticity
c. AD-IA Model
d. ACEA agreement

27. In economics, one kind of good (or service) is said to be a _____ for another kind in so far as the two kinds of goods can be consumed or used in place of one another in at least some of their possible uses.

Classic examples of _____s include margarine and butter, or petroleum and natural gas (used for heating or electricity.) The fact that one good is substitutable for another has immediate economic consequences: insofar as one good can be substituted for another, the demand for the two kinds of good will be bound together by the fact that customers can trade off one good for the other if it becomes advantageous to do so.

a. Private good
b. Substitute good
c. Merit good
d. Veblen goods

Chapter 3. Demand Analysis and Optimal Pricing

28. In economics, the _____ of demand measures the responsiveness of the demand of a good to the change in the income of the people demanding the good. It is calculated as the ratio of the percent change in demand to the percent change in income. For example, if, in response to a 10% increase in income, the demand of a good increased by 20%, the _____ of demand would be 20%/10% = 2.
   a. ACCRA Cost of Living Index
   b. Income elasticity
   c. AD-IA Model
   d. ACEA agreement

29. In economics, a _____ occurs when, due to the economies of scale of a particular industry, the maximum efficiency of production and distribution is realized through a single supplier.

   Natural monopolies arise where the largest supplier in an industry, often the first supplier in a market, has an overwhelming cost advantage over other actual or potential competitors. This tends to be the case in industries where capital costs predominate, creating economies of scale which are large in relation to the size of the market, and hence high barriers to entry; examples include water services and electricity.

   a. Common-pool resource
   b. Collective goods
   c. Privatizing profits and socializing losses
   d. Natural monopoly

30. In economics, a _____ exists when a specific individual or enterprise has sufficient control over a particular product or service to determine significantly the terms on which other individuals shall have access to it. Monopolies are thus characterized by a lack of economic competition for the good or service that they provide and a lack of viable substitute goods. The verb 'monopolize' refers to the process by which a firm gains persistently greater market share than what is expected under perfect competition.
   a. Monopoly
   b. 130-30 fund
   c. 1921 recession
   d. 100-year flood

31. In economics, a firm is said to reap monopoly profits when a lack of viable market competition allows it to set its prices above the equilibrium price for a good or service without losing profits to competitors. Monopoly profit is a type of economic profit, that is, it is a profit greater than the normal profit that is typical in a perfectly competitive industry. The resulting price is known as the _____.
   a. Gross national income
   b. Payment schedule
   c. Gross Dealer Concession
   d. Monopoly price

32. _____ is a term used in economics to describe how an economic quantity is related to economic fluctuations. It is the opposite of procyclical. However, it has more than one meaning.
   a. Mathematical economics
   b. Price revolution
   c. Countercyclical
   d. Law of comparative advantage

33. _____s is the social science that studies the production, distribution, and consumption of goods and services. The term _____s comes from the Ancient Greek oá¼°κονομῖα from oá¼¶κος (oikos, 'house') + vÏŒμος (nomos, 'custom' or 'law'), hence 'rules of the house(hold)'. Current _____ models developed out of the broader field of political economy in the late 19th century, owing to a desire to use an empirical approach more akin to the physical sciences.
   a. Economic
   b. Opportunity cost
   c. Inflation
   d. Energy economics

Chapter 3. Demand Analysis and Optimal Pricing

34. _____ is the increase in the amount of the goods and services produced by an economy over time. It is conventionally measured as the percent rate of increase in real gross domestic product, or real GDP. Growth is usually calculated in real terms, i.e. inflation-adjusted terms, in order to net out the effect of inflation on the price of the goods and services produced.
    a. AD-IA Model
    b. Economic growth
    c. ACCRA Cost of Living Index
    d. ACEA agreement

35. In economics, a _____ is a general slowdown in economic activity over a sustained period of time, or a business cycle contraction. During _____s, many macroeconomic indicators vary in a similar way. Production as measured by Gross Domestic Product (GDP), employment, investment spending, capacity utilization, household incomes and business profits all fall during _____s.
    a. Monetary economics
    b. Treasury View
    c. Leading indicators
    d. Recession

36. _____ is the process of estimation in unknown situations. Prediction is a similar, but more general term. Both can refer to estimation of time series, cross-sectional or longitudinal data.
    a. 130-30 fund
    b. 1921 recession
    c. Forecasting
    d. 100-year flood

37. A _____ refers to any type debt instrument, such as a loan, bond, mortgage that does not have a fixed rate of interest over the life of the instrument. Such debt typically uses an index or other base rate for establishing the interest rate for each relevant period. One of the most common rates to use as the basis for applying interest rates is the London Inter-bank Offered Rate, or LIBOR
    a. Disposal tax effect
    b. Floating interest rate
    c. Moneylender
    d. Money market

38. In microeconomics, _____ is the extra revenue that an additional unit of product will bring. It is the additional income from selling one more unit of a good; sometimes equal to price. It can also be described as the change in total revenue/change in number of units sold.
    a. Market demand schedule
    b. Marginal revenue
    c. Long term
    d. Reservation price

39. _____s are expenses that change in proportion to the activity of a business. In other words, _____ is the sum of marginal costs. It can also be considered normal costs.
    a. Cost allocation
    b. Variable cost
    c. Cost-Volume-Profit Analysis
    d. Quality costs

Chapter 3. Demand Analysis and Optimal Pricing

40. A _____ is:

- Rewrite _____, in generative grammar and computer science
- Standardization, a formal and widely-accepted statement, fact, definition, or qualification
- Operation, a determinate _____ for performing a mathematical operation and obtaining a certain result (Mathematics, Logic)
    - Unary operation
    - Binary operation
- _____ of inference, a function from sets of formulae to formulae (Mathematics, Logic)
- _____ of thumb, principle with broad application that is not intended to be strictly accurate or reliable for every situation. Also often simply referred to as a _____
- Moral, an atomic element of a moral code for guiding choices in human behavior
- Heuristic, a quantized '_____' which shows a tendency or probability for successful function
- A regulation, as in sports
- A Production _____, as in computer science
- Procedural law, a _____ set governing the application of laws to cases
    - A law, which may informally be called a '_____'
    - A court ruling, a decision by a court
- In the U.S. Government, a regulation mandated by Congress, but written or expanded upon by the Executive Branch.
- Norm (sociology), an informal but widely accepted _____, concept, truth, definition, or qualification (social norms, legal norms, coding norms)
- Norm (philosophy), a kind of sentence or a reason to act, feel or believe
- 'Rulership' is the concept of governance by a government:
    - Military _____, governance by a military body
    - Monastic _____, a collection of precepts that guides the life of monks or nuns in a religious order where the superior holds the place of Christ
- Slide _____

- '_____,' a song by Ayumi Hamasaki
- '_____,' a song by rapper Nas
- '_____s,' an album by the band The Whitest Boy Alive
- _____s: Pyaar Ka Superhit Formula, a 2003 Bollywood film
- ruler, an instrument for measuring lengths
- _____, a component of an astrolabe, circumferator or similar instrument
- The _____s, a bestselling self-help book
- _____ Project (Run Up-to-date Linux Everywhere), a project that aims to use up-to-date Linux software on old PCs
- _____ engine, a software system that helps managing business _____s
- Ja _____, a hip hop artist
    - R.U.L.E., a 2005 greatest hits album by rapper Ja _____
- '_____s,' a KMFDM song

a. Demand
b. Rule
c. Procter ' Gamble
d. Technocracy

Chapter 3. Demand Analysis and Optimal Pricing

41. A _____ is a situation that involves losing one quality or aspect of something in return for gaining another quality or aspect. It implies a decision to be made with full comprehension of both the upside and downside of a particular choice.

In economics the term is expressed as opportunity cost, referring the most preferred alternative given up.

    a. Friedman-Savage utility function
    b. Whitemail
    c. Nonmarket
    d. Trade-off

42. In economics, the _____ of an industry is used as an indicator of the relative size of firms in relation to the industry as a whole. It is calculated as the sum of the percent market share of the top n industries. This may also assist in determining the market structure of the industry.

    a. Concentration ratio
    b. Pacman conjecture
    c. Quasi-rent
    d. Monopolization

43. A _____ is an expression that compares quantities relative to each other. The most common examples involve two quantities, but any number of quantities can be compared. _____s are represented mathematically by separating each quantity with a colon, for example the _____ 2:3, which is read as the _____ 'two to three'.

    a. 100-year flood
    b. Ratio
    c. 130-30 fund
    d. Y-intercept

44. In economics and finance, _____ is the change in total cost that arises when the quantity produced changes by one unit. It is the cost of producing one more unit of a good. Mathematically, the _____ function is expressed as the first derivative of the total cost (TC) function with respect to quantity (Q.)

    a. Marginal cost
    b. Quality costs
    c. Variable cost
    d. Khozraschyot

45. In economics, the _____ or marginal physical product is the extra output produced by one more unit of an input (for instance, the difference in output when a firm's labour is increased from five to six units.) Assuming that no other inputs to production change, the _____ of a given input (X) can be expressed as:

    _____ = $\Delta Y/\Delta X$ = (the change of Y)/(the change of X.)

-
  -
    - Pending approval by Thomas Sowell***

In neoclassical economics, this is the mathematical derivative of the production function.... Note that the 'product' (Y) is typically defined ignoring external costs and benefits.

    a. Labor problem
    b. Productive capacity
    c. Factor prices
    d. Marginal product

46. In microeconomics, _____ is quite simply the conversion of inputs into outputs. It is an economic process that uses resources to create a good or service that is suitable for exchange. This can include manufacturing, storing, shipping, and packaging.

Chapter 3. Demand Analysis and Optimal Pricing

a. MET
b. Red Guards
c. Solved
d. Production

47. Discounting is a financial mechanism in which a debtor obtains the right to delay payments to a creditor, for a defined period of time, in exchange for a charge or fee. Essentially, the party that owes money in the present purchases the right to delay the payment until some future date. The _____, or charge, is simply the difference between the original amount owed in the present and the amount that has to be paid in the future to settle the debt.
a. Certified Risk Manager
b. Reliability theory
c. Discount
d. Reinsurance

48. _____ is buying products in large quantities at a lower price per item than is available for smaller quantities. Wholesale is selling or related to selling goods in large quantities for resale to the consumer. Retailing is buying products in bulk at wholesale, and selling them in small quantities at higher prices.
a. Low-cost country sourcing
b. Forward Commitment Procurement
c. Purchase Discount
d. Bulk purchasing

49. _____ is the advantage gained by the initial occupant of a market segment. This advantage may stem from the fact that the first entrant can gain control of resources that followers may not be able to match. Sometimes the first mover is not able to capitalise on its advantage, leaving the opportunity for another firm to gain second-mover advantage.
a. Cross-docking
b. First-mover advantage
c. Business engineering
d. Continuous Improvement Process

50. The _____ is an interest rate a central bank charges depository institutions that borrow reserves from it.

The term _____ has two meanings:

- the same as interest rate; the term 'discount' does not refer to the meaning of the word, but to the purpose of using the quantity, such as computations of present value, e.g. net present value or discounted cash flow

- the annual effective _____, which is the annual interest divided by the capital including that interest; this rate is lower than the interest rate; it corresponds to using the value after a year as the nominal value, and seeing the initial value as the nominal value minus a discount; it is used for Treasury Bills and similar financial instruments

The annual effective _____ is the annual interest divided by the capital including that interest, which is the interest rate divided by 100% plus the interest rate. It is the annual discount factor to be applied to the future cash flow, to find the discount, subtracted from a future value to find the value one year earlier.

For example, suppose there is a government bond that sells for $95 and pays $100 in a year's time.

a. Stochastic volatility
b. Johansen test
c. Perpetuity
d. Discount rate

51. _____ is a term used in business to indicate a state of intense competitive rivalry accompanied by a multi-lateral series of price reduction. One competitor will lower its price, then others will lower their prices to match. If one of them reduces their price again, a new round of reductions starts.

a. Price war
b. Transactional Net Margin Method
c. Discounts and allowances
d. Big ticket item

52. In microeconomic theory, an _____ is a graph showing different bundles of goods, each measured as to quantity, between which a consumer is indifferent. That is, at each point on the curve, the consumer has no preference for one bundle over another. In other words, they are all equally preferred.
   a. Indifference curve
   b. Expenditure minimization problem
   c. Engel curve
   d. Indifference map

53. In economics, _____ is a measure of the relative satisfaction from consumption of various goods and services. Given this measure, one may speak meaningfully of increasing or decreasing _____, and thereby explain economic behavior in terms of attempts to increase one's _____. For illustrative purposes, changes in _____ are sometimes expressed in units called utils.
   a. Utility function
   b. Expected utility hypothesis
   c. Ordinal utility
   d. Utility

54. In economics, the _____ of a good or of a service is the utility of the specific use to which an agent would put a given increase in that good or service, or of the specific use that would be abandoned in response to a given decrease. In other words, _____ is the utility of the marginal use -- which, on the assumption of economic rationality, would be the least urgent use of the good or service, from the best feasible combination of actions in which its use is included. Under the mainstream assumptions, the _____ of a good or service is the posited quantified change in utility obtained by increasing or by decreasing use of that good or service.
   a. 130-30 fund
   b. 1921 recession
   c. 100-year flood
   d. Marginal Utility

55. _____ is a common concept in economics, and gives rise to derived concepts such as consumer debt. Generally _____ is defined by opposition to production. But the precise definition can vary because different schools of economists define production quite differently.
   a. Cash or share options
   b. Federal Reserve Bank Notes
   c. Consumption
   d. Foreclosure data providers

56. In economics, the _____ is the rate at which a consumer is ready to give up one good in exchange for another good while maintaining the same level of satisfaction.

Under the standard assumption of neoclassical economics that goods and services are continuously divisible, the marginal rates of substitution will be the same regardless of the direction of exchange, and will correspond to the slope of an indifference curve (more precisely, to the slope multiplied by -1) passing through the consumption bundle in question, at that point: mathematically, it is the implicit derivative. MRS of Y for X is the amount of Y for which a consumer is willing to exchange for X locally.

   a. Quality bias
   b. Supply and demand
   c. Demand vacuum
   d. Marginal rate of substitution

Chapter 3. Demand Analysis and Optimal Pricing

57. In economics, game theory, and decision theory the _____ theorem or _____ hypothesis predicts that the 'betting preferences' of people with regard to uncertain outcomes (gambles) can be described by a mathematical relation which takes into account the size of a payout (whether in money or other goods), the probability of occurrence, risk aversion, and the different utility of the same payout to people with different assets or personal preferences. It is a more sophisticated theory than simply predicting that choices will be made based on expected value (which takes into account only the size of the payout and the probability of occurrence.)

Daniel Bernoulli described the complete theory in 1738.

    a. Expected utility   b. Ordinal utility
    c. Expected utility hypothesis   d. Utility

58. Procter is a surname, and may also refer to:

- Bryan Waller Procter (pseud. Barry Cornwall), English poet
- Goodwin Procter, American law firm
- _____, consumer products multinational

    a. Bucket shop   b. Tightness
    c. Drawdown   d. Procter ' Gamble

59. _____ is the total money received from the sale of any given quantity of output.

The _____ is calculated by taking the price of the sale times the quantity sold, i.e.

_____ = price X quantity.

    a. Total revenue   b. Market development funds
    c. Ceteris paribus   d. Small numbers game

Chapter 4. Estimating Demand

1. _____ is the process of estimation in unknown situations. Prediction is a similar, but more general term. Both can refer to estimation of time series, cross-sectional or longitudinal data.
   a. Forecasting
   b. 130-30 fund
   c. 100-year flood
   d. 1921 recession

2. _____ is one of the four Ps of the marketing mix. The other three aspects are product, promotion, and place. It is also a key variable in microeconomic price allocation theory.
   a. Point of total assumption
   b. Guaranteed Maximum Price
   c. Premium pricing
   d. Pricing

Chapter 4. Estimating Demand

3. A _____ is:

   - Rewrite _____, in generative grammar and computer science
   - Standardization, a formal and widely-accepted statement, fact, definition, or qualification
   - Operation, a determinate _____ for performing a mathematical operation and obtaining a certain result (Mathematics, Logic)
     - Unary operation
     - Binary operation
   - _____ of inference, a function from sets of formulae to formulae (Mathematics, Logic)
   - _____ of thumb, principle with broad application that is not intended to be strictly accurate or reliable for every situation. Also often simply referred to as a _____
   - Moral, an atomic element of a moral code for guiding choices in human behavior
   - Heuristic, a quantized '_____' which shows a tendency or probability for successful function
   - A regulation, as in sports
   - A Production _____, as in computer science
   - Procedural law, a _____ set governing the application of laws to cases
     - A law, which may informally be called a '_____'
     - A court ruling, a decision by a court
   - In the U.S. Government, a regulation mandated by Congress, but written or expanded upon by the Executive Branch.
   - Norm (sociology), an informal but widely accepted _____, concept, truth, definition, or qualification (social norms, legal norms, coding norms)
   - Norm (philosophy), a kind of sentence or a reason to act, feel or believe
   - 'Rulership' is the concept of governance by a government:
     - Military _____, governance by a military body
     - Monastic _____, a collection of precepts that guides the life of monks or nuns in a religious order where the superior holds the place of Christ
   - Slide _____

   - '_____,' a song by Ayumi Hamasaki
   - '_____,' a song by rapper Nas
   - '_____s,' an album by the band The Whitest Boy Alive
   - _____s: Pyaar Ka Superhit Formula, a 2003 Bollywood film
   - ruler, an instrument for measuring lengths
   - _____, a component of an astrolabe, circumferator or similar instrument
   - The _____s, a bestselling self-help book
   - _____ Project (Run Up-to-date Linux Everywhere), a project that aims to use up-to-date Linux software on old PCs
   - _____ engine, a software system that helps managing business _____s
   - Ja _____, a hip hop artist
     - R.U.L.E., a 2005 greatest hits album by rapper Ja _____
   - '_____s,' a KMFDM song

   a. Procter ' Gamble
   b. Demand
   c. Technocracy
   d. Rule

Chapter 4. Estimating Demand

4. Economics:

   - _____, the desire to own something and the ability to pay for it
   - _____ curve, a graphic representation of a _____ schedule
   - _____ deposit, the money in checking accounts
   - _____ pull theory, the theory that inflation occurs when _____ for goods and services exceeds existing supplies
   - _____ schedule, a table that lists the quantity of a good a person will buy it each different price
   - _____ side economics, the school of economics at believes government spending and tax cuts open economy by raising _____

   a. Production
   b. McKesson ' Robbins scandal
   c. Demand
   d. Variability

5. _____ is the activity of estimating the quantity of a product or service that consumers will purchase. _____ involves techniques including both informal methods, such as educated guesses, and quantitative methods, such as the use of historical sales data or current data from test markets. _____ may be used in making pricing decisions, in assessing future capacity requirements, or in making decisions on whether to enter a new market.

   a. Demand forecasting
   b. Financial Reporting
   c. Finance designations
   d. Cost price

6. _____ is a broad label that refers to any individuals or households that use goods and services generated within the economy. The concept of a _____ is used in different contexts, so that the usage and significance of the term may vary.

   Typically when business people and economists talk of _____s they are talking about person as _____, an aggregated commodity item with little individuality other than that expressed in the buy/not-buy decision.

   a. 1921 recession
   b. 100-year flood
   c. Consumer
   d. 130-30 fund

7. _____s is the social science that studies the production, distribution, and consumption of goods and services. The term _____s comes from the Ancient Greek οἰκονομῐ́α from οἶκος (oikos, 'house') + νόμος (nomos, 'custom' or 'law'), hence 'rules of the house(hold)'. Current _____ models developed out of the broader field of political economy in the late 19th century, owing to a desire to use an empirical approach more akin to the physical sciences.

   a. Inflation
   b. Energy economics
   c. Opportunity cost
   d. Economic

8. In economics, _____ is the difference between a company's total revenue and its opportunity costs. It is the increase in wealth that an investor has from making an investment, taking into consideration all costs associated with that investment including the opportunity cost of capital.

Profit is the factor income of the entrepreneur.

Chapter 4. Estimating Demand

a. Accounting profit
b. Operating profit
c. ACCRA Cost of Living Index
d. Economic profit

9. The _____ is the official currency of 16 of the 27 member states of the European Union (EU.) The states, known collectively as the Eurozone, are Austria, Belgium, Cyprus, Finland, France, Germany, Greece, Ireland, Italy, Luxembourg, Malta, the Netherlands, Portugal, Slovakia, Slovenia, and Spain. The currency is also used in a further five European countries, with and without formal agreements and is consequently used daily by some 327 million Europeans.

a. Import and Export Price Indices
b. Equity capital market
c. IRS Code 3401
d. Euro

10. _____ is an economic concept with commonplace familiarity. It is the price that a good or service is offered at, or will fetch, in the marketplace. It is of interest mainly in the study of microeconomics.

a. Market price
b. Market anomaly
c. Paper trading
d. Noisy market hypothesis

11. A _____ represents the combinations of goods and services that a consumer can purchase given current prices and his income. Consumer theory uses the concepts of a _____ and a preference map to analyze consumer choices. Both concepts have a ready graphical representation in the two-good case.

a. Revealed preference
b. Joint demand
c. Budget constraint
d. Quality bias

12. _____ in economics and business is the result of an exchange and from that trade we assign a numerical monetary value to a good, service or asset. If Alice trades Bob 4 apples for an orange, the _____ of an orange is 4 apples. Inversely, the _____ of an apple is 1/4 oranges.

a. Price war
b. Price book
c. Premium pricing
d. Price

13. The _____ consists of a number of economic theories which describe the nature of the firm, company including its existence, its behaviour, and its relationship with the market.

In simplified terms, the _____ aims to answer these questions:

1. Existence - why do firms emerge, why are not all transactions in the economy mediated over the market?
2. Boundaries - why the boundary between firms and the market is located exactly there? Which transactions are performed internally and which are negotiated on the market?
3. Organization - why are firms structured in such specific way? What is the interplay of formal and informal relationships?

Despite looking simple, these questions are not answered by the established economic theory, which usually views firms as given, and treats them as black boxes without any internal structure.

The First World War period saw a change of emphasis in economic theory away from industry-level analysis which mainly included analysing markets to analysis at the level of the firm, as it became increasingly clear that perfect competition was no longer an adequate model of how firms behaved. Economic theory till then had focussed on trying to understand markets alone and there had been little study on understanding why firms or organisations exist.

Chapter 4. Estimating Demand

a. Theory of the firm
b. Khazzoom-Brookes postulate
c. Technology gap
d. Policy Ineffectiveness Proposition

14. A _____ is a group of people or organizations sharing one or more characteristics that cause them to have similar product and/or service needs. A true _____ meets all of the following criteria: it is distinct from other segments (different segments have different needs), it is homogeneous within the segment (exhibits common needs); it responds similarly to a market stimulus, and it can be reached by a market intervention. The term is also used when consumers with identical product and/or service needs are divided up into groups so they can be charged different amounts.
   a. Market Segmentation Index
   b. Customer to customer
   c. Pricing science
   d. Market segment

15. _____ is a term used to described a tendency or preference towards a particular perspective, ideology or result, especially when the tendency interferes with the ability to be impartial, unprejudiced, or objective. The term _____ed is used to describe an action, judgment, or other outcome influenced by a prejudged perspective. It is also used to refer to a person or body of people whose actions or judgments exhibit _____.
   a. 130-30 fund
   b. 100-year flood
   c. 1921 recession
   d. Bias

16. _____ or cross section (of a study population) in statistics and econometrics is a type of one-dimensional data set. _____ refers to data collected by observing many subjects (such as individuals, firms or countries/regions) at the same point of time, or without regard to differences in time. Analysis of _____ usually consists of comparing the differences among the subjects.
   a. 1921 recession
   b. 130-30 fund
   c. 100-year flood
   d. Cross-sectional data

17. In microeconomics, _____ is quite simply the conversion of inputs into outputs. It is an economic process that uses resources to create a good or service that is suitable for exchange. This can include manufacturing, storing, shipping, and packaging.
   a. Solved
   b. MET
   c. Red Guards
   d. Production

18. In economics, _____ is the ratio of the percent change in one variable to the percent change in another variable. It is a tool for measuring the responsiveness of a function to changes in parameters in a relative way. Commonly analyzed are _____ of substitution, price and wealth.
   a. Elasticity of demand
   b. Elasticity
   c. ACEA agreement
   d. ACCRA Cost of Living Index

19. _____ exists when sales of identical goods or services are transacted at different prices from the same provider. In a theoretical market with perfect information, no transaction costs or prohibition on secondary exchange (or re-selling) to prevent arbitrage, _____ can only be a feature of monopoly and oligopoly markets, where market power can be exercised. Otherwise, the moment the seller tries to sell the same good at different prices, the buyer at the lower price can arbitrage by selling to the consumer buying at the higher price but with a tiny discount.
   a. Price discrimination
   b. Loss leader
   c. Lerner Index
   d. Transfer pricing

Chapter 4. Estimating Demand

20. In finance, _____ refers to quote and trade related-data associated with equity, fixed-income, financial derivatives, currency, and other investment instruments. The term _____ traditionally refers to numerical price data, reported from trading venues, such as stock exchanges. The price data is attached to a ticker symbol and additional data about the trade.
    a. Market anomaly
    b. Payment for order flow
    c. Speculation
    d. Market data

21. A _____ is the procedure of systematically acquiring and recording information about the members of a given population. It is a regularly occurring and official count of a particular population. The term is used mostly in connection with national 'population and door to door _____es' (to be taken every 10 years according to United Nations recommendations), agriculture, and business _____es.
    a. 130-30 fund
    b. 100-year flood
    c. 1921 recession
    d. Census

22. The _____ or gross domestic income (GDI), a basic measure of an economy's economic performance, is the market value of all final goods and services produced within the borders of a nation in a year. _____ can be defined in three ways, all of which are conceptually identical. First, it is equal to the total expenditures for all final goods and services produced within the country in a stipulated period of time (usually a 365-day year.)
    a. Countercyclical
    b. Monopolistic competition
    c. Gross domestic product
    d. Market structure

23. In statistics, _____ refers to techniques for the modeling and analysis of numerical data consisting of values of a dependent variable and of one or more independent variables The dependent variable in the regression equation is modeled as a function of the independent variables, corresponding parameters, and an error term. The error term is treated as a random variable.
    a. 100-year flood
    b. Regression analysis
    c. 130-30 fund
    d. 1921 recession

24. In statistics, _____ has two related meanings:

    - the arithmetic _____
    - the expected value of a random variable, which is also called the population _____.

    It is sometimes stated that the '_____' _____s average. This is incorrect if '_____' is taken in the specific sense of 'arithmetic _____' as there are different types of averages: the _____, median, and mode. Other simple statistical analyses use measures of spread, such as range, interquartile range, or standard deviation. For a real-valued random variable X, the _____ is the expectation of X. Note that not every probability distribution has a defined _____ (or variance); see the Cauchy distribution for an example.

    a. 100-year flood
    b. 1921 recession
    c. Mean
    d. 130-30 fund

25. In probability theory and statistics, _____ is a measure of the variability or dispersion of a population, a data set, or a probability distribution. A low _____ indicates that the data points tend to be very close to the same value (the mean), while high _____ indicates that the data are 'spread out' over a large range of values.

Chapter 4. Estimating Demand

For example, the average height for adult men in the United States is about 70 inches, with a _____ of around 3 inches.

a. Standard deviation
c. 100-year flood
b. 130-30 fund
d. 1921 recession

26. In economics, the _____ can be defined as the graph depicting the relationship between the price of a certain commodity, and the amount of it that consumers are willing and able to purchase at that given price. It is a graphic representation of a demand schedule. The _____ for all consumers together follows from the _____ of every individual consumer: the individual demands at each price are added together.
  a. Wage curve
  c. Cost curve
  b. Kuznets curve
  d. Demand curve

27. The terms '_____' and 'independent variable' are used in similar but subtly different ways in mathematics and statistics as part of the standard terminology in those subjects. They are used to distinguish between two types of quantities being considered, separating them into those available at the start of a process and those being created by it, where the latter (_____s) are dependent on the former (independent variables.)

In traditional calculus, a function is defined as a relation between two terms called variables because their values vary.

  a. 1921 recession
  c. 100-year flood
  b. Dependent variable
  d. 130-30 fund

28. The terms 'dependent variable' and '_____' are used in similar but subtly different ways in mathematics and statistics as part of the standard terminology in those subjects. They are used to distinguish between two types of quantities being considered, separating them into those available at the start of a process and those being created by it, where the latter (dependent variables) are dependent on the former (_____s.)

The _____ is typically the variable being manipulated or changed and the dependent variable is the observed result of the _____ being manipulated.

  a. ACCRA Cost of Living Index
  c. Independent variable
  b. AD-IA Model
  d. ACEA agreement

29. A _____ is an object whose consumption increases the utility of the consumer, for which the quantity demanded exceeds the quantity supplied at zero price. _____s are usually modeled as having diminishing marginal utility. The first individual purchase has high utility; the second has less.
  a. Composite good
  c. Merit good
  b. Pie method
  d. Good

30. In mathematics, a _____ is a constant multiplicative factor of a certain object. For example, in the expression $9x^2$, the _____ of x^2 is 9.

The object can be such things as a variable, a vector, a function, etc.

Chapter 4. Estimating Demand

a. 100-year flood
b. 130-30 fund
c. Coefficient
d. 1921 recession

31. In statistics, the _____, R^2 is used in the context of statistical models whose main purpose is the prediction of future outcomes on the basis of other related information. It is the proportion of variability in a data set that is accounted for by the statistical model. It provides a measure of how well future outcomes are likely to be predicted by the model.
   a. DFFITS
   b. Feasible generalized least squares
   c. Partial leverage
   d. Coefficient of determination

32. In statistics, a _____ is, broadly speaking, a statistic whose sampling distribution is a Student's t-distribution. These are a parametric statistic, most frequently used in frequentist statistical hypothesis testing in Student's t-tests, but can be defined and used independently of hypothesis testing.

Broadly speaking, a _____ is any statistic whose sampling distribution is a Student's t-distribution.

   a. T-statistic
   b. Kurtosis risk
   c. Standardized coefficients
   d. Path coefficients

33. _____ is a statistical phenomenon in which two or more predictor variables in a multiple regression model are highly correlated. In this situation the coefficient estimates may change erratically in response to small changes in the model or the data. _____ does not reduce the predictive power or reliability of the model as a whole; it only affects calculations regarding individual predictors.
   a. Multicollinearity
   b. Generalized additive model
   c. Quantile regression
   d. Total sum of squares

34. In neoclassical economics and microeconomics, _____ describes the perfect being a market in which there are many small firms, all producing homogeneous goods. In the short term, such markets are productively inefficient as output will not occur where mc is equal to ac, but allocatively efficient, as output under _____ will always occur where mc is equal to mr, and therefore where mc equals ar. However, in the long term, such markets are both allocatively and productively efficient.
   a. General equilibrium
   b. Law of supply
   c. Co-operative economics
   d. Perfect competition

35. A _____ is a counterfeit agreement among industries. It is an informal organization of producers that agree to coordinate prices and production. _____s usually occur in an oligopolistic industry, where there is a small number of sellers and usually involve homogeneous products.
   a. Shill
   b. Cartel
   c. 100-year flood
   d. Shanzhai

36. _____ is the transition of a national economy from monopoly control by groups of large businesses to a free market economy. This change rarely arises naturally, and is generally the result of regulation by a governing body.

A modern example of _____ is the economic restructuring of Germany after the fall of the Third Reich in 1945.

Chapter 4. Estimating Demand

a. Decartelization
c. Monopolization
b. Complementary monopoly
d. Market power

37. In economics, the _____ of an industry is used as an indicator of the relative size of firms in relation to the industry as a whole. It is calculated as the sum of the percent market share of the top n industries. This may also assist in determining the market structure of the industry.
   a. Monopolization
   c. Quasi-rent
   b. Pacman conjecture
   d. Concentration ratio

38. A _____ is an expression that compares quantities relative to each other. The most common examples involve two quantities, but any number of quantities can be compared. _____s are represented mathematically by separating each quantity with a colon, for example the _____ 2:3, which is read as the _____ 'two to three'.
   a. 130-30 fund
   c. Ratio
   b. 100-year flood
   d. Y-intercept

39. _____ is a concept with somewhat disparate meanings in several fields. It also has a common meaning which has a loose connection with some of those more definite meanings.

Casually, it is typically used to denote a lack of order, or purpose, or cause.

   a. Randomness
   c. 1921 recession
   b. 100-year flood
   d. 130-30 fund

40. In statistics, _____ indicates the strength and direction of a linear relationship between two random variables. That is in contrast with the usage of the term in colloquial speech, which denotes any relationship, not necessarily linear. In general statistical usage, _____ or co-relation refers to the departure of two random variables from independence.
   a. 100-year flood
   c. Correlation
   b. 1921 recession
   d. 130-30 fund

41. A _____ refers to any type debt instrument, such as a loan, bond, mortgage that does not have a fixed rate of interest over the life of the instrument. Such debt typically uses an index or other base rate for establishing the interest rate for each relevant period. One of the most common rates to use as the basis for applying interest rates is the London Inter-bank Offered Rate, or LIBOR
   a. Floating interest rate
   c. Money market
   b. Disposal tax effect
   d. Moneylender

Chapter 5. Forecasting

1. The _____ is the official currency of 16 of the 27 member states of the European Union (EU.) The states, known collectively as the Eurozone, are Austria, Belgium, Cyprus, Finland, France, Germany, Greece, Ireland, Italy, Luxembourg, Malta, the Netherlands, Portugal, Slovakia, Slovenia, and Spain. The currency is also used in a further five European countries, with and without formal agreements and is consequently used daily by some 327 million Europeans.
   - a. Euro
   - b. Import and Export Price Indices
   - c. Equity capital market
   - d. IRS Code 3401

2. _____ is the process of estimation in unknown situations. Prediction is a similar, but more general term. Both can refer to estimation of time series, cross-sectional or longitudinal data.
   - a. 130-30 fund
   - b. 100-year flood
   - c. Forecasting
   - d. 1921 recession

3. Economics:
   - _____, the desire to own something and the ability to pay for it
   - _____ curve, a graphic representation of a _____ schedule
   - _____ deposit, the money in checking accounts
   - _____ pull theory, the theory that inflation occurs when _____ for goods and services exceeds existing supplies
   - _____ schedule, a table that lists the quantity of a good a person will buy it each different price
   - _____ side economics, the school of economics at believes government spending and tax cuts open economy by raising _____

   - a. McKesson ' Robbins scandal
   - b. Variability
   - c. Production
   - d. Demand

4. _____s is concerned with the tasks of developing and applying quantitative or statistical methods to the study and elucidation of economic principles. _____s combines economic theory with statistics to analyze and test economic relationships. Theoretical _____s considers questions about the statistical properties of estimators and tests, while applied _____s is concerned with the application of _____ methods to assess economic theories.
   - a. Evolutionary economics
   - b. Experimental economics
   - c. Economic
   - d. Econometric

5. The terms 'dependent variable' and '_____' are used in similar but subtly different ways in mathematics and statistics as part of the standard terminology in those subjects. They are used to distinguish between two types of quantities being considered, separating them into those available at the start of a process and those being created by it, where the latter (dependent variables) are dependent on the former (_____s.)

   The _____ is typically the variable being manipulated or changed and the dependent variable is the observed result of the _____ being manipulated.
   - a. AD-IA Model
   - b. Independent variable
   - c. ACEA agreement
   - d. ACCRA Cost of Living Index

6. In economics, _____ are key economic variables that economists used to predict a new phase of the business cycle. A leading indicator is one that changes before the economy does; a lagging indicator is one that changes after the economy has changed. Examples of _____ include stock prices, which often improve or worsen before a similar change in the economy.
   a. Macroeconomics
   b. Gross domestic product
   c. Medium of exchange
   d. Leading indicators

7. A _____ is a public market for the trading of company stock and derivatives at an agreed price; these are securities listed on a stock exchange as well as those only traded privately.

The size of the world _____ was estimated at about $36.6 trillion US at the beginning of October 2008 . The total world derivatives market has been estimated at about $791 trillion face or nominal value, 11 times the size of the entire world economy.

   a. Stock market
   b. Adam Smith
   c. Adolf Hitler
   d. Adolph Fischer

8. The term _____ refers to economy-wide fluctuations in production or economic activity over several months or years. These fluctuations occur around a long-term growth trend, and typically involve shifts over time between periods of relatively rapid economic growth (expansion or boom), and periods of relative stagnation or decline (contraction or recession.)

These fluctuations are often measured using the growth rate of real gross domestic product.

   a. Tobit model
   b. Consumer theory
   c. Nominal value
   d. Business cycle

9. The terms '_____' and 'independent variable' are used in similar but subtly different ways in mathematics and statistics as part of the standard terminology in those subjects. They are used to distinguish between two types of quantities being considered, separating them into those available at the start of a process and those being created by it, where the latter (_____s) are dependent on the former (independent variables.)

In traditional calculus, a function is defined as a relation between two terms called variables because their values vary.

   a. Dependent variable
   b. 1921 recession
   c. 100-year flood
   d. 130-30 fund

10. _____s is the social science that studies the production, distribution, and consumption of goods and services. The term _____s comes from the Ancient Greek oá¼°κονομῐ́α from oá¼¶κος (oikos, 'house') + νÍŒμος (nomos, 'custom' or 'law'), hence 'rules of the house(hold)'. Current _____ models developed out of the broader field of political economy in the late 19th century, owing to a desire to use an empirical approach more akin to the physical sciences.
   a. Inflation
   b. Opportunity cost
   c. Energy economics
   d. Economic

11. _____ is the increase in the amount of the goods and services produced by an economy over time. It is conventionally measured as the percent rate of increase in real gross domestic product, or real GDP. Growth is usually calculated in real terms, i.e. inflation-adjusted terms, in order to net out the effect of inflation on the price of the goods and services produced.
   a. ACCRA Cost of Living Index
   b. AD-IA Model
   c. ACEA agreement
   d. Economic growth

12. _____ or government expenditure is classified by economists into three main types. Government purchases of goods and services for current use are classed as government consumption. Government purchases of goods and services intended to create future benefits, such as infrastructure investment or research spending, are classed as government investment.
   a. 100-year flood
   b. 130-30 fund
   c. Government spending
   d. 1921 recession

13. The _____ or gross domestic income (GDI), a basic measure of an economy's economic performance, is the market value of all final goods and services produced within the borders of a nation in a year. _____ can be defined in three ways, all of which are conceptually identical. First, it is equal to the total expenditures for all final goods and services produced within the country in a stipulated period of time (usually a 365-day year.)
   a. Monopolistic competition
   b. Market structure
   c. Countercyclical
   d. Gross domestic product

14. _____ is a fee paid on borrowed assets. It is the price paid for the use of borrowed money, or, money earned by deposited funds. Assets that are sometimes lent with _____ include money, shares, consumer goods through hire purchase, major assets such as aircraft, and even entire factories in finance lease arrangements.
   a. Asset protection
   b. Insolvency
   c. Interest
   d. Internal debt

15. An _____ is the price a borrower pays for the use of money they do not own, for instance a small company might borrow from a bank to kick start their business, and the return a lender receives for deferring the use of funds, by lending it to the borrower. _____s are normally expressed as a percentage rate over the period of one year.

   _____s targets are also a vital tool of monetary policy and are used to control variables like investment, inflation, and unemployment.

   a. Enterprise value
   b. Interest rate
   c. Arrow-Debreu model
   d. ACCRA Cost of Living Index

16. _____ is a concept with somewhat disparate meanings in several fields. It also has a common meaning which has a loose connection with some of those more definite meanings.

Casually, it is typically used to denote a lack of order, or purpose, or cause.

   a. 100-year flood
   b. 130-30 fund
   c. 1921 recession
   d. Randomness

17. In economics, a _____ is a general slowdown in economic activity over a sustained period of time, or a business cycle contraction. During _____s, many macroeconomic indicators vary in a similar way. Production as measured by Gross Domestic Product (GDP), employment, investment spending, capacity utilization, household incomes and business profits all fall during _____s.
   a. Monetary economics
   c. Treasury View
   b. Leading indicators
   d. Recession

18. The term '_____' refers to the concept of collecting information and attempting to spot a pattern in the information. In some fields of study, the term '_____' has more formally-defined meanings.

   In project management _____ is a mathematical technique that uses historical results to predict future outcome.

   a. Probit model
   c. Quantile regression
   b. Trend analysis
   d. Coefficient of determination

19. _____ is a common concept in economics, and gives rise to derived concepts such as consumer debt. Generally _____ is defined by opposition to production. But the precise definition can vary because different schools of economists define production quite differently.
   a. Federal Reserve Bank Notes
   c. Foreclosure data providers
   b. Consumption
   d. Cash or share options

20. In statistics, _____ refers to techniques for the modeling and analysis of numerical data consisting of values of a dependent variable and of one or more independent variables The dependent variable in the regression equation is modeled as a function of the independent variables, corresponding parameters, and an error term. The error term is treated as a random variable.
   a. 100-year flood
   c. 1921 recession
   b. 130-30 fund
   d. Regression analysis

21. In economics, _____ is a rise in the general level of prices of goods and services in an economy over a period of time. When the general price level rises, each unit of currency buys fewer goods and services; consequently, _____ is also a decline in the real value of money--a loss of purchasing power in the medium of exchange which is also the monetary unit of account in the economy. A chief measure of general price-level _____ is the general _____ rate, which is the percentage change in a general price index (normally the Consumer Price Index) over time.
   a. Energy economics
   c. Opportunity cost
   b. Economic
   d. Inflation

22. _____, in microeconomics, are the cost advantages that a business obtains due to expansion. They are factors that cause a producere;s average cost per unit to fall as scale is increased. _____ is a long run concept and refers to reductions in unit cost as the size of a facility, or scale, increases.
   a. Economic production quantity
   c. Isoquant
   b. Underinvestment employment relationship
   d. Economies of scale

23. In statistics, a _____ is, broadly speaking, a statistic whose sampling distribution is a Student's t-distribution. These are a parametric statistic, most frequently used in frequentist statistical hypothesis testing in Student's t-tests, but can be defined and used independently of hypothesis testing.

Broadly speaking, a _____ is any statistic whose sampling distribution is a Student's t-distribution.

- a. Path coefficients
- b. Standardized coefficients
- c. T-statistic
- d. Kurtosis risk

24. _____s are statistical models used in econometrics. An _____ specifies the statistical relationship that is believed to hold between the various economic quantities pertaining a particular economic phenomena under study. An _____ can be derived from a deterministic economic model by allowing for uncertainty or from an economic model which itself is stochastic.
- a. ACCRA Cost of Living Index
- b. Economic statistics
- c. Event study
- d. Econometric model

25. The _____ is one of several stock market indices, created by nineteenth-century Wall Street Journal editor and Dow Jones ' Company co-founder Charles Dow. It is an index that shows how certain stocks have traded. Dow compiled the index to gauge the performance of the industrial sector of the American stock market.
- a. Fama-French three factor model
- b. Federal Reserve Bank Notes
- c. Commodity fetishism
- d. Dow Jones Industrial Average

26. _____ is the combined income earned by an entire group of persons. '_____' in economics is a broad conceptual term. It may express the proceeds from total output in the economy for producers of that output.
- a. Aggregate income
- b. Independent income
- c. Average propensity to save
- d. Unearned income

27. A _____ is a method of measuring a section of the stock market. Many indices are cited by news or financial services firms and are used to benchmark the performance of portfolios such as mutual funds.

Stock market indices may be classed in many ways.

- a. Lock up period
- b. Scrip issue
- c. Stock market bubble
- d. Stock market Index

28. _____ is exchange of capital, goods, and services across international borders or territories. In most countries, it represents a significant share of gross domestic product (GDP.) While _____ has been present throughout much of history , its economic, social, and political importance has been on the rise in recent centuries.
- a. Import license
- b. Incoterms
- c. Intra-industry trade
- d. International trade

29. _____ is a branch of economics that deals with the performance, structure, and behavior of a national or regional economy as a whole. Along with microeconomics, _____ is one of the two most general fields in economics. It is the study of the behavior and decision-making of entire economies.
- a. New Trade Theory
- b. Tobit model
- c. Macroeconomics
- d. Nominal value

Chapter 5. Forecasting

30. _____ is a branch of economics that studies how individuals, households and firms and some states make decisions to allocate limited resources, typically in markets where goods or services are being bought and sold. _____ examines how these decisions and behaviours affect the supply and demand for goods and services, which determines prices; and how prices, in turn, determine the supply and demand of goods and services.

Whereas macroeconomics involves the 'sum total of economic activity, dealing with the issues of growth, inflation and unemployment, and with national economic policies relating to these issues' and the effects of government actions on them.

- a. New Keynesian economics
- b. Recession
- c. Countercyclical
- d. Microeconomics

31. In economics, _____ is the total amount of money available in an economy at a particular point in time. There are several ways to define 'money', but standard measures usually include currency in circulation and demand deposits.

_____ data are recorded and published, usually by the government or the central bank of the country.

- a. Neutrality of money
- b. Veil of money
- c. Velocity of money
- d. Money supply

32. _____ is a measure of the strength of a brand, product, service relative to competitive offerings. There is often a geographic element to the competitive landscape. In defining _____, you must see to what extent a product, brand, or firm controls a product category in a given geographic area.

- a. Demand shaping
- b. Horizontal territorial allocation
- c. Price elasticity of supply
- d. Market dominance

33. _____ is the planning process used to determine whether a firm's long term investments such as new machinery, replacement machinery, new plants, new products, and research development projects are worth pursuing. It is budget for major capital, or investment, expenditures.

Many formal methods are used in _____, including the techniques such as

- Net present value
- Profitability index
- Internal rate of return
- Modified Internal Rate of Return
- Equivalent annuity

These methods use the incremental cash flows from each potential investment, or project. Techniques based on accounting earnings and accounting rules are sometimes used - though economists consider this to be improper - such as the accounting rate of return, and 'return on investment.' Simplified and hybrid methods are used as well, such as payback period and discounted payback period.

Chapter 5. Forecasting

a. Voting interest
b. Preferred stock
c. Participating preferred stock
d. Capital budgeting

34. In mathematics, a _____ is a constant multiplicative factor of a certain object. For example, in the expression $9x^2$, the _____ of x^2 is 9.

The object can be such things as a variable, a vector, a function, etc.

a. 100-year flood
b. 130-30 fund
c. 1921 recession
d. Coefficient

35. In economics, the _____ is a single mathematical function used to express consumer spending. It was developed by John Maynard Keynes and detailed most famously in his book The General Theory of Employment, Interest, and Money. The function is used to calculate the amount of total consumption in an economy.

a. DAD-SAS model
b. Liquidity preference
c. Procyclical
d. Consumption function

36. In economics and sociology, an _____ is any factor (financial or non-financial) that enables or motivates a particular course of action, or counts as a reason for preferring one choice to the alternatives. It is an expectation that encourages people to behave in a certain way. Since human beings are purposeful creatures, the study of _____ structures is central to the study of all economic activity (both in terms of individual decision-making and in terms of co-operation and competition within a larger institutional structure.)

a. Economic reform
b. Epstein-Zin preferences
c. Incentive
d. Isocost

37. _____ in economics and business is the result of an exchange and from that trade we assign a numerical monetary value to a good, service or asset. If Alice trades Bob 4 apples for an orange, the _____ of an orange is 4 apples. Inversely, the _____ of an apple is 1/4 oranges.

a. Price book
b. Price war
c. Premium pricing
d. Price

38. In statistics, and particularly in econometrics, the _____ of a system of equations is the result of solving the system for the endogenous variables. This gives the latter as a function of the exogenous variables, if any.

Let Y and X be random vectors.

a. Panel data
b. Local independence
c. FWL theorem
d. Reduced form

39. In mathematics, _____ are a set of equations containing multiple variables. _____ are representations of multi-variant sets of relationships (functions) where it is postulated that there exists some set(s) of conditions where these functions (equations) are equal or intersect. In the simplest case, there exist one or more constants or variables, that, when substituted for the unknown terms of the equation(s) produce the same or identical results.

a. 100-year flood
b. 130-30 fund
c. Slutsky equation
d. Simultaneous equations

Chapter 5. Forecasting

40. To _____ is to impose a financial charge or other levy upon a taxpayer by a state or the functional equivalent of a state.

_____es are also imposed by many subnational entities. _____es consist of direct _____ or indirect _____, and may be paid in money or as its labour equivalent (often but not always unpaid.)

   a. Tax
   b. 130-30 fund
   c. 1921 recession
   d. 100-year flood

41. To tax is to impose a financial charge or other levy upon a taxpayer by a state or the functional equivalent of a state.

_____ are also imposed by many subnational entities. _____ consist of direct tax or indirect tax, and may be paid in money or as its labour equivalent (often but not always unpaid.)

   a. 1921 recession
   b. 130-30 fund
   c. Taxes
   d. 100-year flood

42. A _____ is a counterfeit agreement among industries. It is an informal organization of producers that agree to coordinate prices and production. _____s usually occur in an oligopolistic industry, where there is a small number of sellers and usually involve homogeneous products.

   a. 100-year flood
   b. Shanzhai
   c. Cartel
   d. Shill

43. _____ is the transition of a national economy from monopoly control by groups of large businesses to a free market economy. This change rarely arises naturally, and is generally the result of regulation by a governing body.

A modern example of _____ is the economic restructuring of Germany after the fall of the Third Reich in 1945.

   a. Monopolization
   b. Decartelization
   c. Complementary monopoly
   d. Market power

44. A _____ is an object whose consumption increases the utility of the consumer, for which the quantity demanded exceeds the quantity supplied at zero price. _____s are usually modeled as having diminishing marginal utility. The first individual purchase has high utility; the second has less.

   a. Merit good
   b. Pie method
   c. Composite good
   d. Good

45. _____ refers to an action or object coming from outside a system. It is the opposite of endogenous, something generated from within the system.

- In an economic model, an _____ change is one that comes from outside the model and is unexplained by the model. For example, in the simple supply and demand model, a change in consumer tastes or preferences is unexplained by the model and also leads to endogenous changes in demand that lead to changes in the equilibrium price. Put another way, an _____ change involves an alteration of a variable that is autonomous, i.e., unaffected by the workings of the model.

- In linear regression, it means that the variable is independent of all other response values.

- In biology, '_____' refers to an action or object coming from the outside of a system. For example, an _____ contrast agent in medical imaging refers to a liquid injected into the patient intravenously that enhances visibility of a pathology, such as a tumor.

a. ACEA agreement
b. ACCRA Cost of Living Index
c. AD-IA Model
d. Exogenous

46. The _____ consists of a number of economic theories which describe the nature of the firm, company including its existence, its behaviour, and its relationship with the market.

In simplified terms, the _____ aims to answer these questions:

1. Existence - why do firms emerge, why are not all transactions in the economy mediated over the market?
2. Boundaries - why the boundary between firms and the market is located exactly there? Which transactions are performed internally and which are negotiated on the market?
3. Organization - why are firms structured in such specific way? What is the interplay of formal and informal relationships?

Despite looking simple, these questions are not answered by the established economic theory, which usually views firms as given, and treats them as black boxes without any internal structure.

The First World War period saw a change of emphasis in economic theory away from industry-level analysis which mainly included analysing markets to analysis at the level of the firm, as it became increasingly clear that perfect competition was no longer an adequate model of how firms behaved. Economic theory till then had focussed on trying to understand markets alone and there had been little study on understanding why firms or organisations exist.

a. Technology gap
b. Theory of the firm
c. Policy Ineffectiveness Proposition
d. Khazzoom-Brookes postulate

47. In finance, the _____s between two currencies specifies how much one currency is worth in terms of the other. It is the value of a foreign natione;s currency in terms of the home natione;s currency. For example an _____ of 102 Japanese yen to the United States dollar means that JPY 102 is worth the same as USD 1.

Chapter 5. Forecasting

a. Interbank market
c. ACCRA Cost of Living Index
b. ACEA agreement
d. Exchange rate

48. _____ is a branch of applied mathematics that is used in the social sciences (most notably economics), biology, engineering, political science, international relations, computer science, and philosophy. _____ attempts to mathematically capture behavior in strategic situations, in which an individual's success in making choices depends on the choices of others. While initially developed to analyze competitions in which one individual does better at another's expense (zero sum games), it has been expanded to treat a wide class of interactions, which are classified according to several criteria.

a. Dollar auction
c. Proper equilibrium
b. Game theory
d. Discriminatory price auction

49. The phrase _____ refers to the aspect of corporate strategy, corporate finance and management dealing with the buying, selling and combining of different companies that can aid, finance, or help a growing company in a given industry grow rapidly without having to create another business entity.

An acquisition, also known as a takeover or a buyout, is the buying of one company (the 'target') by another. An acquisition may be friendly or hostile.

a. Peace dividend
c. Political economy
b. Productive and unproductive labour
d. Mergers and acquisitions

50. In economics, a model is a theoretical construct that represents economic processes by a set of variables and a set of logical and/or quantitative relationships between them. The _____ is a simplified framework designed to illustrate complex processes, often but not always using mathematical techniques. Frequently, _____s use structural parameters.

a. AD-IA Model
c. ACEA agreement
b. ACCRA Cost of Living Index
d. Economic model

51. The term _____ refers to government debt, expenditures and revenues, or to finance (particularly financial revenue) in general.

- _____ deficit is the budget deficit of federal or local government
- _____ policy is the discretionary spending of governments. Contrasts with monetary policy.
- _____ year and _____ quarter are reporting periods for firms and other agencies.

a. Drawdown
c. Bucket shop
b. Procter ' Gamble
d. Fiscal

52. In economics, _____ is the use of government spending and revenue collection to influence the economy.

_____ can be contrasted with the other main type of economic policy, monetary policy, which attempts to stabilize the economy by controlling interest rates and the supply of money. The two main instruments of _____ are government spending and taxation.

Chapter 5. Forecasting

a. Fiscalism
b. 100-year flood
c. Sustainable investment rule
d. Fiscal policy

53. _____ is the process by which the government, central bank (ii) availability of money, and (iii) cost of money or rate of interest, in order to attain a set of objectives oriented towards the growth and stability of the economy. Monetary theory provides insight into how to craft optimal _____.

_____ is referred to as either being an expansionary policy where an expansionary policy increases the total supply of money in the economy, and a contractionary policy decreases the total money supply.

a. 100-year flood
b. 1921 recession
c. 130-30 fund
d. Monetary policy

54. The _____ is a bank regulation that sets the minimum reserves each bank must hold to customer deposits and notes. It would normally be in the form of fiat currency stored in a bank vault (vault cash), or with a central bank.

The reserve ratio is sometimes used as a tool in the monetary policy, influencing the country's economy, borrowing, and interest rates.

a. Probability of default
b. Private money
c. Fractional-reserve banking
d. Reserve requirement

55. _____ measures the nominal future sum of money that a given sum of money is 'worth' at a specified time in the future assuming a certain interest rate rate of return; it is the present value multiplied by the accumulation function.

The value does not include corrections for inflation or other factors that affect the true value of money in the future. This is used in time value of money calculations.

a. Future value
b. Negative gearing
c. Future-oriented
d. Present value

56. In statistics, _____ has two related meanings:

- the arithmetic _____
- the expected value of a random variable, which is also called the population _____.

It is sometimes stated that the '_____' _____s average. This is incorrect if '_____' is taken in the specific sense of 'arithmetic _____' as there are different types of averages: the _____, median, and mode. Other simple statistical analyses use measures of spread, such as range, interquartile range, or standard deviation. For a real-valued random variable X, the _____ is the expectation of X. Note that not every probability distribution has a defined _____ (or variance); see the Cauchy distribution for an example.

a. Mean
b. 130-30 fund
c. 100-year flood
d. 1921 recession

Chapter 5. Forecasting

57. _____ is the a method of technical and economic research of the systems for purpose to optimize a parity between system's consumer functions or properties and expenses to achieve those functions or properties.

This methodology for continuous perfection of production, industrial technologies, organizational structures was developed by Juryj Sobolev in 1948 at the 'Perm telephone factory'

- 1948 Juryj Sobolev - the first success in application of a method analysis at the 'Perm telephone factory'.
- 1949 - the first application for the invention as result of use of the new method.

Today in economically developed countries practically each enterprise or the company use methodology of the kind of functional-cost analysis as a practice of the quality management, most full satisfying to principles of standards of series ISO 9000.

- Interest of consumer not in products itself, but the advantage which it will receive from its usage.
- The consumer aspires to reduce his expenses
- Functions needed by consumer can be executed in the various ways, and, hence, with various efficiency and expenses. Among possible alternatives of realization of functions exist such in which the parity of quality and the price is the optimal for the consumer.

The goal of _____ is achievement of the highest consumer satisfaction of production at simultaneous decrease in all kinds of industrial expenses Classical _____ has three English synonyms - Value Engineering, Value Management, Value Analysis.

a. Willingness to pay
c. Staple financing
b. Monopoly wage
d. Function cost analysis

58. _____ is a way of expressing knowledge or belief that an event will occur or has occurred. In mathematics the concept has been given an exact meaning in _____ theory, that is used extensively in such areas of study as mathematics, statistics, finance, gambling, science, and philosophy to draw conclusions about the likelihood of potential events and the underlying mechanics of complex systems.

The word _____ does not have a consistent direct definition.

a. 130-30 fund
c. 100-year flood
b. 1921 recession
d. Probability

59. In probability theory and statistics, a _____ identifies either the probability of each value of an unidentified random variable (when the variable is discrete), or the probability of the value falling within a particular interval (when the variable is continuous.) The _____ describes the range of possible values that a random variable can attain and the probability that the value of the random variable is within any (measurable) subset of that range. The Normal distribution, often called the 'bell curve'

When the random variable takes values in the set of real numbers, the _____ is completely described by the cumulative distribution function, whose value at each real x is the probability that the random variable is smaller than or equal to x.

a. 100-year flood
b. 1921 recession
c. Probability distribution
d. 130-30 fund

60. In statistics, a _____ is an interval estimate of a population parameter. Instead of estimating the parameter by a single value, an interval likely to include the parameter is given. Thus, _____s are used to indicate the reliability of an estimate.
    a. Biostatistics
    b. Polynomial regression
    c. Logistic regression
    d. Confidence interval

61. In economics, _____ and economies of scale are related terms that describe what happens as the scale of production increases. They are different terms and should not be used interchangeably.

_____ refers to a technical property of production that examines changes in output subsequent to a proportional change in all inputs (where all inputs increase by a constant factor.)

    a. Necessity good
    b. Customer equity
    c. Constant returns to scale
    d. Returns to scale

62. A _____ is an economic indicator that reacts slowly to economic changes, and therefore has little predictive value. Generally these types of indicators follow an event; they are historical in nature. For example, in a performance measuring system, profit earned by a business is a _____ as it reflects a historical performance; similarly, improved customer satisfaction is the result of initiatives taken in the past.
    a. Skyscraper Index
    b. Nonfarm payrolls
    c. Lagging indicator
    d. Bureau of Labor Statistics

Chapter 6. Production

1. _____ is a broad label that refers to any individuals or households that use goods and services generated within the economy. The concept of a _____ is used in different contexts, so that the usage and significance of the term may vary.

Typically when business people and economists talk of _____s they are talking about person as _____, an aggregated commodity item with little individuality other than that expressed in the buy/not-buy decision.

- a. Consumer
- b. 100-year flood
- c. 1921 recession
- d. 130-30 fund

2. In microeconomics, _____ is quite simply the conversion of inputs into outputs. It is an economic process that uses resources to create a good or service that is suitable for exchange. This can include manufacturing, storing, shipping, and packaging.
- a. Solved
- b. Red Guards
- c. MET
- d. Production

3. A _____ represents the combinations of goods and services that a consumer can purchase given current prices and his income. Consumer theory uses the concepts of a _____ and a preference map to analyze consumer choices. Both concepts have a ready graphical representation in the two-good case.
- a. Revealed preference
- b. Joint demand
- c. Quality bias
- d. Budget constraint

4. _____ is the term denoting either an entrance or changes which are inserted into a system and which activate/modify a process. It is an abstract concept, used in the modeling, system(s) design and system(s) exploitation. It is usually connected with other terms, e.g., _____ field, _____ variable, _____ parameter, _____ value, _____ signal, _____ device and _____ file.
- a. AD-IA Model
- b. ACEA agreement
- c. ACCRA Cost of Living Index
- d. Input

5. In economics and finance, _____ is the change in total cost that arises when the quantity produced changes by one unit. It is the cost of producing one more unit of a good. Mathematically, the _____ function is expressed as the first derivative of the total cost (TC) function with respect to quantity (Q.)
- a. Variable cost
- b. Quality costs
- c. Khozraschyot
- d. Marginal cost

6. In economics, a _____ is a function that specifies the output of a firm, an industry, or an entire economy for all combinations of inputs. A meta-_____ compares the practice of the existing entities converting inputs X into output y to determine the most efficient practice _____ of the existing entities, whether the most efficient feasible practice production or the most efficient actual practice production. In either case, the maximum output of a technologically-determined production process is a mathematical function of input factors of production.
- a. Post-Fordism
- b. Short-run
- c. Constant elasticity of substitution
- d. Production function

7. _____, in economics, is the period of time required for economic agents to reallocate resources, and generally reestablish equilibrium.

The actual length of this period, usually numbered in years or decades, varies widely depending on circumstantial context. During the _____, all factors are variable.

a. Government surplus
b. Long term
c. Producer surplus
d. Temporary equilibrium method

8. In economics, the _____ or marginal physical product is the extra output produced by one more unit of an input (for instance, the difference in output when a firm's labour is increased from five to six units.) Assuming that no other inputs to production change, the _____ of a given input (X) can be expressed as:

_____ = ΔY/ΔX = (the change of Y)/(the change of X.)

- o
  - Pending approval by Thomas Sowell***

In neoclassical economics, this is the mathematical derivative of the production function.... Note that the 'product' (Y) is typically defined ignoring external costs and benefits.

a. Productive capacity
b. Factor prices
c. Labor problem
d. Marginal product

9. A _____ or labor union is an organization of workers who have banded together to achieve common goals in key areas and working conditions. The _____, through its leadership, bargains with the employer on behalf of union members (rank and file members) and negotiates labor contracts (Collective bargaining) with employers. This may include the negotiation of wages, work rules, complaint procedures, rules governing hiring, firing and promotion of workers, benefits, workplace safety and policies.

a. Guaranteed investment contracts
b. Consumer goods
c. Case-Shiller Home Price Indices
d. Trade union

10. In economics, _____ refers to the ability of a person or a country to produce a particular good at a lower marginal cost and opportunity cost than another person or country. It is the ability to produce a product most efficiently given all the other products that could be produced. It can be contrasted with absolute advantage which refers to the ability of a person or a country to produce a particular good at a lower absolute cost than another.

a. Gravity model of trade
b. Triffin dilemma
c. Hot money
d. Comparative advantage

11. In economics, _____ refers to how the marginal contribution of a factor of production usually decreases as more of the factor is used. According to this relationship, in a production system with fixed and variable inputs, beyond some point, each additional unit of the variable input yields smaller and smaller increases in output. Conversely, producing one more unit of output costs more and more in variable inputs.

a. Derivatives law
b. Patent troll
c. Diminishing returns
d. Community property

Chapter 6. Production

12. This concept is also known as the law of diminishing marginal returns, the _____, or the law of increasing opportunity cost.

The concept of diminishing returns can be traced back to the concerns of early economists such as Johann Heinrich von Thünen, Turgot, Thomas Malthus and David Ricardo.

Suppose that one kilogram of seed applied to a plot of land of a fixed size produces one ton of crop.

   a. Fair Labor Standards Act
   b. Bennett Amendment
   c. Lang Law
   d. Law of increasing relative cost

13. In microeconomics, _____ is the term used to refer to total when marginal cost is subtracted from marginal revenue. Under the marginal approach to profit maximization, to maximize profits, a firm should continue to produce a good until _____ is zero. Profit Maximization - The Marginal Approach.

   a. Holding period return
   b. Marginal profit
   c. Lehman scale
   d. Corporate synergy

14. In microeconomics, _____ is the extra revenue that an additional unit of product will bring. It is the additional income from selling one more unit of a good; sometimes equal to price. It can also be described as the change in total revenue/change in number of units sold.

   a. Long term
   b. Market demand schedule
   c. Reservation price
   d. Marginal revenue

15. The marginal revenue productivity theory of wages, also referred to as the _____ of labor, is the change in total revenue earned by a firm that results from employing one more unit of labor. It is a neoclassical model that determines, under some conditions, the optimal number of workers to employ at an exogenously determined market wage rate.

The _____ of a worker is equal to the product of the marginal product of labor (MP) and the marginal revenue (MR), given by MR×MP = _____.

   a. Marginal revenue productivity theory of wages
   b. Marginal revenue product
   c. Real prices and ideal prices
   d. Coal depletion

16. _____s is the social science that studies the production, distribution, and consumption of goods and services. The term _____s comes from the Ancient Greek oá¼°κονομῖα from oá¼¶κος (oikos, 'house') + vÏŒμος (nomos, 'custom' or 'law'), hence 'rules of the house(hold)'. Current _____ models developed out of the broader field of political economy in the late 19th century, owing to a desire to use an empirical approach more akin to the physical sciences.

   a. Inflation
   b. Economic
   c. Opportunity cost
   d. Energy economics

17. A _____ is a situation that involves losing one quality or aspect of something in return for gaining another quality or aspect. It implies a decision to be made with full comprehension of both the upside and downside of a particular choice.

In economics the term is expressed as opportunity cost, referring the most preferred alternative given up.

Chapter 6. Production

    a. Whitemail   b. Nonmarket
    c. Friedman-Savage utility function   d. Trade-off

18. In production, returns to scale refers to changes in output subsequent to a proportional change in all inputs (where all inputs increase by a constant factor.) If output increases by that same proportional change then there are _____ If output increases by less than that proportional change, there are decreasing returns to scale (DRS.)

    a. Consumer sovereignty   b. Constant returns to scale
    c. Long term   d. Lexicographic preferences

19. In calculus, a function f defined on a subset of the real numbers with real values is called _____, if for all x and y such that x >≤ y one has f(x) >≤ f(y), so f preserves the order. In layman's terms, the sign of the slope is always positive (the curve tending upwards) or zero (i.e., non-decreasing, or asymptotic, or depicted as a horizontal, flat line) Likewise, a function is called monotonically decreasing (non-increasing) if, whenever x >≤ y, then f(x) >≥ f(y), so it reverses the order.

    a. 100-year flood   b. Monotonic
    c. 1921 recession   d. 130-30 fund

20. In economics, _____ and economies of scale are related terms that describe what happens as the scale of production increases. They are different terms and should not be used interchangeably.

_____ refers to a technical property of production that examines changes in output subsequent to a proportional change in all inputs (where all inputs increase by a constant factor.)

    a. Constant returns to scale   b. Returns to scale
    c. Necessity good   d. Customer equity

21. Economics:

- _____ ,the desire to own something and the ability to pay for it
- _____ curve, a graphic representation of a _____ schedule
- _____ deposit, the money in checking accounts
- _____ pull theory, the theory that inflation occurs when _____ for goods and services exceeds existing supplies
- _____ schedule, a table that lists the quantity of a good a person will buy it each different price
- _____ side economics, the school of economics at believes government spending and tax cuts open economy by raising _____

    a. Variability   b. McKesson ' Robbins scandal
    c. Production   d. Demand

22. In economics, _____ is the percentage change of output (GDP or revenue for a single firm) divided by the percentage change of an input.

It is calculated as marginal product of an input to its average product. It is a local measure, defined at a point.

Chapter 6. Production

a. Eco commerce
b. Inventory turnover ratio
c. Accumulated other comprehensive income
d. Output elasticity

23. In economics, _____ is the ratio of the percent change in one variable to the percent change in another variable. It is a tool for measuring the responsiveness of a function to changes in parameters in a relative way. Commonly analyzed are _____ of substitution, price and wealth.

a. ACEA agreement
b. ACCRA Cost of Living Index
c. Elasticity of demand
d. Elasticity

24. To _____ is to impose a financial charge or other levy upon a taxpayer by a state or the functional equivalent of a state.

_____es are also imposed by many subnational entities. _____es consist of direct _____ or indirect _____, and may be paid in money or as its labour equivalent (often but not always unpaid.)

a. Tax
b. 1921 recession
c. 100-year flood
d. 130-30 fund

25. In economics, the _____ functional form of production functions is widely used to represent the relationship of an output to inputs. It was proposed by Knut Wicksell (1851-1926), and tested against statistical evidence by Charles Cobb and Paul Douglas in 1900-1928.

For production, the function is

$$Y = AL^{\alpha}K^{\beta},$$

where:

- Y = total production (the monetary value of all goods produced in a year)
- L = labor input
- K = capital input
- A = total factor productivity
- α and β are the output elasticities of labor and capital, respectively. These values are constants determined by available technology.

Output elasticity measures the responsiveness of output to a change in levels of either labor or capital used in production, ceteris paribus. For example if α = 0.15, a 1% increase in labor would lead to approximately a 0.15% increase in output.

a. Growth accounting
b. Social savings
c. Cobb-Douglas
d. Demand-pull theory

Chapter 6. Production

26. In economics, an _____ is a contour line drawn through the set of points at which the same quantity of output is produced while changing the quantities of two or more inputs. While an indifference curve helps to answer the utility-maximizing problem of consumers, the _____ deals with the cost-minimization problem of producers. _____s are typically drawn on capital-labor graphs, showing the tradeoff between capital and labor in the production function, and the decreasing marginal returns of both inputs.
    a. Underinvestment employment relationship
    b. Economic production quantity
    c. Economies of scale
    d. Isoquant

27. In economics, the _____ or the Technical Rate of Substitution (TRS) is the amount by which the quantity of one input has to be reduced ($-\Delta x_2$) when one extra unit of another input is used ($\Delta x_1 = 1$), so that output remains constant ($y = \bar{y}$.)

$$MRTS(x_1, x_2) = \frac{\Delta x_2}{\Delta x_1} = -\frac{MP_1}{MP_2}$$

where MP_1 and MP_2 are the marginal products of input 1 and input 2, respectively.

Along an isoquant, the MRTS shows the rate at which one input (e.g. capital or labor) may be substituted for another, while maintaining the same level of output.

    a. Household production function
    b. Pork cycle
    c. Producer surplus
    d. Marginal rate of technical substitution

28. In economics, game theory, and decision theory the _____ theorem or _____ hypothesis predicts that the 'betting preferences' of people with regard to uncertain outcomes (gambles) can be described by a mathematical relation which takes into account the size of a payout (whether in money or other goods), the probability of occurrence, risk aversion, and the different utility of the same payout to people with different assets or personal preferences. It is a more sophisticated theory than simply predicting that choices will be made based on expected value (which takes into account only the size of the payout and the probability of occurrence.)

Daniel Bernoulli described the complete theory in 1738.

    a. Utility
    b. Expected utility
    c. Ordinal utility
    d. Expected utility hypothesis

29. In economics, the _____ is the rate at which a consumer is ready to give up one good in exchange for another good while maintaining the same level of satisfaction.

Under the standard assumption of neoclassical economics that goods and services are continuously divisible, the marginal rates of substitution will be the same regardless of the direction of exchange, and will correspond to the slope of an indifference curve (more precisely, to the slope multiplied by -1) passing through the consumption bundle in question, at that point: mathematically, it is the implicit derivative. MRS of Y for X is the amount of Y for which a consumer is willing to exchange for X locally.

Chapter 6. Production

a. Quality bias
c. Supply and demand
b. Demand vacuum
d. Marginal rate of substitution

30. In economics, _____ is a measure of the relative satisfaction from consumption of various goods and services. Given this measure, one may speak meaningfully of increasing or decreasing _____, and thereby explain economic behavior in terms of attempts to increase one's _____. For illustrative purposes, changes in _____ are sometimes expressed in units called utils.

a. Expected utility hypothesis
c. Ordinal utility
b. Utility function
d. Utility

31. In economics an _____ line represents a combination of inputs which all cost the same amount. Although similar to the budget constraint in consumer theory, the use of the _____ pertains to cost-minimization in production, as opposed to utility-maximization. The typical _____ line represents the ratio of costs of labour and capital, so the formula is often written as:

$$rK + wL = C$$

Where w represents the wage of labour, and r represents the rental rate of capital.

a. Inventory analysis
c. Incentive
b. Epstein-Zin preferences
d. Isocost

32. The _____ consists of a number of economic theories which describe the nature of the firm, company including its existence, its behaviour, and its relationship with the market.

In simplified terms, the _____ aims to answer these questions:

1. Existence - why do firms emerge, why are not all transactions in the economy mediated over the market?
2. Boundaries - why the boundary between firms and the market is located exactly there? Which transactions are performed internally and which are negotiated on the market?
3. Organization - why are firms structured in such specific way? What is the interplay of formal and informal relationships?

Despite looking simple, these questions are not answered by the established economic theory, which usually views firms as given, and treats them as black boxes without any internal structure.

The First World War period saw a change of emphasis in economic theory away from industry-level analysis which mainly included analysing markets to analysis at the level of the firm, as it became increasingly clear that perfect competition was no longer an adequate model of how firms behaved. Economic theory till then had focussed on trying to understand markets alone and there had been little study on understanding why firms or organisations exist.

a. Khazzoom-Brookes postulate
c. Policy Ineffectiveness Proposition
b. Technology gap
d. Theory of the firm

Chapter 6. Production

33. In economics, the _____ of an industry is used as an indicator of the relative size of firms in relation to the industry as a whole. It is calculated as the sum of the percent market share of the top n industries. This may also assist in determining the market structure of the industry.
    a. Pacman conjecture
    b. Monopolization
    c. Quasi-rent
    d. Concentration ratio

34. _____ is a term used in game theory. A game is said to have _____ if all players know all moves that have taken place.

    Chess is an example of a game with _____ as each player can see all of the pieces on the board at all times.

    a. Game theory
    b. Parity game
    c. Perfect rationality
    d. Perfect information

35. A _____ is an expression that compares quantities relative to each other. The most common examples involve two quantities, but any number of quantities can be compared. _____s are represented mathematically by separating each quantity with a colon, for example the _____ 2:3, which is read as the _____ 'two to three'.
    a. 100-year flood
    b. 130-30 fund
    c. Ratio
    d. Y-intercept

36. In economics, _____ are business expenses that are not dependent on the activities of the business They tend to be time-related, such as salaries or rents being paid per month. This is in contrast to variable costs, which are volume-related (and are paid per quantity.)

    In management accounting, _____ are defined as expenses that do not change in proportion to the activity of a business, within the relevant period or scale of production.

    a. Quality costs
    b. Cost-Volume-Profit Analysis
    c. Cost of poor quality
    d. Fixed costs

37. _____ or cross section (of a study population) in statistics and econometrics is a type of one-dimensional data set. _____ refers to data collected by observing many subjects (such as individuals, firms or countries/regions) at the same point of time, or without regard to differences in time. Analysis of _____ usually consists of comparing the differences among the subjects.
    a. 100-year flood
    b. 1921 recession
    c. 130-30 fund
    d. Cross-sectional data

38. _____ are usually numerical time-series, i.e., sets of data (covering periods of time) for part or all of a single economy or the international economy. When they are time-series the data sets are usually monthly but can be quarterly and annual. The data may be adjusted in various ways (for ease of further analysis), most commonly adjusted or unadjusted for seasonal fluctuations.
    a. ACCRA Cost of Living Index
    b. ACEA agreement
    c. AD-IA Model
    d. Economic data

Chapter 6. Production

39. _____, in microeconomics, are the cost advantages that a business obtains due to expansion. They are factors that cause a producere;s average cost per unit to fall as scale is increased. _____ is a long run concept and refers to reductions in unit cost as the size of a facility, or scale, increases.
- a. Economic production quantity
- b. Isoquant
- c. Economies of scale
- d. Underinvestment employment relationship

40. In statistics, _____ refers to techniques for the modeling and analysis of numerical data consisting of values of a dependent variable and of one or more independent variables The dependent variable in the regression equation is modeled as a function of the independent variables, corresponding parameters, and an error term. The error term is treated as a random variable.
- a. 130-30 fund
- b. 1921 recession
- c. 100-year flood
- d. Regression analysis

Chapter 7. Cost Analysis

1. _____ is a process of attributing cost to particular cost centres. For example the wage of the driver of the purchasing department can be allocated to the purchasing department cost centre. It is not necessary to share the wage cost over several different cost centers.
   - a. Repugnancy costs
   - b. Marginal cost
   - c. Quality costs
   - d. Cost allocation

2. In economics and finance, _____ is the change in total cost that arises when the quantity produced changes by one unit. It is the cost of producing one more unit of a good. Mathematically, the _____ function is expressed as the first derivative of the total cost (TC) function with respect to quantity (Q.)
   - a. Quality costs
   - b. Variable cost
   - c. Khozraschyot
   - d. Marginal cost

3. A _____ is an object whose consumption increases the utility of the consumer, for which the quantity demanded exceeds the quantity supplied at zero price. _____s are usually modeled as having diminishing marginal utility. The first individual purchase has high utility; the second has less.
   - a. Good
   - b. Merit good
   - c. Pie method
   - d. Composite good

4. _____s is the social science that studies the production, distribution, and consumption of goods and services. The term _____s comes from the Ancient Greek οἰκονομία from οἶκος (oikos, 'house') + νόμος (nomos, 'custom' or 'law'), hence 'rules of the house(hold)'. Current _____ models developed out of the broader field of political economy in the late 19th century, owing to a desire to use an empirical approach more akin to the physical sciences.
   - a. Inflation
   - b. Energy economics
   - c. Opportunity cost
   - d. Economic

5. In economics, _____ is the difference between a company's total revenue and its opportunity costs. It is the increase in wealth that an investor has from making an investment, taking into consideration all costs associated with that investment including the opportunity cost of capital.

   Profit is the factor income of the entrepreneur.

   - a. Accounting profit
   - b. Operating profit
   - c. ACCRA Cost of Living Index
   - d. Economic profit

6. _____ or economic opportunity loss is the value of the next best alternative foregone as the result of making a decision. _____ analysis is an important part of a company's decision-making processes but is not treated as an actual cost in any financial statement. The next best thing that a person can engage in is referred to as the _____ of doing the best thing and ignoring the next best thing to be done.
   - a. Industrial organization
   - b. Economic
   - c. Opportunity cost
   - d. Economic ideology

7. _____s are expenses that change in proportion to the activity of a business. In other words, _____ is the sum of marginal costs. It can also be considered normal costs.
   - a. Cost allocation
   - b. Variable cost
   - c. Cost-Volume-Profit Analysis
   - d. Quality costs

Chapter 7. Cost Analysis

8. _____ is the difference between price and the costs of bringing to market whatever it is that is accounted as an enterprise (whether by harvest, extraction, manufacture, or purchase) in terms of the component costs of delivered goods and/or services and any operating or other expenses.

A key difficulty in measuring profit is in defining costs. Pure economic monetary profits can be zero or negative even in competitive equilibrium when accounted monetized costs exceed monetized price.

a. Operating profit
b. Economic profit
c. Accounting profit
d. ACCRA Cost of Living Index

9. In economics, _____ are business expenses that are not dependent on the activities of the business They tend to be time-related, such as salaries or rents being paid per month. This is in contrast to variable costs, which are volume-related (and are paid per quantity.)

In management accounting, _____ are defined as expenses that do not change in proportion to the activity of a business, within the relevant period or scale of production.

a. Cost of poor quality
b. Cost-Volume-Profit Analysis
c. Fixed costs
d. Quality costs

10. In economics and business decision-making, _____ are costs that cannot be recovered once they have been incurred. _____ are sometimes contrasted with variable costs, which are the costs that will change due to the proposed course of action, and prospective costs which are costs that will be incurred if an action is taken.

In traditional microeconomic theory, only variable costs are relevant to a decision.

a. Halo effect
b. Hyperbolic discounting
c. Post-purchase rationalization
d. Sunk costs

64   *Chapter 7. Cost Analysis*

11. A _____ is:

- Rewrite _____, in generative grammar and computer science
- Standardization, a formal and widely-accepted statement, fact, definition, or qualification
- Operation, a determinate _____ for performing a mathematical operation and obtaining a certain result (Mathematics, Logic)
    - Unary operation
    - Binary operation
- _____ of inference, a function from sets of formulae to formulae (Mathematics, Logic)
- _____ of thumb, principle with broad application that is not intended to be strictly accurate or reliable for every situation. Also often simply referred to as a _____
- Moral, an atomic element of a moral code for guiding choices in human behavior
- Heuristic, a quantized '_____' which shows a tendency or probability for successful function
- A regulation, as in sports
- A Production _____, as in computer science
- Procedural law, a _____ set governing the application of laws to cases
    - A law, which may informally be called a '_____'
    - A court ruling, a decision by a court
- In the U.S. Government, a regulation mandated by Congress, but written or expanded upon by the Executive Branch.
- Norm (sociology), an informal but widely accepted _____, concept, truth, definition, or qualification (social norms, legal norms, coding norms)
- Norm (philosophy), a kind of sentence or a reason to act, feel or believe
- 'Rulership' is the concept of governance by a government:
    - Military _____, governance by a military body
    - Monastic _____, a collection of precepts that guides the life of monks or nuns in a religious order where the superior holds the place of Christ
- Slide _____

- '_____,' a song by Ayumi Hamasaki
- '_____,' a song by rapper Nas
- '_____s,' an album by the band The Whitest Boy Alive
- _____s: Pyaar Ka Superhit Formula, a 2003 Bollywood film
- ruler, an instrument for measuring lengths
- _____, a component of an astrolabe, circumferator or similar instrument
- The _____s, a bestselling self-help book
- _____ Project (Run Up-to-date Linux Everywhere), a project that aims to use up-to-date Linux software on old PCs
- _____ engine, a software system that helps managing business _____s
- Ja _____, a hip hop artist
    - R.U.L.E., a 2005 greatest hits album by rapper Ja _____
- '_____s,' a KMFDM song

a. Procter ' Gamble   b. Rule
c. Technocracy   d. Demand

Chapter 7. Cost Analysis

12. The _____ is a federally owned corporation in the United States created by congressional charter in May 1933 to provide navigation, flood control, electricity generation, fertilizer manufacturing, and economic development in the Tennessee Valley, a region particularly impacted by the Great Depression. The _____ was envisioned not only as an electricity provider, but also as a regional economic development agency that would use federal experts and electricity to rapidly modernize the region's economy and society.

The _____'s jurisdiction covers most of Tennessee, parts of Alabama, Mississippi, and Kentucky, and small slices of Georgia, North Carolina, and Virginia.

   a. Tennessee Valley Authority
   c. 100-year flood
   b. 1921 recession
   d. 130-30 fund

13. In economics, and cost accounting, _____ describes the total economic cost of production and is made up of variable costs, which vary according to the quantity of a good produced and include inputs such as labor and raw materials, plus fixed costs, which are independent of the quantity of a good produced and include inputs (capital) that cannot be varied in the short term, such as buildings and machinery. _____ in economics includes the total opportunity cost of each factor of production in addition to fixed and variable costs.

The rate at which _____ changes as the amount produced changes is called marginal cost.

   a. 100-year flood
   c. 130-30 fund
   b. 1921 recession
   d. Total cost

14. _____, in economics, is the period of time required for economic agents to reallocate resources, and generally reestablish equilibrium.

The actual length of this period, usually numbered in years or decades, varies widely depending on circumstantial context. During the _____, all factors are variable.

   a. Temporary equilibrium method
   c. Government surplus
   b. Producer surplus
   d. Long term

15. In microeconomics, _____ is quite simply the conversion of inputs into outputs. It is an economic process that uses resources to create a good or service that is suitable for exchange. This can include manufacturing, storing, shipping, and packaging.
   a. Production
   c. Red Guards
   b. MET
   d. Solved

16. In economics, _____ is equal to total cost divided by the number of goods produced (the output quantity, Q.) It is also equal to the sum of average variable costs (total variable costs divided by Q) plus average fixed costs (total fixed costs divided by Q.) _____s may be dependent on the time period considered (increasing production may be expensive or impossible in the short term, for example.)
   a. Average variable cost
   c. Explicit cost
   b. Average fixed cost
   d. Average cost

Chapter 7. Cost Analysis

17. _____ is an economics term to describe a firms variable costs (labor, electricity, etc.) divided by the quantity (Q) of total units of output.

$$AVC = \frac{TVC}{Q}$$

Where:

- TVC = Total Variable Cost
- _____ = Average variable cost
- Q = Quantity of Units Produced

_____ plus average fixed cost equals average total cost:

_____ + AFC = ATC.

a. Explicit cost
c. Inventory valuation
b. Average fixed cost
d. Average variable cost

18. In economics, the concept of the _____ refers to the decision-making time frame of a firm in which at least one factor of production is fixed. Costs which are fixed in the _____ have no impact on a firms decisions. For example a firm can raise output by increasing the amount of labour through overtime.
a. Hicks-neutral technical change
c. Product Pipeline
b. Productivity model
d. Short-run

19. This concept is also known as the law of diminishing marginal returns, the _____, or the law of increasing opportunity cost.

The concept of diminishing returns can be traced back to the concerns of early economists such as Johann Heinrich von Thünen, Turgot, Thomas Malthus and David Ricardo.

Suppose that one kilogram of seed applied to a plot of land of a fixed size produces one ton of crop.

a. Bennett Amendment
c. Fair Labor Standards Act
b. Lang Law
d. Law of increasing relative cost

20. In economics, the _____ or marginal physical product is the extra output produced by one more unit of an input (for instance, the difference in output when a firm's labour is increased from five to six units.) Assuming that no other inputs to production change, the _____ of a given input (X) can be expressed as:

Chapter 7. Cost Analysis

_____ = ΔY/ΔX = (the change of Y)/(the change of X.)

-
  - o
    - Pending approval by Thomas Sowell***

In neoclassical economics, this is the mathematical derivative of the production function.... Note that the 'product' (Y) is typically defined ignoring external costs and benefits.

a. Marginal product
c. Factor prices
b. Productive capacity
d. Labor problem

21. In economics, _____ refers to how the marginal contribution of a factor of production usually decreases as more of the factor is used. According to this relationship, in a production system with fixed and variable inputs, beyond some point, each additional unit of the variable input yields smaller and smaller increases in output. Conversely, producing one more unit of output costs more and more in variable inputs.

a. Patent troll
c. Community property
b. Derivatives law
d. Diminishing returns

22. _____ is an economics term used to describe the total fixed costs (TFC) divided by the quantity (Q) of units produced.

$$AFC = \frac{TFC}{Q}$$

_____ is a per-unit measure of fixed costs. As the total number of goods produced increases, the _____ decreases because the same amount of fixed costs are being spread over a larger number of units.

a. Average variable cost
c. Average fixed cost
b. Explicit cost
d. Inventory valuation

23. In calculus, a function f defined on a subset of the real numbers with real values is called _____, if for all x and y such that x >≤ y one has f(x) >≤ f(y), so f preserves the order. In layman's terms, the sign of the slope is always positive (the curve tending upwards) or zero (i.e., non-decreasing, or asymptotic, or depicted as a horizontal, flat line) Likewise, a function is called monotonically decreasing (non-increasing) if, whenever x >≤ y, then f(x) >≥ f(y), so it reverses the order.

a. Monotonic
c. 100-year flood
b. 1921 recession
d. 130-30 fund

24. In economic models, the _____ time frame assumes no fixed factors of production. Firms can enter or leave the marketplace, and the cost (and availability) of land, labor, raw materials, and capital goods can be assumed to vary. In contrast, in the short-run time frame, certain factors are assumed to be fixed, because there is not sufficient time for them to change.

a. Long-run
b. Diseconomies of scale
c. Price/performance ratio
d. Productivity world

25. In economics, _____ and economies of scale are related terms that describe what happens as the scale of production increases. They are different terms and should not be used interchangeably.

_____ refers to a technical property of production that examines changes in output subsequent to a proportional change in all inputs (where all inputs increase by a constant factor.)

a. Customer equity
b. Returns to scale
c. Constant returns to scale
d. Necessity good

26. In economics, _____ refers to the ability of a person or a country to produce a particular good at a lower marginal cost and opportunity cost than another person or country. It is the ability to produce a product most efficiently given all the other products that could be produced. It can be contrasted with absolute advantage which refers to the ability of a person or a country to produce a particular good at a lower absolute cost than another.

a. Triffin dilemma
b. Comparative advantage
c. Hot money
d. Gravity model of trade

27.

_____ is, in very basic words, a position a firm occupies against its competitors.

According to Michael Porter, the three methods for creating a sustainable _____ are through:

1. Cost leadership - Cost advantage occurs when a firm delivers the same services as its competitors but at a lower cost;

2. Differentiation - Differentiation advantage occurs when a firm delivers greater services for the same price of its competitors. They are collectively known as positional advantages because they denote the firm's position in its industry as a leader in either superior services or cost;

3. Focus (economics) - A focused approach requires the firm to concentrate on a narrow, exclusive competitive segment (market niche), hoping to achieve a local rather than industry wide _____. There are cost focus seekers, who aim to obtain a local cost advantage over competition and differentiation focuser, who are looking for a local difference.

a. Six Forces Model
b. Chaos theory in organizational development
c. National Diamond
d. Competitive advantage

28. _____ is exchange of capital, goods, and services across international borders or territories. In most countries, it represents a significant share of gross domestic product (GDP.) While _____ has been present throughout much of history, its economic, social, and political importance has been on the rise in recent centuries.

Chapter 7. Cost Analysis

a. Intra-industry trade
c. Incoterms
b. Import license
d. International trade

29. A _____ or labor union is an organization of workers who have banded together to achieve common goals in key areas and working conditions. The _____, through its leadership, bargains with the employer on behalf of union members (rank and file members) and negotiates labor contracts (Collective bargaining) with employers. This may include the negotiation of wages, work rules, complaint procedures, rules governing hiring, firing and promotion of workers, benefits, workplace safety and policies.
   a. Guaranteed investment contracts
   c. Trade union
   b. Case-Shiller Home Price Indices
   d. Consumer goods

30. In finance, the _____s between two currencies specifies how much one currency is worth in terms of the other. It is the value of a foreign natione;s currency in terms of the home natione;s currency. For example an _____ of 102 Japanese yen to the United States dollar means that JPY 102 is worth the same as USD 1.
   a. ACCRA Cost of Living Index
   c. ACEA agreement
   b. Interbank market
   d. Exchange rate

31. In production, returns to scale refers to changes in output subsequent to a proportional change in all inputs (where all inputs increase by a constant factor.) If output increases by that same proportional change then there are _____ If output increases by less than that proportional change, there are decreasing returns to scale (DRS.)
   a. Long term
   c. Consumer sovereignty
   b. Lexicographic preferences
   d. Constant returns to scale

32. _____, in microeconomics, are the cost advantages that a business obtains due to expansion. They are factors that cause a producere;s average cost per unit to fall as scale is increased. _____ is a long run concept and refers to reductions in unit cost as the size of a facility, or scale, increases.
   a. Economic production quantity
   c. Isoquant
   b. Underinvestment employment relationship
   d. Economies of scale

33. _____ is the production of large amounts of standardized products, including and especially on assembly lines. The concepts of _____ are applied to various kinds of products, from fluids and particulates handled in bulk to discrete solid parts to assemblies of such parts

_____ of assemblies typically uses electric-motor-powered moving tracks or conveyor belts to move partially complete products to workers, who perform simple repetitive tasks.

   a. Mass production
   c. 1921 recession
   b. 100-year flood
   d. 130-30 fund

34. _____ or cross section (of a study population) in statistics and econometrics is a type of one-dimensional data set. _____ refers to data collected by observing many subjects (such as individuals, firms or countries/regions) at the same point of time, or without regard to differences in time. Analysis of _____ usually consists of comparing the differences among the subjects.
   a. 100-year flood
   c. 1921 recession
   b. 130-30 fund
   d. Cross-sectional data

Chapter 7. Cost Analysis

35. The terms 'dependent variable' and '_____' are used in similar but subtly different ways in mathematics and statistics as part of the standard terminology in those subjects. They are used to distinguish between two types of quantities being considered, separating them into those available at the start of a process and those being created by it, where the latter (dependent variables) are dependent on the former (_____s.)

The _____ is typically the variable being manipulated or changed and the dependent variable is the observed result of the _____ being manipulated.

  a. Independent variable
  b. ACEA agreement
  c. ACCRA Cost of Living Index
  d. AD-IA Model

36. In economics, a _____ occurs when, due to the economies of scale of a particular industry, the maximum efficiency of production and distribution is realized through a single supplier.

Natural monopolies arise where the largest supplier in an industry, often the first supplier in a market, has an overwhelming cost advantage over other actual or potential competitors. This tends to be the case in industries where capital costs predominate, creating economies of scale which are large in relation to the size of the market, and hence high barriers to entry; examples include water services and electricity.

  a. Collective goods
  b. Privatizing profits and socializing losses
  c. Common-pool resource
  d. Natural monopoly

37. In statistics, _____ refers to techniques for the modeling and analysis of numerical data consisting of values of a dependent variable and of one or more independent variables The dependent variable in the regression equation is modeled as a function of the independent variables, corresponding parameters, and an error term. The error term is treated as a random variable.
  a. 100-year flood
  b. 1921 recession
  c. 130-30 fund
  d. Regression analysis

38. In economics, a _____ is a graph of the costs of production as a function of total quantity produced. In a free market economy, productively efficient firms use these curves to find the optimal point of production, where they make the most profits. There are a few different types of _____s, each relevant to a different area of economics.
  a. Phillips curve
  b. Kuznets curve
  c. Demand curve
  d. Cost curve

39. In economics, _____ is the ratio of the percent change in one variable to the percent change in another variable. It is a tool for measuring the responsiveness of a function to changes in parameters in a relative way. Commonly analyzed are _____ of substitution, price and wealth.
  a. Elasticity of demand
  b. ACCRA Cost of Living Index
  c. ACEA agreement
  d. Elasticity

40. In economics, a _____ exists when a specific individual or enterprise has sufficient control over a particular product or service to determine significantly the terms on which other individuals shall have access to it. Monopolies are thus characterized by a lack of economic competition for the good or service that they provide and a lack of viable substitute goods. The verb 'monopolize' refers to the process by which a firm gains persistently greater market share than what is expected under perfect competition.

a. Monopoly
b. 130-30 fund
c. 100-year flood
d. 1921 recession

41. The _____ consists of a number of economic theories which describe the nature of the firm, company including its existence, its behaviour, and its relationship with the market.

In simplified terms, the _____ aims to answer these questions:

1. Existence - why do firms emerge, why are not all transactions in the economy mediated over the market?
2. Boundaries - why the boundary between firms and the market is located exactly there? Which transactions are performed internally and which are negotiated on the market?
3. Organization - why are firms structured in such specific way? What is the interplay of formal and informal relationships?

Despite looking simple, these questions are not answered by the established economic theory, which usually views firms as given, and treats them as black boxes without any internal structure.

The First World War period saw a change of emphasis in economic theory away from industry-level analysis which mainly included analysing markets to analysis at the level of the firm, as it became increasingly clear that perfect competition was no longer an adequate model of how firms behaved. Economic theory till then had focussed on trying to understand markets alone and there had been little study on understanding why firms or organisations exist.

a. Policy Ineffectiveness Proposition
b. Technology gap
c. Khazzoom-Brookes postulate
d. Theory of the firm

42. In economics, an _____ is a way of representing various distributions of resources. Edgeworth made his presentation in his famous book, Mathematical Psychics: An essay on the application of mathematics to the moral sciences, 1881. Edgeworth's original two axis depiction was developed into the now familiar box diagram by Pareto in 1906 and was popularized in a later exposition by Bowley.

a. International Social Security Association
b. Equivalent variation
c. ACCRA Cost of Living Index
d. Edgeworth box

43. _____ are conceptually similar to economies of scale. Whereas economies of scale primarily refer to efficiencies associated with supply-side changes, such as increasing or decreasing the scale of production, of a single product type, _____ refer to efficiencies primarily associated with demand-side changes, such as increasing or decreasing the scope of marketing and distribution, of different types of products. _____ are one of the main reasons for such marketing strategies as product bundling, product lining, and family branding.

a. Economies of scale
b. Isoquant
c. Economic production quantity
d. Economies of scope

Chapter 7. Cost Analysis

44. Procter is a surname, and may also refer to:

- Bryan Waller Procter (pseud. Barry Cornwall), English poet
- Goodwin Procter, American law firm
- _____, consumer products multinational

a. Tightness
c. Procter ' Gamble
b. Bucket shop
d. Drawdown

45. _____ is a branch of applied mathematics that is used in the social sciences (most notably economics), biology, engineering, political science, international relations, computer science, and philosophy. _____ attempts to mathematically capture behavior in strategic situations, in which an individual's success in making choices depends on the choices of others. While initially developed to analyze competitions in which one individual does better at another's expense (zero sum games), it has been expanded to treat a wide class of interactions, which are classified according to several criteria.

a. Discriminatory price auction
c. Dollar auction
b. Game theory
d. Proper equilibrium

46. An _____ is a manufacturing process in which parts (usually interchangeable parts) are added to a product in a sequential manner using optimally planned logistics to create a finished product much faster than with handcrafting-type methods. The _____ developed by Ford Motor Company between 1908 and 1915 made _____s famous in the following decade through the social ramifications of mass production, such as the affordability of the Ford Model T and the introduction of high wages for Ford workers. However, the various preconditions for the development at Ford stretched far back into the 19th century, from the gradual realization of the dream of interchangeability, to the concept of reinventing workflow and job descriptions using analytical methods.

a. ACCRA Cost of Living Index
c. AD-IA Model
b. ACEA agreement
d. Assembly line

47. The _____ or gross domestic income (GDI), a basic measure of an economy's economic performance, is the market value of all final goods and services produced within the borders of a nation in a year. _____ can be defined in three ways, all of which are conceptually identical. First, it is equal to the total expenditures for all final goods and services produced within the country in a stipulated period of time (usually a 365-day year.)

a. Market structure
c. Countercyclical
b. Monopolistic competition
d. Gross domestic product

48. _____ or the economics of information is a branch of microeconomic theory that studies how information affects an economy and economic decisions. Information has special characteristics. It is easy to create but hard to trust.

a. ACEA agreement
c. Information economics
b. ACCRA Cost of Living Index
d. AD-IA Model

49. _____ in economics and business is the result of an exchange and from that trade we assign a numerical monetary value to a good, service or asset. If Alice trades Bob 4 apples for an orange, the _____ of an orange is 4 apples. Inversely, the _____ of an apple is 1/4 oranges.

Chapter 7. Cost Analysis

a. Price book
b. Premium pricing
c. Price war
d. Price

50. _____ is a term used in business to indicate a state of intense competitive rivalry accompanied by a multi-lateral series of price reduction. One competitor will lower its price, then others will lower their prices to match. If one of them reduces their price again, a new round of reductions starts.

a. Price war
b. Discounts and allowances
c. Transactional Net Margin Method
d. Big ticket item

51. In economics, the _____ functional form of production functions is widely used to represent the relationship of an output to inputs. It was proposed by Knut Wicksell (1851-1926), and tested against statistical evidence by Charles Cobb and Paul Douglas in 1900-1928.

For production, the function is

$$Y = AL^{\alpha}K^{\beta},$$

where:

- Y = total production (the monetary value of all goods produced in a year)
- L = labor input
- K = capital input
- A = total factor productivity
- α and β are the output elasticities of labor and capital, respectively. These values are constants determined by available technology.

Output elasticity measures the responsiveness of output to a change in levels of either labor or capital used in production, ceteris paribus. For example if α = 0.15, a 1% increase in labor would lead to approximately a 0.15% increase in output.

a. Growth accounting
b. Demand-pull theory
c. Cobb-Douglas
d. Social savings

52. Economics:

- _____, the desire to own something and the ability to pay for it
- _____ curve, a graphic representation of a _____ schedule
- _____ deposit, the money in checking accounts
- _____ pull theory, the theory that inflation occurs when _____ for goods and services exceeds existing supplies
- _____ schedule, a table that lists the quantity of a good a person will buy it each different price
- _____ side economics, the school of economics at believes government spending and tax cuts open economy by raising _____

Chapter 7. Cost Analysis

a. McKesson ' Robbins scandal
b. Variability
c. Production
d. Demand

53. In economics, _____ is the process by which a firm determines the price and output level that returns the greatest profit. There are several approaches to this problem. The total revenue--total cost method relies on the fact that profit equals revenue minus cost, and the marginal revenue--marginal cost method is based on the fact that total profit in a perfectly competitive market reaches its maximum point where marginal revenue equals marginal cost.

a. Normal profit
b. 100-year flood
c. Profit maximization
d. Profit margin

54. A _____ is a counterfeit agreement among industries. It is an informal organization of producers that agree to coordinate prices and production. _____s usually occur in an oligopolistic industry, where there is a small number of sellers and usually involve homogeneous products.

a. Cartel
b. Shill
c. 100-year flood
d. Shanzhai

55. _____ is the transition of a national economy from monopoly control by groups of large businesses to a free market economy. This change rarely arises naturally, and is generally the result of regulation by a governing body.

A modern example of _____ is the economic restructuring of Germany after the fall of the Third Reich in 1945.

a. Complementary monopoly
b. Market power
c. Monopolization
d. Decartelization

56. An _____ is a decision such that no other available decision options will lead to a better outcome. It is an important concept in decision theory. In order to compare the different decision outcomes, one commonly assigns a relative utility to each of them.

a. Optimal decision
b. Influence diagram
c. Expected value of sample information
d. Intertemporal choice

57. _____ or amortisation is the process of increasing an amount over a period of time. The word comes from Middle English amortisen to kill, alienate in mortmain, from Anglo-French amorteser, alteration of amortir, from Vulgar Latin admortire to kill, from Latin ad- + mort-, mors death. Particular instances of the term include:

- _____, the allocation of a lump sum amount to different time periods, particularly for loans and other forms of finance, including related interest or other finance charges.
    - _____ schedule, a table detailing each periodic payment on a loan (typically a mortgage), as generated by an _____ calculator.
    - Negative _____, an _____ schedule where the loan amount actually increases through not paying the full interest
- Amortized analysis, analyzing the execution cost of algorithms over a sequence of operations.
- _____ of capital expenditures of certain assets under accounting rules, particularly intangible assets, in a manner analogous to depreciation.
- _____ (tax law)

Chapter 7. Cost Analysis

_____ is also used in the context of zoning regulations and describes the time in which a property owner has to relocate when the property's use constitutes a preexisting nonconforming use under zoning regulations.

a. Economic miracle
b. Amortization
c. Augmentation
d. Oslo Agreements

58. In management accounting, _____ establishes budget and actual cost of operations, processes, departments or product and the analysis of variances, profitability or social use of funds. Managers use _____ to support decision-making to cut a company's costs and improve profitability. As a form of management accounting, _____ need not follow standards such as GAAP, because its primary use is for internal managers, rather than outside users, and what to compute is instead decided pragmatically.

a. Quality costs
b. Khozraschyot
c. Total absorption costing
d. Cost accounting

59. The phrase _____ and acquisitions refers to the aspect of corporate strategy, corporate finance and management dealing with the buying, selling and combining of different companies that can aid, finance, or help a growing company in a given industry grow rapidly without having to create another business entity.

An acquisition, also known as a takeover or a buyout, is the buying of one company (the 'target') by another. An acquisition may be friendly or hostile.

a. Peace dividend
b. Mergers
c. Differential accumulation
d. Political economy

60. The phrase _____ refers to the aspect of corporate strategy, corporate finance and management dealing with the buying, selling and combining of different companies that can aid, finance, or help a growing company in a given industry grow rapidly without having to create another business entity.

An acquisition, also known as a takeover or a buyout, is the buying of one company (the 'target') by another. An acquisition may be friendly or hostile.

a. Peace dividend
b. Productive and unproductive labour
c. Mergers and acquisitions
d. Political economy

61. _____ refers to the pricing of contributions (assets, tangible and intangible, services, and funds) transferred within an organization. For example, goods from the production division may be sold to the marketing division, or goods from a parent company may be sold to a foreign subsidiary. Since the prices are set within an organization (i.e. controlled), the typical market mechanisms that establish prices for such transactions between third parties may not apply.

a. Transfer pricing
b. Rational pricing
c. Two-part tariff
d. San Francisco congestion pricing

62. _____ is one of the four Ps of the marketing mix. The other three aspects are product, promotion, and place. It is also a key variable in microeconomic price allocation theory.

a. Premium pricing
b. Point of total assumption
c. Guaranteed Maximum Price
d. Pricing

Chapter 8. Decision Making under Uncertainty

1. In economics, a _____ is a general slowdown in economic activity over a sustained period of time, or a business cycle contraction. During _____s, many macroeconomic indicators vary in a similar way. Production as measured by Gross Domestic Product (GDP), employment, investment spending, capacity utilization, household incomes and business profits all fall during _____s.
   - a. Monetary economics
   - b. Leading indicators
   - c. Treasury View
   - d. Recession

2. _____ is a branch of economics that deals with the performance, structure, and behavior of a national or regional economy as a whole. Along with microeconomics, _____ is one of the two most general fields in economics. It is the study of the behavior and decision-making of entire economies.
   - a. Tobit model
   - b. Macroeconomics
   - c. Nominal value
   - d. New Trade Theory

3. In economic models, the _____ time frame assumes no fixed factors of production. Firms can enter or leave the marketplace, and the cost (and availability) of land, labor, raw materials, and capital goods can be assumed to vary. In contrast, in the short-run time frame, certain factors are assumed to be fixed, because there is not sufficient time for them to change.
   - a. Long-run
   - b. Price/performance ratio
   - c. Diseconomies of scale
   - d. Productivity world

4. A _____ is a set of exclusive rights granted by a state to an inventor or his assignee for a limited period of time in exchange for a disclosure of an invention.

   The procedure for granting _____s, the requirements placed on the _____ee and the extent of the exclusive rights vary widely between countries according to national laws and international agreements. Typically, however, a _____ application must include one or more claims defining the invention which must be new, inventive, and useful or industrially applicable.
   - a. Bank regulation
   - b. Long service leave
   - c. Bona fide occupational qualification
   - d. Patent

5. _____ is a term used in game theory. A game is said to have _____ if all players know all moves that have taken place.

   Chess is an example of a game with _____ as each player can see all of the pieces on the board at all times.
   - a. Perfect information
   - b. Game theory
   - c. Perfect rationality
   - d. Parity game

6. _____ in economics and business is the result of an exchange and from that trade we assign a numerical monetary value to a good, service or asset. If Alice trades Bob 4 apples for an orange, the _____ of an orange is 4 apples. Inversely, the _____ of an apple is 1/4 oranges.
   - a. Price book
   - b. Price war
   - c. Premium pricing
   - d. Price

Chapter 8. Decision Making under Uncertainty

7. _____ is a way of expressing knowledge or belief that an event will occur or has occurred. In mathematics the concept has been given an exact meaning in _____ theory, that is used extensively in such areas of study as mathematics, statistics, finance, gambling, science, and philosophy to draw conclusions about the likelihood of potential events and the underlying mechanics of complex systems.

The word _____ does not have a consistent direct definition.

a. Probability
b. 100-year flood
c. 1921 recession
d. 130-30 fund

8. In statistics the _____ of an event i is the number n_i of times the event occurred in the experiment or the study. These frequencies are often graphically represented in histograms.

We speak of absolute frequencies, when the counts n_i themselves are given and of (relative) frequencies, when those are normalized by the total number of events:

$$f_i = \frac{n_i}{N} = \frac{n_i}{\sum_i n_i}.$$

Taking the f_i for all i and tabulating or plotting them leads to a _____ distribution.

a. 130-30 fund
b. 1921 recession
c. 100-year flood
d. Frequency

9. In probability theory and statistics, the _____ (or expectation value or mean and for continuous random variables with a density function it is the probability density -weighted integral of the possible values.

The term '_____' can be misleading.

a. ACCRA Cost of Living Index
b. AD-IA Model
c. ACEA agreement
d. Expected value

10. In probability theory and statistics, a _____ identifies either the probability of each value of an unidentified random variable (when the variable is discrete), or the probability of the value falling within a particular interval (when the variable is continuous.) The _____ describes the range of possible values that a random variable can attain and the probability that the value of the random variable is within any (measurable) subset of that range. The Normal distribution, often called the 'bell curve'

When the random variable takes values in the set of real numbers, the _____ is completely described by the cumulative distribution function, whose value at each real x is the probability that the random variable is smaller than or equal to x.

a. 1921 recession
b. 130-30 fund
c. 100-year flood
d. Probability distribution

Chapter 8. Decision Making under Uncertainty

11. _____ is the a method of technical and economic research of the systems for purpose to optimize a parity between system's consumer functions or properties and expenses to achieve those functions or properties.

This methodology for continuous perfection of production, industrial technologies, organizational structures was developed by Juryj Sobolev in 1948 at the 'Perm telephone factory'

- 1948 Juryj Sobolev - the first success in application of a method analysis at the 'Perm telephone factory'.
- 1949 - the first application for the invention as result of use of the new method.

Today in economically developed countries practically each enterprise or the company use methodology of the kind of functional-cost analysis as a practice of the quality management, most full satisfying to principles of standards of series ISO 9000.

- Interest of consumer not in products itself, but the advantage which it will receive from its usage.
- The consumer aspires to reduce his expenses
- Functions needed by consumer can be executed in the various ways, and, hence, with various efficiency and expenses. Among possible alternatives of realization of functions exist such in which the parity of quality and the price is the optimal for the consumer.

The goal of _____ is achievement of the highest consumer satisfaction of production at simultaneous decrease in all kinds of industrial expenses Classical _____ has three English synonyms - Value Engineering, Value Management, Value Analysis.

a. Function cost analysis
b. Willingness to pay
c. Staple financing
d. Monopoly wage

12. The _____ is a theorem in probability that describes the long-term stability of the mean of a random variable. Given a random variable with a finite expected value, if its values are repeatedly sampled, as the number of these observations increases, the sample mean will tend to approach and stay close to the expected value (the average for the population.)

The LLN can easily be illustrated using the rolls of a die.

a. 130-30 fund
b. 1921 recession
c. 100-year flood
d. Law of large numbers

13. In probability theory and statistics, _____ is a measure of the variability or dispersion of a population, a data set, or a probability distribution. A low _____ indicates that the data points tend to be very close to the same value (the mean), while high _____ indicates that the data are 'spread out' over a large range of values.

For example, the average height for adult men in the United States is about 70 inches, with a _____ of around 3 inches.

Chapter 8. Decision Making under Uncertainty

   a. 100-year flood
   b. 130-30 fund
   c. Standard deviation
   d. 1921 recession

14. _____ is a term used to collectively describe topics relating to the operations of firms with interests in multiple countries. Such firms are sometimes called multinational corporations . Well known MNCs include fast food companies McDonald's and Yum Brands, vehicle manufacturers such as General Motors and Toyota, consumer electronics companies like Samsung, LG and Sony, and energy companies such as ExxonMobil and BP.
   a. AD-IA Model
   b. International business
   c. ACCRA Cost of Living Index
   d. ACEA agreement

15. In finance, the _____s between two currencies specifies how much one currency is worth in terms of the other. It is the value of a foreign natione;s currency in terms of the home natione;s currency. For example an _____ of 102 Japanese yen to the United States dollar means that JPY 102 is worth the same as USD 1.
   a. ACEA agreement
   b. Interbank market
   c. ACCRA Cost of Living Index
   d. Exchange rate

16. In economics, _____ are business expenses that are not dependent on the activities of the business They tend to be time-related, such as salaries or rents being paid per month. This is in contrast to variable costs, which are volume-related (and are paid per quantity.)

In management accounting, _____ are defined as expenses that do not change in proportion to the activity of a business, within the relevant period or scale of production.

   a. Fixed costs
   b. Cost-Volume-Profit Analysis
   c. Cost of poor quality
   d. Quality costs

17. _____ is a type of risk faced by investors, corporations, and governments. It is a risk that can be understood and managed with proper aforethought and investment.

Broadly, _____ refers to the complications businesses and governments may face as a result of what are commonly referred to as political decisions--or e;any political change that alters the expected outcome and value of a given economic action by changing the probability of achieving business objectives.e; .

   a. Capital adequacy ratio
   b. Black-Derman-Toy model
   c. Pull to par
   d. Political risk

18. Procter is a surname, and may also refer to:

   - Bryan Waller Procter (pseud. Barry Cornwall), English poet
   - Goodwin Procter, American law firm
   - _____, consumer products multinational

   a. Drawdown
   b. Bucket shop
   c. Tightness
   d. Procter ' Gamble

Chapter 8. Decision Making under Uncertainty

19. The phrase _____, according to the Organization for Economic Co-operation and Development, refers to 'creative work undertaken on a systematic basis in order to increase the stock of knowledge, including knowledge of man, culture and society, and the use of this stock of knowledge to devise new applications [sic]'

New product design and development is more than often a crucial factor in the survival of a company. In an industry that is fast changing, firms must continually revise their design and range of products. This is necessary due to continuous technology change and development as well as other competitors and the changing preference of customers.

   a. Research and development
   b. 100-year flood
   c. 1921 recession
   d. 130-30 fund

20. _____ is a concept in economics, finance, and psychology related to the behaviour of consumers and investors under uncertainty. _____ is the reluctance of a person to accept a bargain with an uncertain payoff rather than another bargain with a more certain, but possibly lower, expected payoff. For example, a risk-averse investor might choose to put his or her money into a bank account with a low but guaranteed interest rate, rather than into a stock that is likely to have high returns, but also has a chance of becoming worthless.

   a. Risk theory
   b. Reinsurance
   c. Compound annual growth rate
   d. Risk aversion

21. In economics, _____ behavior is in between risk aversion and risk seeking. If offered either â,¬50 or a 50% chance of â,¬100, a risk averse person will take the â,¬50, a risk seeking person will take the 50% chance of â,¬100, and a _____ person would have no preference between the two options.

In finance, when pricing an asset, a common technique is to figure out the probability of a future cash flow, then to discount that cash flow at the risk free rate.

   a. Risk neutral
   b. Transaction risk
   c. Currency risk
   d. Taleb distribution

22. Economics:

   - _____ ,the desire to own something and the ability to pay for it
   - _____ curve,a graphic representation of a _____ schedule
   - _____ deposit, the money in checking accounts
   - _____ pull theory,the theory that inflation occurs when _____ for goods and services exceeds existing supplies
   - _____ schedule,a table that lists the quantity of a good a person will buy it each different price
   - _____ side economics,the school of economics at believes government spending and tax cuts open economy by raising _____

   a. Variability
   b. Production
   c. Demand
   d. McKesson ' Robbins scandal

Chapter 8. Decision Making under Uncertainty

23. _____, in law and economics, is a form of risk management primarily used to hedge against the risk of a contingent loss. _____ is defined as the equitable transfer of the risk of a loss, from one entity to another, in exchange for a premium, and can be thought of as a guaranteed small loss to prevent a large, possibly devastating loss. An insurer is a company selling the _____; an insured or policyholder is the person or entity buying the _____.
   - a. ACEA agreement
   - b. ACCRA Cost of Living Index
   - c. AD-IA Model
   - d. Insurance

24. Discounting is a financial mechanism in which a debtor obtains the right to delay payments to a creditor, for a defined period of time, in exchange for a charge or fee. Essentially, the party that owes money in the present purchases the right to delay the payment until some future date. The _____, or charge, is simply the difference between the original amount owed in the present and the amount that has to be paid in the future to settle the debt.
   - a. Reinsurance
   - b. Certified Risk Manager
   - c. Reliability theory
   - d. Discount

25. A _____ is an entity formed between two or more parties to undertake economic activity together. The parties agree to create a new entity by both contributing equity, and they then share in the revenues, expenses, and control of the enterprise. The venture can be for one specific project only, or a continuing business relationship such as the Fuji Xerox _____.
   - a. Property right
   - b. Nexus of contracts
   - c. Business valuation
   - d. Joint venture

26. _____ is the identification, assessment, and prioritization of risks followed by coordinated and economical application of resources to minimize, monitor, and control the probability and/or impact of unfortunate events.. Risks can come from uncertainty in financial markets, project failures, legal liabilities, credit risk, accidents, natural causes and disasters as well as deliberate attacks from an adversary. Several _____ standards have been developed including the Project Management Institute, the National Institute of Science ' Technology, actuarial societies, and ISO standards.
   - a. Kanban
   - b. Penny stock
   - c. Regression toward the mean
   - d. Risk management

27. An _____ is a person who has possession of an enterprise and assumes significant accountability for the inherent risks and the outcome. It is an ambitious leader who combines land, labor, and capital to create and market new goods or services. The term is a loanword from French and was first defined by the Irish economist Richard Cantillon.
   - a. Expansionary policies
   - b. Entrepreneur
   - c. ACEA agreement
   - d. ACCRA Cost of Living Index

28. In economics, game theory, and decision theory the _____ theorem or _____ hypothesis predicts that the 'betting preferences' of people with regard to uncertain outcomes (gambles) can be described by a mathematical relation which takes into account the size of a payout (whether in money or other goods), the probability of occurrence, risk aversion, and the different utility of the same payout to people with different assets or personal preferences. It is a more sophisticated theory than simply predicting that choices will be made based on expected value (which takes into account only the size of the payout and the probability of occurrence.)

Daniel Bernoulli described the complete theory in 1738.

a. Expected utility hypothesis
b. Utility
c. Ordinal utility
d. Expected utility

29. In economics, _____ is a measure of the relative satisfaction from consumption of various goods and services. Given this measure, one may speak meaningfully of increasing or decreasing _____, and thereby explain economic behavior in terms of attempts to increase one's _____. For illustrative purposes, changes in _____ are sometimes expressed in units called utils.
   a. Utility
   b. Expected utility hypothesis
   c. Utility function
   d. Ordinal utility

30. _____ is an offer (often competitive) of setting a price one is willing to pay for something. A price offer is called a bid. The term may be used in context of auctions, stock exchange, card games, or real estate transactions.
   a. Bidding
   b. Normal good
   c. Central limit order book
   d. Bord halfpenny

31. _____ is the acquisition of goods and/or services at the best possible total cost of ownership, in the right quantity and quality, at the right time, in the right place and from the right source for the direct benefit or use of corporations or individuals, generally via a contract. Simple _____ may involve nothing more than repeat purchasing. Complex _____ could involve finding long term partners - or even 'co-destiny' suppliers that might fundamentally commit one organization to another.
   a. Sole proprietorship
   b. Golden umbrella
   c. Pre-emerging markets
   d. Procurement

32. _____ is a measure of the strength of a brand, product, service relative to competitive offerings. There is often a geographic element to the competitive landscape. In defining _____, you must see to what extent a product, brand, or firm controls a product category in a given geographic area.
   a. Horizontal territorial allocation
   b. Demand shaping
   c. Market dominance
   d. Price elasticity of supply

Chapter 9. The Value of Information

1. Economics:

   - _____, the desire to own something and the ability to pay for it
   - _____ curve, a graphic representation of a _____ schedule
   - _____ deposit, the money in checking accounts
   - _____ pull theory, the theory that inflation occurs when _____ for goods and services exceeds existing supplies
   - _____ schedule, a table that lists the quantity of a good a person will buy it each different price
   - _____ side economics, the school of economics at believes government spending and tax cuts open economy by raising _____

   a. Variability
   c. McKesson ' Robbins scandal
   b. Production
   d. Demand

2. The _____ is one of several stock market indices, created by nineteenth-century Wall Street Journal editor and Dow Jones ' Company co-founder Charles Dow. It is an index that shows how certain stocks have traded. Dow compiled the index to gauge the performance of the industrial sector of the American stock market.
   a. Commodity fetishism
   b. Federal Reserve Bank Notes
   c. Fama-French three factor model
   d. Dow Jones Industrial Average

3. _____s is concerned with the tasks of developing and applying quantitative or statistical methods to the study and elucidation of economic principles. _____s combines economic theory with statistics to analyze and test economic relationships. Theoretical _____s considers questions about the statistical properties of estimators and tests, while applied _____s is concerned with the application of _____ methods to assess economic theories.
   a. Evolutionary economics
   b. Experimental economics
   c. Econometric
   d. Economic

4. The _____ is the official currency of 16 of the 27 member states of the European Union (EU.) The states, known collectively as the Eurozone, are Austria, Belgium, Cyprus, Finland, France, Germany, Greece, Ireland, Italy, Luxembourg, Malta, the Netherlands, Portugal, Slovakia, Slovenia, and Spain. The currency is also used in a further five European countries, with and without formal agreements and is consequently used daily by some 327 million Europeans.
   a. Equity capital market
   b. IRS Code 3401
   c. Euro
   d. Import and Export Price Indices

5. In economics, _____ are key economic variables that economists used to predict a new phase of the business cycle. A leading indicator is one that changes before the economy does; a lagging indicator is one that changes after the economy has changed. Examples of _____ include stock prices, which often improve or worsen before a similar change in the economy.
   a. Macroeconomics
   b. Gross domestic product
   c. Medium of exchange
   d. Leading indicators

6. In economics, a _____ is a general slowdown in economic activity over a sustained period of time, or a business cycle contraction. During _____s, many macroeconomic indicators vary in a similar way. Production as measured by Gross Domestic Product (GDP), employment, investment spending, capacity utilization, household incomes and business profits all fall during _____s.

a. Treasury View
b. Recession
c. Leading indicators
d. Monetary economics

7. A _____ is a public market for the trading of company stock and derivatives at an agreed price; these are securities listed on a stock exchange as well as those only traded privately.

The size of the world _____ was estimated at about $36.6 trillion US at the beginning of October 2008 . The total world derivatives market has been estimated at about $791 trillion face or nominal value, 11 times the size of the entire world economy.

a. Stock market
b. Adolf Hitler
c. Adolph Fischer
d. Adam Smith

8. _____ is the a method of technical and economic research of the systems for purpose to optimize a parity between system's consumer functions or properties and expenses to achieve those functions or properties.

This methodology for continuous perfection of production, industrial technologies, organizational structures was developed by Juryj Sobolev in 1948 at the 'Perm telephone factory'

- 1948 Juryj Sobolev - the first success in application of a method analysis at the 'Perm telephone factory' .
- 1949 - the first application for the invention as result of use of the new method.

Today in economically developed countries practically each enterprise or the company use methodology of the kind of functional-cost analysis as a practice of the quality management, most full satisfying to principles of standards of series ISO 9000.

- Interest of consumer not in products itself, but the advantage which it will receive from its usage.
- The consumer aspires to reduce his expenses
- Functions needed by consumer can be executed in the various ways, and, hence, with various efficiency and expenses. Among possible alternatives of realization of functions exist such in which the parity of quality and the price is the optimal for the consumer.

The goal of _____ is achievement of the highest consumer satisfaction of production at simultaneous decrease in all kinds of industrial expenses Classical _____ has three English synonyms - Value Engineering, Value Management, Value Analysis.

a. Staple financing
b. Monopoly wage
c. Function cost analysis
d. Willingness to pay

9. _____ is an offer (often competitive) of setting a price one is willing to pay for something. A price offer is called a bid. The term may be used in context of auctions, stock exchange, card games, or real estate transactions.

a. Central limit order book
b. Bord halfpenny
c. Normal good
d. Bidding

10. _____ is the acquisition of goods and/or services at the best possible total cost of ownership, in the right quantity and quality, at the right time, in the right place and from the right source for the direct benefit or use of corporations or individuals, generally via a contract. Simple _____ may involve nothing more than repeat purchasing. Complex _____ could involve finding long term partners - or even 'co-destiny' suppliers that might fundamentally commit one organization to another.

a. Golden umbrella
b. Pre-emerging markets
c. Procurement
d. Sole proprietorship

11. _____ is the process of estimation in unknown situations. Prediction is a similar, but more general term. Both can refer to estimation of time series, cross-sectional or longitudinal data.

a. 130-30 fund
b. 1921 recession
c. 100-year flood
d. Forecasting

12. In probability theory and statistics, the _____ (or expectation value or mean and for continuous random variables with a density function it is the probability density -weighted integral of the possible values.

The term '_____' can be misleading.

a. ACCRA Cost of Living Index
b. AD-IA Model
c. Expected value
d. ACEA agreement

13. _____ is the probability of some event A, given the occurrence of some other event B. _____ is written $P(A|B)$, and is read 'the probability of A, given B'.

Joint probability is the probability of two events in conjunction. That is, it is the probability of both events together.

a. Memorylessness
b. Conditional probability
c. Marginal likelihood
d. Density function

14. _____ is a term used in game theory. A game is said to have _____ if all players know all moves that have taken place.

Chess is an example of a game with _____ as each player can see all of the pieces on the board at all times.

a. Game theory
b. Parity game
c. Perfect information
d. Perfect rationality

15. In Bayesian inference, a _____ distribution, often called simply the prior, is a probability distribution representing knowledge or belief about an unknown quantity a priori, that is, before any data have been observed. The unknown quantity could be a parameter, hypothesis or latent variable.

The posterior probability is then the conditional probability taking the data into account.

Chapter 9. The Value of Information

a. Hyperprior
b. Bayesian experimental design
c. Bayesian average
d. Prior probability

16. _____ is a way of expressing knowledge or belief that an event will occur or has occurred. In mathematics the concept has been given an exact meaning in _____ theory, that is used extensively in such areas of study as mathematics, statistics, finance, gambling, science, and philosophy to draw conclusions about the likelihood of potential events and the underlying mechanics of complex systems.

The word _____ does not have a consistent direct definition.

a. 1921 recession
b. 130-30 fund
c. 100-year flood
d. Probability

17. A _____ refers to any type debt instrument, such as a loan, bond, mortgage that does not have a fixed rate of interest over the life of the instrument. Such debt typically uses an index or other base rate for establishing the interest rate for each relevant period. One of the most common rates to use as the basis for applying interest rates is the London Inter-bank Offered Rate, or LIBOR

a. Disposal tax effect
b. Money market
c. Moneylender
d. Floating interest rate

18. _____ is a concept with somewhat disparate meanings in several fields. It also has a common meaning which has a loose connection with some of those more definite meanings.

Casually, it is typically used to denote a lack of order, or purpose, or cause.

a. 130-30 fund
b. Randomness
c. 100-year flood
d. 1921 recession

19. In economics, _____ behavior is in between risk aversion and risk seeking. If offered either â‚¬50 or a 50% chance of â‚¬100, a risk averse person will take the â‚¬50, a risk seeking person will take the 50% chance of â‚¬100, and a _____ person would have no preference between the two options.

In finance, when pricing an asset, a common technique is to figure out the probability of a future cash flow, then to discount that cash flow at the risk free rate.

a. Currency risk
b. Transaction risk
c. Risk neutral
d. Taleb distribution

20. A _____ or labor union is an organization of workers who have banded together to achieve common goals in key areas and working conditions. The _____, through its leadership, bargains with the employer on behalf of union members (rank and file members) and negotiates labor contracts (Collective bargaining) with employers. This may include the negotiation of wages, work rules, complaint procedures, rules governing hiring, firing and promotion of workers, benefits, workplace safety and policies.

a. Case-Shiller Home Price Indices
b. Consumer goods
c. Guaranteed investment contracts
d. Trade union

Chapter 9. The Value of Information

21. In economics, _____ refers to the ability of a person or a country to produce a particular good at a lower marginal cost and opportunity cost than another person or country. It is the ability to produce a product most efficiently given all the other products that could be produced. It can be contrasted with absolute advantage which refers to the ability of a person or a country to produce a particular good at a lower absolute cost than another.
- a. Hot money
- b. Comparative advantage
- c. Triffin dilemma
- d. Gravity model of trade

22. _____ in economics and business is the result of an exchange and from that trade we assign a numerical monetary value to a good, service or asset. If Alice trades Bob 4 apples for an orange, the _____ of an orange is 4 apples. Inversely, the _____ of an apple is 1/4 oranges.
- a. Price war
- b. Premium pricing
- c. Price book
- d. Price

23. A _____ is a counterfeit agreement among industries. It is an informal organization of producers that agree to coordinate prices and production. _____s usually occur in an oligopolistic industry, where there is a small number of sellers and usually involve homogeneous products.
- a. Shill
- b. 100-year flood
- c. Cartel
- d. Shanzhai

24. _____ is the transition of a national economy from monopoly control by groups of large businesses to a free market economy. This change rarely arises naturally, and is generally the result of regulation by a governing body.

A modern example of _____ is the economic restructuring of Germany after the fall of the Third Reich in 1945.

- a. Market power
- b. Complementary monopoly
- c. Monopolization
- d. Decartelization

25. In probability theory and statistics, _____ is a measure of the variability or dispersion of a population, a data set, or a probability distribution. A low _____ indicates that the data points tend to be very close to the same value (the mean), while high _____ indicates that the data are 'spread out' over a large range of values.

For example, the average height for adult men in the United States is about 70 inches, with a _____ of around 3 inches.

- a. 130-30 fund
- b. 100-year flood
- c. 1921 recession
- d. Standard deviation

26. In economics and especially in the theory of competition, _____ are obstacles in the path of a firm that make it difficult to enter a given market.

_____ are the source of a firm's pricing power - the ability of a firm to raise prices without losing all its customers.

The term refers to hindrances that an individual may face while trying to gain entrance into a profession or trade.

Chapter 9. The Value of Information

a. Limit price
b. Group boycott
c. Barriers to entry
d. Social dumping

27. In economics, the _____ of an industry is used as an indicator of the relative size of firms in relation to the industry as a whole. It is calculated as the sum of the percent market share of the top n industries. This may also assist in determining the market structure of the industry.
a. Pacman conjecture
b. Quasi-rent
c. Monopolization
d. Concentration ratio

28. _____ is a common market structure where many competing producers sell products that are differentiated from one another (ie. the products are substitutes, but are not exactly alike.) Many markets are monopolistically competitive, common examples include the markets for restaurants, cereal, clothing, shoes and service industries in large cities.
a. Financial crisis
b. Mathematical economics
c. Perfect competition
d. Monopolistic competition

29. An _____ is a market form in which a market or industry is dominated by a small number of sellers (oligopolists.) Because there are few participants in this type of market, each oligopolist is aware of the actions of the others. The decisions of one firm influence, and are influenced by, the decisions of other firms.
a. Oligopsony
b. ACEA agreement
c. Oligopoly
d. ACCRA Cost of Living Index

30. In neoclassical economics and microeconomics, _____ describes the perfect being a market in which there are many small firms, all producing homogeneous goods. In the short term, such markets are productively inefficient as output will not occur where mc is equal to ac, but allocatively efficient, as output under _____ will always occur where mc is equal to mr, and therefore where mc equals ar. However, in the long term, such markets are both allocatively and productively efficient.
a. General equilibrium
b. Law of supply
c. Co-operative economics
d. Perfect competition

31. In economics, a _____ exists when a specific individual or enterprise has sufficient control over a particular product or service to determine significantly the terms on which other individuals shall have access to it. Monopolies are thus characterized by a lack of economic competition for the good or service that they provide and a lack of viable substitute goods. The verb 'monopolize' refers to the process by which a firm gains persistently greater market share than what is expected under perfect competition.
a. 100-year flood
b. 1921 recession
c. Monopoly
d. 130-30 fund

32. A _____ is an expression that compares quantities relative to each other. The most common examples involve two quantities, but any number of quantities can be compared. _____s are represented mathematically by separating each quantity with a colon, for example the _____ 2:3, which is read as the _____ 'two to three'.
a. 130-30 fund
b. 100-year flood
c. Ratio
d. Y-intercept

33. In economics, _____ describes the state of a market with respect to competition.

- Perfect competition, in which the market consists of a very large number of firms producing a homogeneous product.
- Monopolistic competition where there are a large number of independent firms which have a very small proportion of the market share.
- Oligopoly, in which a market is dominated by a small number of firms which own more than 40% of the market share.
- Oligopsony, a market dominated by many sellers and a few buyers.
- Monopoly, where there is only one provider of a product or service.
- Natural monopoly, a monopoly in which economies of scale cause efficiency to increase continuously with the size of the firm. A firm is a natural monopoly if it is able to serve the entire market demand at a lower cost than any combination of two or more smaller, more specialized firms.
- Monopsony, when there is only one buyer in a market.

The imperfectly competitive structure is quite identical to the realistic market conditions where some monopolistic competitors, monopolists, oligopolists, and duopolists exist and dominate the market conditions. The elements of _____ include the number and size distribution of firms, entry conditions, and the extent of differentiation.

These somewhat abstract concerns tend to determine some but not all details of a specific concrete market system where buyers and sellers actually meet and commit to trade.

a. Human capital
b. Market structure
c. Monopolistic competition
d. Labour economics

34. In economics, a _____ occurs when, due to the economies of scale of a particular industry, the maximum efficiency of production and distribution is realized through a single supplier.

Natural monopolies arise where the largest supplier in an industry, often the first supplier in a market, has an overwhelming cost advantage over other actual or potential competitors. This tends to be the case in industries where capital costs predominate, creating economies of scale which are large in relation to the size of the market, and hence high barriers to entry; examples include water services and electricity.

a. Privatizing profits and socializing losses
b. Collective goods
c. Common-pool resource
d. Natural monopoly

35. In economic models, the _____ time frame assumes no fixed factors of production. Firms can enter or leave the marketplace, and the cost (and availability) of land, labor, raw materials, and capital goods can be assumed to vary. In contrast, in the short-run time frame, certain factors are assumed to be fixed, because there is not sufficient time for them to change.

a. Diseconomies of scale
b. Price/performance ratio
c. Productivity world
d. Long-run

Chapter 10. Perfect Competition

1. _____s (economically referred to as land or raw materials) occur naturally within environments that exist relatively undisturbed by mankind, in a natural form. A _____'s is often characterized by amounts of biodiversity existent in various ecosystems.

Mining, petroleum extraction, fishing, hunting, and forestry are generally considered natural-resource industries.

- a. 100-year flood
- b. 130-30 fund
- c. 1921 recession
- d. Natural resource

2. _____ is the change in population over time, and can be quantified as the change in the number of individuals in a population using 'per unit time' for measurement. The term _____ can technically refer to any species, but almost always refers to humans, and it is often used informally for the more specific demographic term _____ rate , and is often used to refer specifically to the growth of the population of the world.

Simple models of _____ include the Malthusian Growth Model and the logistic model.

- a. Population growth
- b. 100-year flood
- c. Population dynamics
- d. 130-30 fund

3. A _____ is a counterfeit agreement among industries. It is an informal organization of producers that agree to coordinate prices and production. _____s usually occur in an oligopolistic industry, where there is a small number of sellers and usually involve homogeneous products.
- a. Shanzhai
- b. Cartel
- c. 100-year flood
- d. Shill

4. _____ is the transition of a national economy from monopoly control by groups of large businesses to a free market economy. This change rarely arises naturally, and is generally the result of regulation by a governing body.

A modern example of _____ is the economic restructuring of Germany after the fall of the Third Reich in 1945.

- a. Market power
- b. Monopolization
- c. Complementary monopoly
- d. Decartelization

5. Economics:

   - _____,the desire to own something and the ability to pay for it
   - _____ curve,a graphic representation of a _____ schedule
   - _____ deposit, the money in checking accounts
   - _____ pull theory,the theory that inflation occurs when _____ for goods and services exceeds existing supplies
   - _____ schedule,a table that lists the quantity of a good a person will buy it each different price
   - _____ side economics,the school of economics at believes government spending and tax cuts open economy by raising _____

Chapter 10. Perfect Competition

a. Production
b. Variability
c. McKesson ' Robbins scandal
d. Demand

6. In economics and especially in the theory of competition, _____ are obstacles in the path of a firm that make it difficult to enter a given market.

_____ are the source of a firm's pricing power - the ability of a firm to raise prices without losing all its customers.

The term refers to hindrances that an individual may face while trying to gain entrance into a profession or trade.

a. Social dumping
b. Barriers to entry
c. Group boycott
d. Limit price

7. In economics, _____ describes the state of a market with respect to competition.

- Perfect competition, in which the market consists of a very large number of firms producing a homogeneous product.
- Monopolistic competition where there are a large number of independent firms which have a very small proportion of the market share.
- Oligopoly, in which a market is dominated by a small number of firms which own more than 40% of the market share.
- Oligopsony, a market dominated by many sellers and a few buyers.
- Monopoly, where there is only one provider of a product or service.
- Natural monopoly, a monopoly in which economies of scale cause efficiency to increase continuously with the size of the firm. A firm is a natural monopoly if it is able to serve the entire market demand at a lower cost than any combination of two or more smaller, more specialized firms.
- Monopsony, when there is only one buyer in a market.

The imperfectly competitive structure is quite identical to the realistic market conditions where some monopolistic competitors, monopolists, oligopolists, and duopolists exist and dominate the market conditions. The elements of _____ include the number and size distribution of firms, entry conditions, and the extent of differentiation.

These somewhat abstract concerns tend to determine some but not all details of a specific concrete market system where buyers and sellers actually meet and commit to trade.

a. Labour economics
b. Monopolistic competition
c. Human capital
d. Market structure

8. _____ is a common market structure where many competing producers sell products that are differentiated from one another (ie. the products are substitutes, but are not exactly alike.) Many markets are monopolistically competitive, common examples include the markets for restaurants, cereal, clothing, shoes and service industries in large cities.

a. Perfect competition
b. Monopolistic competition
c. Mathematical economics
d. Financial crisis

Chapter 10. Perfect Competition

9. In economics, a _____ exists when a specific individual or enterprise has sufficient control over a particular product or service to determine significantly the terms on which other individuals shall have access to it. Monopolies are thus characterized by a lack of economic competition for the good or service that they provide and a lack of viable substitute goods. The verb 'monopolize' refers to the process by which a firm gains persistently greater market share than what is expected under perfect competition.

- a. 100-year flood
- b. 1921 recession
- c. 130-30 fund
- d. Monopoly

10. An _____ is a market form in which a market or industry is dominated by a small number of sellers (oligopolists.) Because there are few participants in this type of market, each oligopolist is aware of the actions of the others. The decisions of one firm influence, and are influenced by, the decisions of other firms.

- a. ACEA agreement
- b. ACCRA Cost of Living Index
- c. Oligopoly
- d. Oligopsony

11. In neoclassical economics and microeconomics, _____ describes the perfect being a market in which there are many small firms, all producing homogeneous goods. In the short term, such markets are productively inefficient as output will not occur where mc is equal to ac, but allocatively efficient, as output under _____ will always occur where mc is equal to mr, and therefore where mc equals ar. However, in the long term, such markets are both allocatively and productively efficient.

- a. Co-operative economics
- b. General equilibrium
- c. Law of supply
- d. Perfect competition

12. In economic models, the _____ time frame assumes no fixed factors of production. Firms can enter or leave the marketplace, and the cost (and availability) of land, labor, raw materials, and capital goods can be assumed to vary. In contrast, in the short-run time frame, certain factors are assumed to be fixed, because there is not sufficient time for them to change.

- a. Long-run
- b. Productivity world
- c. Diseconomies of scale
- d. Price/performance ratio

13. _____ is an economic model based on price, utility and quantity in a market. It predicts that in a competitive market, price will function to equalize the quantity demanded by consumers, and the quantity supplied by producers, resulting in an economic equilibrium of price and quantity. The model incorporates other factors changing equilibrium as a shift of demand and/or supply.

- a. Joint demand
- b. Rational addiction
- c. Deferred gratification
- d. Supply and Demand

14. In economics, the _____ can be defined as the graph depicting the relationship between the price of a certain commodity, and the amount of it that consumers are willing and able to purchase at that given price. It is a graphic representation of a demand schedule. The _____ for all consumers together follows from the _____ of every individual consumer: the individual demands at each price are added together.

- a. Kuznets curve
- b. Cost curve
- c. Wage curve
- d. Demand curve

15. A _____ is an object whose consumption increases the utility of the consumer, for which the quantity demanded exceeds the quantity supplied at zero price. _____s are usually modeled as having diminishing marginal utility. The first individual purchase has high utility; the second has less.

Chapter 10. Perfect Competition

    a. Composite good
    b. Merit good
    c. Pie method
    d. Good

16. _____ is the term denoting either an entrance or changes which are inserted into a system and which activate/modify a process. It is an abstract concept, used in the modeling, system(s) design and system(s) exploitation. It is usually connected with other terms, e.g., _____ field, _____ variable, _____ parameter, _____ value, _____ signal, _____ device and _____ file.
    a. AD-IA Model
    b. Input
    c. ACCRA Cost of Living Index
    d. ACEA agreement

17. _____ in economics and business is the result of an exchange and from that trade we assign a numerical monetary value to a good, service or asset. If Alice trades Bob 4 apples for an orange, the _____ of an orange is 4 apples. Inversely, the _____ of an apple is 1/4 oranges.
    a. Price book
    b. Premium pricing
    c. Price war
    d. Price

18. In marketing, _____ is the process of distinguishing the differences of a product or offering from others, to make it more attractive to a particular target market. This involves differentiating it from competitors' products as well as one's own product offerings.

Differentiation is a source of competitive advantage.

    a. Product differentiation
    b. Market segment
    c. Technology acceptance model
    d. Pricing science

19. In economics, the concept of the _____ refers to the decision-making time frame of a firm in which at least one factor of production is fixed. Costs which are fixed in the _____ have no impact on a firms decisions. For example a firm can raise output by increasing the amount of labour through overtime.
    a. Hicks-neutral technical change
    b. Productivity model
    c. Product Pipeline
    d. Short-run

20. Competitive market equilibrium is the traditional concept of economic equilibrium, appropriate for the analysis of commodity markets with flexible prices and many traders, and serving as the benchmark of efficiency in economic analysis. It relies crucially on the assumption of a competitive environment where each trader decides upon a quantity that is so small compared to the total quantity traded in the market that their individual transactions have no influence on the prices.Competitive markets are an ideal, a standard that other market structures are evaluated by.

A _____ consists of a vector of prices and an allocation such that given the prices, each trader by maximizing his objective function (profit, preferences) subject to his technological possibilities and resource constraints plans to trade into his part of the proposed allocation, and such that the prices make all net trades compatible with one another ('clear the market') by equating aggregate supply and demand for the commodities which are traded.

    a. Product-Market Growth Matrix
    b. Partial equilibrium
    c. Market system
    d. Competitive equilibrium

Chapter 10. Perfect Competition

21. _____ is a branch of applied mathematics that is used in the social sciences (most notably economics), biology, engineering, political science, international relations, computer science, and philosophy. _____ attempts to mathematically capture behavior in strategic situations, in which an individual's success in making choices depends on the choices of others. While initially developed to analyze competitions in which one individual does better at another's expense (zero sum games), it has been expanded to treat a wide class of interactions, which are classified according to several criteria.
    a. Dollar auction
    b. Discriminatory price auction
    c. Proper equilibrium
    d. Game theory

22. The _____ is an economic law stated as: 'In an efficient market all identical goods must have only one price.' The _____ relates to the outcome of free trade and globalization. It is the theory that some day all areas of the world will make the same amount of money as every other part of the world for equal work/product quality.

    The intuition for this law is that all sellers will flock to the highest prevailing price, and all buyers to the lowest current market price.

    a. Law of one price
    b. Precaria
    c. Loss of use
    d. Leave of absence

23. In microeconomics, _____ is the extra revenue that an additional unit of product will bring. It is the additional income from selling one more unit of a good; sometimes equal to price. It can also be described as the change in total revenue/change in number of units sold.
    a. Marginal revenue
    b. Reservation price
    c. Market demand schedule
    d. Long term

24. Monopoly power is an example of market failure which occurs when one or more of the participants has the ability to influence the price or other outcomes in some general or specialized market. The most commonly discussed form of market power is that of a monopoly, but other forms such as monopsony, and more moderate versions of these two extremes, exist. Market participants that have market power are sometimes referred to as 'price makers', while those without are sometimes called '_____'.
    a. Market power
    b. Monopolization
    c. Market concentration
    d. Price takers

25. In economics, _____ is the ratio of the percent change in one variable to the percent change in another variable. It is a tool for measuring the responsiveness of a function to changes in parameters in a relative way. Commonly analyzed are _____ of substitution, price and wealth.
    a. ACEA agreement
    b. Elasticity of demand
    c. ACCRA Cost of Living Index
    d. Elasticity

26. The _____ is the apparent contradiction that although water is on the whole more useful, in terms of survival, than diamonds, diamonds command a higher price in the market. The economist Adam Smith is often considered to be the classic presenter of this paradox. Nicolaus Copernicus, John Locke, John Law and others had previously tried to explain the disparity.
    a. 100-year flood
    b. St. Petersburg paradox
    c. 130-30 fund
    d. Paradox of value

Chapter 10. Perfect Competition

27. In economics, economic equilibrium is simply a state of the world where economic forces are balanced and in the absence of external influences the (equilibrium) values of economic variables will not change. It is the point at which quantity demanded and quantity supplied are equal. _____, for example, refers to a condition where a market price is established through competition such that the amount of goods or services sought by buyers is equal to the amount of goods or services produced by sellers.
   a. Regulated market
   b. Marketization
   c. Market equilibrium
   d. Product-Market Growth Matrix

28. In economics, the _____ of an industry is used as an indicator of the relative size of firms in relation to the industry as a whole. It is calculated as the sum of the percent market share of the top n industries. This may also assist in determining the market structure of the industry.
   a. Pacman conjecture
   b. Monopolization
   c. Quasi-rent
   d. Concentration ratio

29. A _____ is an expression that compares quantities relative to each other. The most common examples involve two quantities, but any number of quantities can be compared. _____s are represented mathematically by separating each quantity with a colon, for example the _____ 2:3, which is read as the _____ 'two to three'.
   a. Y-intercept
   b. 100-year flood
   c. 130-30 fund
   d. Ratio

30. _____ was a survey conducted by the U.S. Department of Justice to gauge the prevalence of alcohol and illegal drug use among prior arrestees. It was a reformulation of the prior Drug Use Forecasting (DUF) program, focused on five drugs in particular: cocaine, marijuana, methamphetamine, opiates, and PCP.

Participants were randomly selected from arrest records in major metropolitan areas; because no personally identifying information is taken from each record chosen, the resulting data can be correlated to arrest rates, but not to the total population of persons charged.

   a. ACCRA Cost of Living Index
   b. AD-IA Model
   c. ACEA agreement
   d. Arrestee Drug Abuse Monitoring

31. In economics, the _____ is the term economists use to describe the self-regulating nature of the marketplace. The _____ is a metaphor coined by the economist Adam Smith in The Wealth of Nations.

Adam Smith mentions the metaphor in Book IV of The Wealth of Nations, arguing that people in any society will certainly employ their capital in foreign trading only if the profits available by that method far exceed those available locally, and that in such a case it is better for society as a whole if they so did.

   a. ACCRA Cost of Living Index
   b. ACEA agreement
   c. AD-IA Model
   d. Invisible hand

32. _____ was a Scottish moral philosopher and a pioneer of political economy. One of the key figures of the Scottish Enlightenment, Smith is the author of The Theory of Moral Sentiments and An Inquiry into the Nature and Causes of the Wealth of Nations. The latter, usually abbreviated as The Wealth of Nations, is considered his magnum opus and the first modern work of economics.

Chapter 10. Perfect Competition

a. Adolf Hitler
b. Alan Greenspan
c. Adam Smith
d. Adolph Fischer

33. In economics and sociology, an _____ is any factor (financial or non-financial) that enables or motivates a particular course of action, or counts as a reason for preferring one choice to the alternatives. It is an expectation that encourages people to behave in a certain way. Since human beings are purposeful creatures, the study of _____ structures is central to the study of all economic activity (both in terms of individual decision-making and in terms of co-operation and competition within a larger institutional structure.)
   a. Isocost
   b. Economic reform
   c. Epstein-Zin preferences
   d. Incentive

34. _____ is a broad label that refers to any individuals or households that use goods and services generated within the economy. The concept of a _____ is used in different contexts, so that the usage and significance of the term may vary.

Typically when business people and economists talk of _____s they are talking about person as _____, an aggregated commodity item with little individuality other than that expressed in the buy/not-buy decision.

   a. 130-30 fund
   b. 1921 recession
   c. Consumer
   d. 100-year flood

35. _____ is a term which is used in economics to refer to the rule or sovereignty of purchasers in markets as to production of goods. It is the power of consumers to decide what gets produced. People use the this term to describe the consumer as the 'king,' or ruler, of the market, the one who determines what products will be produced.
   a. Schedule delay
   b. Consumer sovereignty
   c. Reservation price
   d. Microeconomic reform

36. The term surplus is used in economics for several related quantities. The _____ is the amount that consumers benefit by being able to purchase a product for a price that is less than they would be willing to pay. The producer surplus is the amount that producers benefit by selling at a market price mechanism that is higher than they would be willing to sell for.
   a. Marginal rate of technical substitution
   b. Necessity good
   c. Microeconomic reform
   d. Consumer surplus

37. _____s is the social science that studies the production, distribution, and consumption of goods and services. The term _____s comes from the Ancient Greek οἰκονομία from οἶκος (oikos, 'house') + νόμος (nomos, 'custom' or 'law'), hence 'rules of the house(hold)'. Current _____ models developed out of the broader field of political economy in the late 19th century, owing to a desire to use an empirical approach more akin to the physical sciences.
   a. Energy economics
   b. Inflation
   c. Opportunity cost
   d. Economic

38. The term surplus is used in economics for several related quantities. The consumer surplus is the amount that consumers benefit by being able to purchase a product for a price that is less than they would be willing to pay. The _____ is the amount that producers benefit by selling at a market price mechanism that is higher than they would be willing to sell for.

Chapter 10. Perfect Competition

a. Long term
c. Returns to scale
b. Producer surplus
d. Schedule delay

39. A _____ provision refers to any program which seeks to provide a minimum level of income, service or other support for many marginalized groups such as the poor, elderly, and disabled people. _____ programs are undertaken by governments as well as non-governmental organizations (NGOs.) _____ payments and services are typically provided at the expense of taxpayers generally, funded by benefactors, or by compulsory enrollment of the poor themselves.

a. 130-30 fund
c. 100-year flood
b. 1921 recession
d. Social welfare

40. _____ is exchange of capital, goods, and services across international borders or territories. In most countries, it represents a significant share of gross domestic product (GDP.) While _____ has been present throughout much of history , its economic, social, and political importance has been on the rise in recent centuries.

a. Incoterms
c. Intra-industry trade
b. Import license
d. International trade

41. _____ is the concept or idea of fairness in economics, particularly as to taxation or welfare economics.

In welfare economics, _____ may be distinguished from economic efficiency in overall evaluation of social welfare. Although '_____' has broader uses, it may be posed as a counterpart to economic inequality in yielding a 'good' distribution of welfare.

a. ACCRA Cost of Living Index
c. Equity
b. AD-IA Model
d. ACEA agreement

42. In economics, game theory, and decision theory the _____ theorem or _____ hypothesis predicts that the 'betting preferences' of people with regard to uncertain outcomes (gambles) can be described by a mathematical relation which takes into account the size of a payout (whether in money or other goods), the probability of occurrence, risk aversion, and the different utility of the same payout to people with different assets or personal preferences. It is a more sophisticated theory than simply predicting that choices will be made based on expected value (which takes into account only the size of the payout and the probability of occurrence.)

Daniel Bernoulli described the complete theory in 1738.

a. Ordinal utility
c. Expected utility hypothesis
b. Utility
d. Expected utility

43. In economics, _____ is a measure of the relative satisfaction from consumption of various goods and services. Given this measure, one may speak meaningfully of increasing or decreasing _____, and thereby explain economic behavior in terms of attempts to increase one's _____. For illustrative purposes, changes in _____ are sometimes expressed in units called utils.

a. Ordinal utility
c. Utility function
b. Expected utility hypothesis
d. Utility

44. _____ is used to assign the available resources in an economic way. It is part of resource management.

Chapter 10. Perfect Competition

In strategic planning, is a plan for using available resources, for example human resources, especially in the near term, to achieve goals for the future.

- a. 100-year flood
- b. Resource allocation
- c. 1921 recession
- d. 130-30 fund

45. The phrase _____ refers to the aspect of corporate strategy, corporate finance and management dealing with the buying, selling and combining of different companies that can aid, finance, or help a growing company in a given industry grow rapidly without having to create another business entity.

An acquisition, also known as a takeover or a buyout, is the buying of one company (the 'target') by another. An acquisition may be friendly or hostile.

- a. Peace dividend
- b. Political economy
- c. Productive and unproductive labour
- d. Mergers and acquisitions

46. _____ is a measure of the strength of a brand, product, service relative to competitive offerings. There is often a geographic element to the competitive landscape. In defining _____, you must see to what extent a product, brand, or firm controls a product category in a given geographic area.

- a. Demand shaping
- b. Price elasticity of supply
- c. Horizontal territorial allocation
- d. Market dominance

47. In economics, a _____ exists when the production or use of goods and services by the market is not efficient. That is, there exists another outcome where all involved can be made better off. _____s can be viewed as scenarios where individuals' pursuit of pure self-interest leads to results that are not efficient - that can be improved upon from the societal point-of-view.

- a. Fixed exchange rate
- b. General equilibrium
- c. Financial economics
- d. Market failure

48. _____ is a term that encompasses the notion of individuals and firms striving for a greater share of a market to sell or buy goods and services. Merriam-Webster defines competition in business as 'the effort of two or more parties acting independently to secure the business of a third party by offering the most favorable terms.' It was described by Adam Smith in The Wealth of Nations (1776) and later economists as allocating productive resources to their most highly-valued uses. and encouraging efficiency.

- a. Competition in economics
- b. Price fixing
- c. Moral victory
- d. Strategic entry deterrence

49. _____ is one of the four Ps of the marketing mix. The other three aspects are product, promotion, and place. It is also a key variable in microeconomic price allocation theory.

- a. Pricing
- b. Point of total assumption
- c. Guaranteed Maximum Price
- d. Premium pricing

Chapter 10. Perfect Competition

50. In economics, _____ refers to the ability of a person or a country to produce a particular good at a lower marginal cost and opportunity cost than another person or country. It is the ability to produce a product most efficiently given all the other products that could be produced. It can be contrasted with absolute advantage which refers to the ability of a person or a country to produce a particular good at a lower absolute cost than another.
- a. Gravity model of trade
- b. Triffin dilemma
- c. Comparative advantage
- d. Hot money

51. _____ is a type of trade policy that allows traders to act and transact without interference from government. Thus, the policy permits trading partners mutual gains from trade, with goods and services produced according to the theory of comparative advantage.

Under a _____ policy, prices are a reflection of true supply and demand, and are the sole determinant of resource allocation.

- a. 100-year flood
- b. 1921 recession
- c. 130-30 fund
- d. Free trade

52. In economics and finance, _____ is the practice of taking advantage of a price differential between two or more markets: striking a combination of matching deals that capitalize upon the imbalance, the profit being the difference between the market prices. When used by academics, an _____ is a transaction that involves no negative cash flow at any probabilistic or temporal state and a positive cash flow in at least one state; in simple terms, a risk-free profit. A person who engages in _____ is called an arbitrageur--such as a bank or brokerage firm.
- a. Options Price Reporting Authority
- b. Alternext
- c. Electronic trading
- d. Arbitrage

53. In finance, the _____s between two currencies specifies how much one currency is worth in terms of the other. It is the value of a foreign natione;s currency in terms of the home natione;s currency. For example an _____ of 102 Japanese yen to the United States dollar means that JPY 102 is worth the same as USD 1.
- a. Interbank market
- b. ACCRA Cost of Living Index
- c. ACEA agreement
- d. Exchange rate

54. The General Agreement on Tariffs and Trade was the outcome of the failure of negotiating governments to create the International Trade Organization (ITO.) _____ was formed in 1947 and lasted until 1994, when it was replaced by the World Trade Organization. The Bretton Woods Conference had introduced the idea for an organization to regulate trade as part of a larger plan for economic recovery after World War II.
- a. General Agreement on Tariffs and Trade
- b. Dutch-Scandinavian Economic Pact
- c. GATT
- d. General Agreement on Trade in Services

55. _____ is the economic policy of restraining trade between states, through methods such as tariffs on imported goods, restrictive quotas, and a variety of other restrictive government regulations designed to discourage imports, and prevent foreign take-over of local markets and companies. This policy is closely aligned with anti-globalization, and contrasts with free trade, where government barriers to trade are kept to a minimum. The term is mostly used in the context of economics, where _____ refers to policies or doctrines which 'protect' businesses and workers within a country by restricting or regulating trade with foreign nations.

Chapter 10. Perfect Competition

a. Digital economy
b. Knowledge economy
c. Protectionism
d. Google economy

56. A _____ is a duty imposed on goods when they are moved across a political boundary. They are usually associated with protectionism, the economic policy of restraining trade between nations. For political reasons, _____s are usually imposed on imported goods, although they may also be imposed on exported goods.

a. 100-year flood
b. 1921 recession
c. 130-30 fund
d. Tariff

57. A _____ is a general term that describes any government policy or regulation that restricts international trade. The barriers can take many forms, including the following terms that include many restrictions in international trade within multiple countries that import and export any items of trade.

- Import duty
- Import licenses
- Export licenses
- Import quotas
- Tariffs
- Subsidies
- Non-tariff barriers to trade
- Voluntary Export Restraints
- Local Content Requirements
- Embargo

Most _____s work on the same principle: the imposition of some sort of cost on trade that raises the price of the traded products. If two or more nations repeatedly use _____s against each other, then a trade war results.

a. Trade barrier
b. Certificate of origin
c. National Foreign Trade Council
d. Global financial system

58. In economics, a _____ is a loss of economic efficiency that can occur when equilibrium for a good or service is not Pareto optimal. In other words, either people who would have more marginal benefit than marginal cost are not buying the good or service, or people who would have more marginal cost than marginal benefit are buying the product.

Causes of _____ can include monopoly pricing, externalities, taxes or subsidies, and binding price ceilings or floors.

a. Distributive efficiency
b. Deadweight loss
c. Contract curve
d. Leapfrogging

1. In economics, a _____ exists when a specific individual or enterprise has sufficient control over a particular product or service to determine significantly the terms on which other individuals shall have access to it. Monopolies are thus characterized by a lack of economic competition for the good or service that they provide and a lack of viable substitute goods. The verb 'monopolize' refers to the process by which a firm gains persistently greater market share than what is expected under perfect competition.

a. 130-30 fund
b. 1921 recession
c. 100-year flood
d. Monopoly

2. In economics, a _____ occurs when, due to the economies of scale of a particular industry, the maximum efficiency of production and distribution is realized through a single supplier.

Natural monopolies arise where the largest supplier in an industry, often the first supplier in a market, has an overwhelming cost advantage over other actual or potential competitors. This tends to be the case in industries where capital costs predominate, creating economies of scale which are large in relation to the size of the market, and hence high barriers to entry; examples include water services and electricity.

a. Privatizing profits and socializing losses
b. Natural monopoly
c. Common-pool resource
d. Collective goods

3. In economics and especially in the theory of competition, _____ are obstacles in the path of a firm that make it difficult to enter a given market.

_____ are the source of a firm's pricing power - the ability of a firm to raise prices without losing all its customers.

The term refers to hindrances that an individual may face while trying to gain entrance into a profession or trade.

a. Group boycott
b. Social dumping
c. Limit price
d. Barriers to entry

4. A _____ is a counterfeit agreement among industries. It is an informal organization of producers that agree to coordinate prices and production. _____s usually occur in an oligopolistic industry, where there is a small number of sellers and usually involve homogeneous products.

a. 100-year flood
b. Cartel
c. Shill
d. Shanzhai

5. _____ is the transition of a national economy from monopoly control by groups of large businesses to a free market economy. This change rarely arises naturally, and is generally the result of regulation by a governing body.

A modern example of _____ is the economic restructuring of Germany after the fall of the Third Reich in 1945.

a. Market power
b. Complementary monopoly
c. Monopolization
d. Decartelization

Chapter 11. Monopoly

6. _____ is the acquisition of goods and/or services at the best possible total cost of ownership, in the right quantity and quality, at the right time, in the right place and from the right source for the direct benefit or use of corporations or individuals, generally via a contract. Simple _____ may involve nothing more than repeat purchasing. Complex _____ could involve finding long term partners - or even 'co-destiny' suppliers that might fundamentally commit one organization to another.
   a. Golden umbrella
   b. Sole proprietorship
   c. Pre-emerging markets
   d. Procurement

7. Economics:

   - _____, the desire to own something and the ability to pay for it
   - _____ curve, a graphic representation of a _____ schedule
   - _____ deposit, the money in checking accounts
   - _____ pull theory, the theory that inflation occurs when _____ for goods and services exceeds existing supplies
   - _____ schedule, a table that lists the quantity of a good a person will buy it each different price
   - _____ side economics, the school of economics at believes government spending and tax cuts open economy by raising _____

   a. Production
   b. Variability
   c. Demand
   d. McKesson ' Robbins scandal

8. _____s is the social science that studies the production, distribution, and consumption of goods and services. The term _____s comes from the Ancient Greek oá¼°κονομῖα from oá¼¶κος (oikos, 'house') + vĨœµος (nomos, 'custom' or 'law'), hence 'rules of the house(hold)'. Current _____ models developed out of the broader field of political economy in the late 19th century, owing to a desire to use an empirical approach more akin to the physical sciences.
   a. Inflation
   b. Opportunity cost
   c. Energy economics
   d. Economic

9. In economics, _____ is the difference between a company's total revenue and its opportunity costs. It is the increase in wealth that an investor has from making an investment, taking into consideration all costs associated with that investment including the opportunity cost of capital.

Profit is the factor income of the entrepreneur.

   a. Operating profit
   b. ACCRA Cost of Living Index
   c. Accounting profit
   d. Economic profit

10. The _____ or gross domestic income (GDI), a basic measure of an economy's economic performance, is the market value of all final goods and services produced within the borders of a nation in a year. _____ can be defined in three ways, all of which are conceptually identical. First, it is equal to the total expenditures for all final goods and services produced within the country in a stipulated period of time (usually a 365-day year.)
    a. Countercyclical
    b. Monopolistic competition
    c. Market structure
    d. Gross domestic product

Chapter 11. Monopoly

11. _____ in economics and business is the result of an exchange and from that trade we assign a numerical monetary value to a good, service or asset. If Alice trades Bob 4 apples for an orange, the _____ of an orange is 4 apples. Inversely, the _____ of an apple is 1/4 oranges.
   a. Price
   b. Price book
   c. Premium pricing
   d. Price war

12. _____ is an offer (often competitive) of setting a price one is willing to pay for something. A price offer is called a bid. The term may be used in context of auctions, stock exchange, card games, or real estate transactions.
   a. Central limit order book
   b. Normal good
   c. Bidding
   d. Bord halfpenny

13. In economics, the _____ can be defined as the graph depicting the relationship between the price of a certain commodity, and the amount of it that consumers are willing and able to purchase at that given price. It is a graphic representation of a demand schedule. The _____ for all consumers together follows from the _____ of every individual consumer: the individual demands at each price are added together.
   a. Wage curve
   b. Kuznets curve
   c. Cost curve
   d. Demand curve

14. In economics, _____ is the ratio of the percent change in one variable to the percent change in another variable. It is a tool for measuring the responsiveness of a function to changes in parameters in a relative way. Commonly analyzed are _____ of substitution, price and wealth.
   a. ACCRA Cost of Living Index
   b. Elasticity
   c. ACEA agreement
   d. Elasticity of demand

15. _____ is a common market structure where many competing producers sell products that are differentiated from one another (ie. the products are substitutes, but are not exactly alike.) Many markets are monopolistically competitive, common examples include the markets for restaurants, cereal, clothing, shoes and service industries in large cities.
   a. Mathematical economics
   b. Monopolistic competition
   c. Financial crisis
   d. Perfect competition

16. _____ is one of the four Ps of the marketing mix. The other three aspects are product, promotion, and place. It is also a key variable in microeconomic price allocation theory.
   a. Premium pricing
   b. Pricing
   c. Guaranteed Maximum Price
   d. Point of total assumption

Chapter 11. Monopoly 105

17. A _____ is:

- Rewrite _____, in generative grammar and computer science
- Standardization, a formal and widely-accepted statement, fact, definition, or qualification
- Operation, a determinate _____ for performing a mathematical operation and obtaining a certain result (Mathematics, Logic)
    - Unary operation
    - Binary operation
- _____ of inference, a function from sets of formulae to formulae (Mathematics, Logic)
- _____ of thumb, principle with broad application that is not intended to be strictly accurate or reliable for every situation. Also often simply referred to as a _____
- Moral, an atomic element of a moral code for guiding choices in human behavior
- Heuristic, a quantized '_____' which shows a tendency or probability for successful function
- A regulation, as in sports
- A Production _____, as in computer science
- Procedural law, a _____ set governing the application of laws to cases
    - A law, which may informally be called a '_____'
    - A court ruling, a decision by a court
- In the U.S. Government, a regulation mandated by Congress, but written or expanded upon by the Executive Branch.
- Norm (sociology), an informal but widely accepted _____, concept, truth, definition, or qualification (social norms, legal norms, coding norms)
- Norm (philosophy), a kind of sentence or a reason to act, feel or believe
- 'Rulership' is the concept of governance by a government:
    - Military _____, governance by a military body
    - Monastic _____, a collection of precepts that guides the life of monks or nuns in a religious order where the superior holds the place of Christ
- Slide _____

- '_____,' a song by Ayumi Hamasaki
- '_____,' a song by rapper Nas
- '_____s,' an album by the band The Whitest Boy Alive
- _____s: Pyaar Ka Superhit Formula, a 2003 Bollywood film
- ruler, an instrument for measuring lengths
- _____, a component of an astrolabe, circumferator or similar instrument
- The _____s, a bestselling self-help book
- _____ Project (Run Up-to-date Linux Everywhere), a project that aims to use up-to-date Linux software on old PCs
- _____ engine, a software system that helps managing business _____s
- Ja _____, a hip hop artist
    - R.U.L.E., a 2005 greatest hits album by rapper Ja _____
- '_____s,' a KMFDM song

a. Technocracy
c. Rule
b. Procter ' Gamble
d. Demand

18. The _____ consists of a number of economic theories which describe the nature of the firm, company including its existence, its behaviour, and its relationship with the market.

In simplified terms, the _____ aims to answer these questions:

1. Existence - why do firms emerge, why are not all transactions in the economy mediated over the market?
2. Boundaries - why the boundary between firms and the market is located exactly there? Which transactions are performed internally and which are negotiated on the market?
3. Organization - why are firms structured in such specific way? What is the interplay of formal and informal relationships?

Despite looking simple, these questions are not answered by the established economic theory, which usually views firms as given, and treats them as black boxes without any internal structure.

The First World War period saw a change of emphasis in economic theory away from industry-level analysis which mainly included analysing markets to analysis at the level of the firm, as it became increasingly clear that perfect competition was no longer an adequate model of how firms behaved. Economic theory till then had focussed on trying to understand markets alone and there had been little study on understanding why firms or organisations exist.

a. Khazzoom-Brookes postulate
c. Theory of the firm
b. Policy Ineffectiveness Proposition
d. Technology gap

19. The _____ is an independent agency of the United States government, established in 1914 by the _____ Act. Its principal mission is the promotion of 'consumer protection' and the elimination and prevention of what regulators perceive to be harmfully 'anti-competitive' business practices, such as coercive monopoly.

The _____ Act was one of President Wilson's major acts against trusts.

a. 100-year flood
c. 1921 recession
b. 130-30 fund
d. Federal Trade Commission

20. A _____ is a set of exclusive rights granted by a state to an inventor or his assignee for a limited period of time in exchange for a disclosure of an invention.

The procedure for granting _____s, the requirements placed on the _____ee and the extent of the exclusive rights vary widely between countries according to national laws and international agreements. Typically, however, a _____ application must include one or more claims defining the invention which must be new, inventive, and useful or industrially applicable.

a. Long service leave
c. Bank regulation
b. Bona fide occupational qualification
d. Patent

21. The _____ describes a firm's market power. It is defined by:

Chapter 11. Monopoly

$$L = \frac{P - MC}{P}$$

where P is the market price set by the firm and MC is the firm's marginal cost. The index ranges from a high of 1 to a low of 0, with higher numbers implying greater market power.

a. Two-part tariff
b. Lerner index
c. Break even analysis
d. Discounts and allowances

22. In economics and business decision-making, _____ are costs that cannot be recovered once they have been incurred. _____ are sometimes contrasted with variable costs, which are the costs that will change due to the proposed course of action, and prospective costs which are costs that will be incurred if an action is taken.

In traditional microeconomic theory, only variable costs are relevant to a decision.

a. Halo effect
b. Post-purchase rationalization
c. Hyperbolic discounting
d. Sunk costs

23. _____ are conceptually similar to economies of scale. Whereas economies of scale primarily refer to efficiencies associated with supply-side changes, such as increasing or decreasing the scale of production, of a single product type, _____ refer to efficiencies primarily associated with demand-side changes, such as increasing or decreasing the scope of marketing and distribution, of different types of products. _____ are one of the main reasons for such marketing strategies as product bundling, product lining, and family branding.

a. Economic production quantity
b. Isoquant
c. Economies of scale
d. Economies of scope

24. In economics and finance, _____ is the change in total cost that arises when the quantity produced changes by one unit. It is the cost of producing one more unit of a good. Mathematically, the _____ function is expressed as the first derivative of the total cost (TC) function with respect to quantity (Q.)

a. Quality costs
b. Variable cost
c. Khozraschyot
d. Marginal cost

25. _____s (economically referred to as land or raw materials) occur naturally within environments that exist relatively undisturbed by mankind, in a natural form. A _____'s is often characterized by amounts of biodiversity existent in various ecosystems.

Mining, petroleum extraction, fishing, hunting, and forestry are generally considered natural-resource industries.

a. 130-30 fund
b. 1921 recession
c. Natural resource
d. 100-year flood

26. In marketing, _____ is the process of distinguishing the differences of a product or offering from others, to make it more attractive to a particular target market. This involves differentiating it from competitors' products as well as one's own product offerings.

Differentiation is a source of competitive advantage.

a. Market segment
b. Technology acceptance model
c. Pricing science
d. Product differentiation

27. A _____, statutory monopoly, or de jure monopoly is a monopoly that is protected by law from competition. A statutory monopoly may take the form of a government monopoly where the state owns the particular means of production or government-granted monopoly where a private interest is protected from competition such as being granted exclusive rights to offer a particular service in a specific region while agreeing to have their policies and prices regulated. This type of monopoly is usually contrasted with de facto monopoly which is a broad category for monopolies that are not created by government.

a. Financial risk
b. Boom and bust
c. Market moving information
d. Legal Monopoly

28. A limit price is the price set by a monopolist to discourage economic entry into a market, and is illegal in many countries. The limit price is the price that the entrant would face upon entering as long as the incumbent firm did not decrease output. The limit price is often lower than the average cost of production or just low enough to make entering not profitable. The quantity produced by the incumbent firm to act as a deterrent to entry is usually larger than would be optimal for a monopolist, but might still produce higher economic profits than would be earned under perfect competition. The problem with _____ as strategic behavior is that once the entrant has entered the market, the quantity used as a threat to deter entry is no longer the incumbent firm's best response.

a. Predatory pricing
b. Conscious parallelism
c. Third line forcing
d. Limit pricing

29. In economics, a firm is said to reap monopoly profits when a lack of viable market competition allows it to set its prices above the equilibrium price for a good or service without losing profits to competitors. Monopoly profit is a type of economic profit, that is, it is a profit greater than the normal profit that is typical in a perfectly competitive industry. The resulting price is known as the _____.

a. Monopoly Price
b. Payment schedule
c. Gross Dealer Concession
d. Gross national income

30. In neoclassical economics and microeconomics, _____ describes the perfect being a market in which there are many small firms, all producing homogeneous goods. In the short term, such markets are productively inefficient as output will not occur where mc is equal to ac, but allocatively efficient, as output under _____ will always occur where mc is equal to mr, and therefore where mc equals ar. However, in the long term, such markets are both allocatively and productively efficient.

a. Perfect competition
b. Law of supply
c. General equilibrium
d. Co-operative economics

31. In economics, economic equilibrium is simply a state of the world where economic forces are balanced and in the absence of external influences the (equilibrium) values of economic variables will not change. It is the point at which quantity demanded and quantity supplied are equal. _____, for example, refers to a condition where a market price is established through competition such that the amount of goods or services sought by buyers is equal to the amount of goods or services produced by sellers.

Chapter 11. Monopoly

a. Market equilibrium
c. Marketization
b. Product-Market Growth Matrix
d. Regulated market

32. _____ is a broad label that refers to any individuals or households that use goods and services generated within the economy. The concept of a _____ is used in different contexts, so that the usage and significance of the term may vary.

Typically when business people and economists talk of _____s they are talking about person as _____, an aggregated commodity item with little individuality other than that expressed in the buy/not-buy decision.

a. 1921 recession
c. 100-year flood
b. 130-30 fund
d. Consumer

33. _____ is a term which is used in economics to refer to the rule or sovereignty of purchasers in markets as to production of goods. It is the power of consumers to decide what gets produced. People use the this term to describe the consumer as the 'king,' or ruler, of the market, the one who determines what products will be produced.

a. Schedule delay
c. Reservation price
b. Microeconomic reform
d. Consumer sovereignty

34. The term surplus is used in economics for several related quantities. The _____ is the amount that consumers benefit by being able to purchase a product for a price that is less than they would be willing to pay. The producer surplus is the amount that producers benefit by selling at a market price mechanism that is higher than they would be willing to sell for.

a. Microeconomic reform
c. Marginal rate of technical substitution
b. Necessity good
d. Consumer surplus

35. Competition law, known in the United States as _____ law, has three main elements:

- prohibiting agreements or practices that restrict free trading and competition between business entities. This includes in particular the repression of cartels.
- banning abusive behaviour by a firm dominating a market, or anti-competitive practices that tend to lead to such a dominant position. Practices controlled in this way may include predatory pricing, tying, price gouging, refusal to deal, and many others.
- supervising the mergers and acquisitions of large corporations, including some joint ventures. Transactions that are considered to threaten the competitive process can be prohibited altogether, or approved subject to 'remedies' such as an obligation to divest part of the merged business or to offer licences or access to facilities to enable other businesses to continue competing.

The substance and practice of competition law varies from jurisdiction to jurisdiction. Protecting the interests of consumers (consumer welfare) and ensuring that entrepreneurs have an opportunity to compete in the market economy are often treated as important objectives. Competition law is closely connected with law on deregulation of access to markets, state aids and subsidies, the privatisation of state owned assets and the establishment of independent sector regulators. In recent decades, competition law has been viewed as a way to provide better public services.

a. United Kingdom competition law
b. Intellectual property law
c. Anti-Inflation Act
d. Antitrust

36. _____, known in the United States as antitrust law, has three main elements:

- prohibiting agreements or practices that restrict free trading and competition between business entities. This includes in particular the repression of cartels.
- banning abusive behaviour by a firm dominating a market, or anti-competitive practices that tend to lead to such a dominant position. Practices controlled in this way may include predatory pricing, tying, price gouging, refusal to deal, and many others.
- supervising the mergers and acquisitions of large corporations, including some joint ventures. Transactions that are considered to threaten the competitive process can be prohibited altogether, or approved subject to 'remedies' such as an obligation to divest part of the merged business or to offer licences or access to facilities to enable other businesses to continue competing.

The substance and practice of _____ varies from jurisdiction to jurisdiction. Protecting the interests of consumers (consumer welfare) and ensuring that entrepreneurs have an opportunity to compete in the market economy are often treated as important objectives. _____ is closely connected with law on deregulation of access to markets, state aids and subsidies, the privatisation of state owned assets and the establishment of independent sector regulators. In recent decades, _____ has been viewed as a way to provide better public services.

a. Hostile work environment
b. Fee simple
c. Due diligence
d. Competition law

37. In economics, a _____ is a loss of economic efficiency that can occur when equilibrium for a good or service is not Pareto optimal. In other words, either people who would have more marginal benefit than marginal cost are not buying the good or service, or people who would have more marginal cost than marginal benefit are buying the product.

Causes of _____ can include monopoly pricing, externalities, taxes or subsidies, and binding price ceilings or floors.

a. Distributive efficiency
b. Leapfrogging
c. Contract curve
d. Deadweight loss

38. The phrase _____ refers to the aspect of corporate strategy, corporate finance and management dealing with the buying, selling and combining of different companies that can aid, finance, or help a growing company in a given industry grow rapidly without having to create another business entity.

An acquisition, also known as a takeover or a buyout, is the buying of one company (the 'target') by another. An acquisition may be friendly or hostile.

a. Mergers and acquisitions
b. Peace dividend
c. Political economy
d. Productive and unproductive labour

Chapter 11. Monopoly

39. In 1940, President Franklin Roosevelt split the authority into two agencies, the Civil Aeronautics Administration (CAA) and the _____ The CAA was responsible for air traffic control, safety programs, and airway development. The _____ was entrusted with safety rulemaking, accident investigation, and economic regulation of the airlines.
   a. Civil Aeronautics Board
   b. 1921 recession
   c. 100-year flood
   d. 130-30 fund

40. _____ is the removal or simplification of government rules and regulations that constrain the operation of market forces. _____ does not mean elimination of laws against fraud, but eliminating or reducing government control of how business is done, thereby moving toward a more free market.

   The stated rationale for '_____' is often that fewer and simpler regulations will lead to a raised level of competitiveness, therefore higher productivity, more efficiency and lower prices overall.

   a. Deregulation
   b. Secular basis
   c. Fundamental psychological law
   d. Macroeconomic policy instruments

41. In economic models, the _____ time frame assumes no fixed factors of production. Firms can enter or leave the marketplace, and the cost (and availability) of land, labor, raw materials, and capital goods can be assumed to vary. In contrast, in the short-run time frame, certain factors are assumed to be fixed, because there is not sufficient time for them to change.
   a. Productivity world
   b. Price/performance ratio
   c. Diseconomies of scale
   d. Long-run

42. _____ exists when sales of identical goods or services are transacted at different prices from the same provider. In a theoretical market with perfect information, no transaction costs or prohibition on secondary exchange (or re-selling) to prevent arbitrage, _____ can only be a feature of monopoly and oligopoly markets, where market power can be exercised. Otherwise, the moment the seller tries to sell the same good at different prices, the buyer at the lower price can arbitrage by selling to the consumer buying at the higher price but with a tiny discount.
   a. Loss leader
   b. Transfer pricing
   c. Lerner Index
   d. Price discrimination

43. _____ is exchange of capital, goods, and services across international borders or territories. In most countries, it represents a significant share of gross domestic product (GDP.) While _____ has been present throughout much of history, its economic, social, and political importance has been on the rise in recent centuries.
   a. Import license
   b. Incoterms
   c. Intra-industry trade
   d. International trade

44. The phrase _____ and acquisitions refers to the aspect of corporate strategy, corporate finance and management dealing with the buying, selling and combining of different companies that can aid, finance, or help a growing company in a given industry grow rapidly without having to create another business entity.

   An acquisition, also known as a takeover or a buyout, is the buying of one company (the 'target') by another. An acquisition may be friendly or hostile.

a. Political economy
b. Peace dividend
c. Differential accumulation
d. Mergers

Chapter 12. Oligopoly

1. The _____ consists of a number of economic theories which describe the nature of the firm, company including its existence, its behaviour, and its relationship with the market.

In simplified terms, the _____ aims to answer these questions:

1. Existence - why do firms emerge, why are not all transactions in the economy mediated over the market?
2. Boundaries - why the boundary between firms and the market is located exactly there? Which transactions are performed internally and which are negotiated on the market?
3. Organization - why are firms structured in such specific way? What is the interplay of formal and informal relationships?

Despite looking simple, these questions are not answered by the established economic theory, which usually views firms as given, and treats them as black boxes without any internal structure.

The First World War period saw a change of emphasis in economic theory away from industry-level analysis which mainly included analysing markets to analysis at the level of the firm, as it became increasingly clear that perfect competition was no longer an adequate model of how firms behaved. Economic theory till then had focussed on trying to understand markets alone and there had been little study on understanding why firms or organisations exist.

a. Technology gap
c. Theory of the firm
b. Policy Ineffectiveness Proposition
d. Khazzoom-Brookes postulate

2. A _____ is a place of residence or refuge and comfort. It is usually a place in which an individual or a family can rest and be able to store personal property. Most modern-day households contain sanitary facilities and a means of preparing food.
a. Home
c. 1921 recession
b. 130-30 fund
d. 100-year flood

3. An _____ is a market form in which a market or industry is dominated by a small number of sellers (oligopolists.) Because there are few participants in this type of market, each oligopolist is aware of the actions of the others. The decisions of one firm influence, and are influenced by, the decisions of other firms.
a. ACCRA Cost of Living Index
c. Oligopsony
b. ACEA agreement
d. Oligopoly

4. In economics and especially in the theory of competition, _____ are obstacles in the path of a firm that make it difficult to enter a given market.

_____ are the source of a firm's pricing power - the ability of a firm to raise prices without losing all its customers.

The term refers to hindrances that an individual may face while trying to gain entrance into a profession or trade.

a. Group boycott
c. Social dumping
b. Limit price
d. Barriers to entry

5. _____ is the acquisition of goods and/or services at the best possible total cost of ownership, in the right quantity and quality, at the right time, in the right place and from the right source for the direct benefit or use of corporations or individuals, generally via a contract. Simple _____ may involve nothing more than repeat purchasing. Complex _____ could involve finding long term partners - or even 'co-destiny' suppliers that might fundamentally commit one organization to another.
   a. Sole proprietorship
   b. Golden umbrella
   c. Pre-emerging markets
   d. Procurement

6. In economics, _____ describes the state of a market with respect to competition.

   - Perfect competition, in which the market consists of a very large number of firms producing a homogeneous product.
   - Monopolistic competition where there are a large number of independent firms which have a very small proportion of the market share.
   - Oligopoly, in which a market is dominated by a small number of firms which own more than 40% of the market share.
   - Oligopsony, a market dominated by many sellers and a few buyers.
   - Monopoly, where there is only one provider of a product or service.
   - Natural monopoly, a monopoly in which economies of scale cause efficiency to increase continuously with the size of the firm. A firm is a natural monopoly if it is able to serve the entire market demand at a lower cost than any combination of two or more smaller, more specialized firms.
   - Monopsony, when there is only one buyer in a market.

The imperfectly competitive structure is quite identical to the realistic market conditions where some monopolistic competitors, monopolists, oligopolists, and duopolists exist and dominate the market conditions. The elements of _____ include the number and size distribution of firms, entry conditions, and the extent of differentiation.

These somewhat abstract concerns tend to determine some but not all details of a specific concrete market system where buyers and sellers actually meet and commit to trade.

   a. Market structure
   b. Human capital
   c. Monopolistic competition
   d. Labour economics

7. The phrase _____ refers to the aspect of corporate strategy, corporate finance and management dealing with the buying, selling and combining of different companies that can aid, finance, or help a growing company in a given industry grow rapidly without having to create another business entity.

An acquisition, also known as a takeover or a buyout, is the buying of one company (the 'target') by another. An acquisition may be friendly or hostile.

   a. Productive and unproductive labour
   b. Political economy
   c. Peace dividend
   d. Mergers and acquisitions

8. _____ is an offer (often competitive) of setting a price one is willing to pay for something. A price offer is called a bid. The term may be used in context of auctions, stock exchange, card games, or real estate transactions.
   a. Bord halfpenny
   b. Normal good
   c. Central limit order book
   d. Bidding

Chapter 12. Oligopoly

9. In economic models, the _____ time frame assumes no fixed factors of production. Firms can enter or leave the marketplace, and the cost (and availability) of land, labor, raw materials, and capital goods can be assumed to vary. In contrast, in the short-run time frame, certain factors are assumed to be fixed, because there is not sufficient time for them to change.
   a. Price/performance ratio
   b. Productivity world
   c. Diseconomies of scale
   d. Long-run

10. In economics, a _____ exists when a specific individual or enterprise has sufficient control over a particular product or service to determine significantly the terms on which other individuals shall have access to it. Monopolies are thus characterized by a lack of economic competition for the good or service that they provide and a lack of viable substitute goods. The verb 'monopolize' refers to the process by which a firm gains persistently greater market share than what is expected under perfect competition.
   a. Monopoly
   b. 1921 recession
   c. 100-year flood
   d. 130-30 fund

11. _____ is a measure of the strength of a brand, product, service relative to competitive offerings. There is often a geographic element to the competitive landscape. In defining _____, you must see to what extent a product, brand, or firm controls a product category in a given geographic area.
   a. Demand shaping
   b. Price elasticity of supply
   c. Horizontal territorial allocation
   d. Market dominance

12. _____ was a survey conducted by the U.S. Department of Justice to gauge the prevalence of alcohol and illegal drug use among prior arrestees. It was a reformulation of the prior Drug Use Forecasting (DUF) program, focused on five drugs in particular: cocaine, marijuana, methamphetamine, opiates, and PCP.

    Participants were randomly selected from arrest records in major metropolitan areas; because no personally identifying information is taken from each record chosen, the resulting data can be correlated to arrest rates, but not to the total population of persons charged.

   a. ACEA agreement
   b. ACCRA Cost of Living Index
   c. AD-IA Model
   d. Arrestee Drug Abuse Monitoring

13. _____ is a neologism coined to describe cooperative competition. Co-opetition occurs when companies work together for parts of their business where they do not believe they have competitive advantage, and where they believe they can share common costs. For instance, the cooperation between Peugeot and Toyota on shared components for a new city car for Europe in 2005.
   a. Coopetition
   b. Yield management
   c. Subscription
   d. Freebie marketing

14. _____ is a branch of applied mathematics that is used in the social sciences (most notably economics), biology, engineering, political science, international relations, computer science, and philosophy. _____ attempts to mathematically capture behavior in strategic situations, in which an individual's success in making choices depends on the choices of others. While initially developed to analyze competitions in which one individual does better at another's expense (zero sum games), it has been expanded to treat a wide class of interactions, which are classified according to several criteria.

a. Game theory
b. Dollar auction
c. Proper equilibrium
d. Discriminatory price auction

15. A _____ is an object whose consumption increases the utility of the consumer, for which the quantity demanded exceeds the quantity supplied at zero price. _____ s are usually modeled as having diminishing marginal utility. The first individual purchase has high utility; the second has less.
    a. Merit good
    b. Good
    c. Pie method
    d. Composite good

16. A _____ is the procedure of systematically acquiring and recording information about the members of a given population. It is a regularly occurring and official count of a particular population. The term is used mostly in connection with national 'population and door to door _____ es' (to be taken every 10 years according to United Nations recommendations), agriculture, and business _____ es.
    a. 130-30 fund
    b. 1921 recession
    c. Census
    d. 100-year flood

17. In economics, the _____ of an industry is used as an indicator of the relative size of firms in relation to the industry as a whole. It is calculated as the sum of the percent market share of the top n industries. This may also assist in determining the market structure of the industry.
    a. Pacman conjecture
    b. Quasi-rent
    c. Monopolization
    d. Concentration ratio

18. A true _____ is a specific type of oligopoly where only two producers exist in one market. In reality, this definition is generally used where only two firms have dominant control over a market. In the field of industrial organization, it is the most commonly studied form of oligopoly due to its simplicity.
    a. 130-30 fund
    b. 100-year flood
    c. Megacorpstate
    d. Duopoly

19. In economics, _____ is a function of the number of firms and their respective shares of the total production (alternatively, total capacity or total reserves) in a market. Alternative terms are Industry concentration and Seller concentration.

    _____ is related to the concept of industrial concentration, which concerns the distribution of production within an industry, as opposed to a market.

    a. Market concentration
    b. Quasi-rent
    c. Decartelization
    d. Monopolization

20. A _____ is an expression that compares quantities relative to each other. The most common examples involve two quantities, but any number of quantities can be compared. _____ s are represented mathematically by separating each quantity with a colon, for example the _____ 2:3, which is read as the _____ 'two to three'.
    a. 130-30 fund
    b. 100-year flood
    c. Ratio
    d. Y-intercept

Chapter 12. Oligopoly

21. Economics:

    - _____, the desire to own something and the ability to pay for it
    - _____ curve, a graphic representation of a _____ schedule
    - _____ deposit, the money in checking accounts
    - _____ pull theory, the theory that inflation occurs when _____ for goods and services exceeds existing supplies
    - _____ schedule, a table that lists the quantity of a good a person will buy it each different price
    - _____ side economics, the school of economics at believes government spending and tax cuts open economy by raising _____

    a. Demand
    b. McKesson ' Robbins scandal
    c. Production
    d. Variability

22. The _____ or gross domestic income (GDI), a basic measure of an economy's economic performance, is the market value of all final goods and services produced within the borders of a nation in a year. _____ can be defined in three ways, all of which are conceptually identical. First, it is equal to the total expenditures for all final goods and services produced within the country in a stipulated period of time (usually a 365-day year.)

    a. Countercyclical
    b. Monopolistic competition
    c. Market structure
    d. Gross domestic product

23. _____ is a common market structure where many competing producers sell products that are differentiated from one another (ie. the products are substitutes, but are not exactly alike.) Many markets are monopolistically competitive, common examples include the markets for restaurants, cereal, clothing, shoes and service industries in large cities.

    a. Perfect competition
    b. Financial crisis
    c. Mathematical economics
    d. Monopolistic competition

24. In competition law the _____ defines the market in which one or more goods compete. Therefore, the _____ defines whether two or more products can be considered substitute goods and whether they constitute a particular and separate market for competition analysis.

The _____ combines the product market and the geographic market, defined as follows:

1. A relevant product market comprises all those products and/or services which are regarded as interchangeable or substitutable by the consumer by reason of the products' characteristics, their prices and their intended use;
2. A relevant geographic market comprises the area in which the firms concerned are involved in the supply of products or services and in which the conditions of competition are sufficiently homogeneous.

The notion of _____ is used in order to identify the products and undertakings which are directly competing in a business. Therefore, the _____ is the market where the competition takes place.

a. Greenfield agreement
b. Competition law
c. Community property
d. Relevant market

25. In economics, _____ is the ratio of the percent change in one variable to the percent change in another variable. It is a tool for measuring the responsiveness of a function to changes in parameters in a relative way. Commonly analyzed are _____ of substitution, price and wealth.
   a. ACEA agreement
   b. ACCRA Cost of Living Index
   c. Elasticity of demand
   d. Elasticity

26. In economics, an _____ is any good (e.g. a commodity) or service brought into one country from another country in a legitimate fashion, typically for use in trade. It is a good that is brought in from another country for sale. _____ goods or services are provided to domestic consumers by foreign producers. An _____ in the receiving country is an export to the sending country.
   a. Incoterms
   b. Import
   c. Import quota
   d. Economic integration

27. In neoclassical economics and microeconomics, _____ describes the perfect being a market in which there are many small firms, all producing homogeneous goods. In the short term, such markets are productively inefficient as output will not occur where mc is equal to ac, but allocatively efficient, as output under _____ will always occur where mc is equal to mr, and therefore where mc equals ar. However, in the long term, such markets are both allocatively and productively efficient.
   a. Co-operative economics
   b. Law of supply
   c. General equilibrium
   d. Perfect competition

28. _____ in economics and business is the result of an exchange and from that trade we assign a numerical monetary value to a good, service or asset. If Alice trades Bob 4 apples for an orange, the _____ of an orange is 4 apples. Inversely, the _____ of an apple is 1/4 oranges.
   a. Price war
   b. Premium pricing
   c. Price book
   d. Price

29. A _____ is a counterfeit agreement among industries. It is an informal organization of producers that agree to coordinate prices and production. _____s usually occur in an oligopolistic industry, where there is a small number of sellers and usually involve homogeneous products.
   a. Shanzhai
   b. Cartel
   c. 100-year flood
   d. Shill

30. _____ is the transition of a national economy from monopoly control by groups of large businesses to a free market economy. This change rarely arises naturally, and is generally the result of regulation by a governing body.

A modern example of _____ is the economic restructuring of Germany after the fall of the Third Reich in 1945.

   a. Complementary monopoly
   b. Market power
   c. Monopolization
   d. Decartelization

31. The phrase _____ and acquisitions refers to the aspect of corporate strategy, corporate finance and management dealing with the buying, selling and combining of different companies that can aid, finance, or help a growing company in a given industry grow rapidly without having to create another business entity.

Chapter 12. Oligopoly

An acquisition, also known as a takeover or a buyout, is the buying of one company (the 'target') by another. An acquisition may be friendly or hostile.

a. Political economy
b. Differential accumulation
c. Peace dividend
d. Mergers

32. The terms '_____' and 'independent variable' are used in similar but subtly different ways in mathematics and statistics as part of the standard terminology in those subjects. They are used to distinguish between two types of quantities being considered, separating them into those available at the start of a process and those being created by it, where the latter (_____s) are dependent on the former (independent variables.)

In traditional calculus, a function is defined as a relation between two terms called variables because their values vary.

a. 130-30 fund
b. 100-year flood
c. 1921 recession
d. Dependent variable

33. The terms 'dependent variable' and '_____' are used in similar but subtly different ways in mathematics and statistics as part of the standard terminology in those subjects. They are used to distinguish between two types of quantities being considered, separating them into those available at the start of a process and those being created by it, where the latter (dependent variables) are dependent on the former (_____s.)

The _____ is typically the variable being manipulated or changed and the dependent variable is the observed result of the _____ being manipulated.

a. Independent variable
b. AD-IA Model
c. ACEA agreement
d. ACCRA Cost of Living Index

34. _____ is the removal or simplification of government rules and regulations that constrain the operation of market forces. _____ does not mean elimination of laws against fraud, but eliminating or reducing government control of how business is done, thereby moving toward a more free market.

The stated rationale for '_____' is often that fewer and simpler regulations will lead to a raised level of competitiveness, therefore higher productivity, more efficiency and lower prices overall.

a. Secular basis
b. Fundamental psychological law
c. Macroeconomic policy instruments
d. Deregulation

35. _____ is the economic policy of restraining trade between states, through methods such as tariffs on imported goods, restrictive quotas, and a variety of other restrictive government regulations designed to discourage imports, and prevent foreign take-over of local markets and companies. This policy is closely aligned with anti-globalization, and contrasts with free trade, where government barriers to trade are kept to a minimum. The term is mostly used in the context of economics, where _____ refers to policies or doctrines which 'protect' businesses and workers within a country by restricting or regulating trade with foreign nations.

a. Google economy
c. Knowledge economy
b. Protectionism
d. Digital economy

36. Discounting is a financial mechanism in which a debtor obtains the right to delay payments to a creditor, for a defined period of time, in exchange for a charge or fee. Essentially, the party that owes money in the present purchases the right to delay the payment until some future date. The _____, or charge, is simply the difference between the original amount owed in the present and the amount that has to be paid in the future to settle the debt.
   a. Reinsurance
   b. Discount
   c. Certified Risk Manager
   d. Reliability theory

37. In economics, the _____ can be defined as the graph depicting the relationship between the price of a certain commodity, and the amount of it that consumers are willing and able to purchase at that given price. It is a graphic representation of a demand schedule. The _____ for all consumers together follows from the _____ of every individual consumer: the individual demands at each price are added together.
   a. Kuznets curve
   b. Wage curve
   c. Demand curve
   d. Cost curve

38. In microeconomics, _____ is the extra revenue that an additional unit of product will bring. It is the additional income from selling one more unit of a good; sometimes equal to price. It can also be described as the change in total revenue/change in number of units sold.
   a. Market demand schedule
   b. Long term
   c. Reservation price
   d. Marginal revenue

39. The _____ curve theory is an economic theory regarding oligopoly and monopolistic competition. When it was created, the idea fundamentally challenged classical economic tenets such as efficient markets and rapidly-changing prices, ideas that underly basic supply and demand models. _____ was an initial attempt to explain sticky prices.
   a. Kinked demand curve
   b. Marginal demand
   c. Precautionary demand
   d. Kinked demand

40. In economics, _____ is a rise in the general level of prices of goods and services in an economy over a period of time. When the general price level rises, each unit of currency buys fewer goods and services; consequently, _____ is also a decline in the real value of money--a loss of purchasing power in the medium of exchange which is also the monetary unit of account in the economy. A chief measure of general price-level _____ is the general _____ rate, which is the percentage change in a general price index (normally the Consumer Price Index) over time.
   a. Opportunity cost
   b. Energy economics
   c. Economic
   d. Inflation

41. _____ is a term used in business to indicate a state of intense competitive rivalry accompanied by a multi-lateral series of price reduction. One competitor will lower its price, then others will lower their prices to match. If one of them reduces their price again, a new round of reductions starts.
   a. Transactional Net Margin Method
   b. Big ticket item
   c. Discounts and allowances
   d. Price war

42. Procter is a surname, and may also refer to:

- Bryan Waller Procter (pseud. Barry Cornwall), English poet
- Goodwin Procter, American law firm
- _____, consumer products multinational

a. Procter ' Gamble
c. Drawdown
b. Tightness
d. Bucket shop

43. Competition law, known in the United States as _____ law, has three main elements:

- prohibiting agreements or practices that restrict free trading and competition between business entities. This includes in particular the repression of cartels.
- banning abusive behaviour by a firm dominating a market, or anti-competitive practices that tend to lead to such a dominant position. Practices controlled in this way may include predatory pricing, tying, price gouging, refusal to deal, and many others.
- supervising the mergers and acquisitions of large corporations, including some joint ventures. Transactions that are considered to threaten the competitive process can be prohibited altogether, or approved subject to 'remedies' such as an obligation to divest part of the merged business or to offer licences or access to facilities to enable other businesses to continue competing.

The substance and practice of competition law varies from jurisdiction to jurisdiction. Protecting the interests of consumers (consumer welfare) and ensuring that entrepreneurs have an opportunity to compete in the market economy are often treated as important objectives. Competition law is closely connected with law on deregulation of access to markets, state aids and subsidies, the privatisation of state owned assets and the establishment of independent sector regulators. In recent decades, competition law has been viewed as a way to provide better public services.

a. United Kingdom competition law
c. Antitrust
b. Anti-Inflation Act
d. Intellectual property law

44. _____, known in the United States as antitrust law, has three main elements:

- prohibiting agreements or practices that restrict free trading and competition between business entities. This includes in particular the repression of cartels.
- banning abusive behaviour by a firm dominating a market, or anti-competitive practices that tend to lead to such a dominant position. Practices controlled in this way may include predatory pricing, tying, price gouging, refusal to deal, and many others.
- supervising the mergers and acquisitions of large corporations, including some joint ventures. Transactions that are considered to threaten the competitive process can be prohibited altogether, or approved subject to 'remedies' such as an obligation to divest part of the merged business or to offer licences or access to facilities to enable other businesses to continue competing.

The substance and practice of _____ varies from jurisdiction to jurisdiction. Protecting the interests of consumers (consumer welfare) and ensuring that entrepreneurs have an opportunity to compete in the market economy are often treated as important objectives. _____ is closely connected with law on deregulation of access to markets, state aids and subsidies, the privatisation of state owned assets and the establishment of independent sector regulators. In recent decades, _____ has been viewed as a way to provide better public services.

- a. Due diligence
- b. Fee simple
- c. Hostile work environment
- d. Competition law

45. _____s (economically referred to as land or raw materials) occur naturally within environments that exist relatively undisturbed by mankind, in a natural form. A _____'s is often characterized by amounts of biodiversity existent in various ecosystems.

Mining, petroleum extraction, fishing, hunting, and forestry are generally considered natural-resource industries.

- a. 1921 recession
- b. Natural resource
- c. 100-year flood
- d. 130-30 fund

46. In marketing, _____ is the process of distinguishing the differences of a product or offering from others, to make it more attractive to a particular target market. This involves differentiating it from competitors' products as well as one's own product offerings.

Differentiation is a source of competitive advantage.

- a. Product differentiation
- b. Pricing science
- c. Market segment
- d. Technology acceptance model

47. _____s is the social science that studies the production, distribution, and consumption of goods and services. The term _____s comes from the Ancient Greek oá¼°κονομῖα from oá¼¶κος (oikos, 'house') + vĬŒμος (nomos, 'custom' or 'law'), hence 'rules of the house(hold)'. Current _____ models developed out of the broader field of political economy in the late 19th century, owing to a desire to use an empirical approach more akin to the physical sciences.

- a. Energy economics
- b. Economic
- c. Opportunity cost
- d. Inflation

48. In economics, _____ is the difference between a company's total revenue and its opportunity costs. It is the increase in wealth that an investor has from making an investment, taking into consideration all costs associated with that investment including the opportunity cost of capital.

Profit is the factor income of the entrepreneur.

- a. ACCRA Cost of Living Index
- b. Accounting profit
- c. Operating profit
- d. Economic profit

Chapter 12. Oligopoly

49. The _____ is an independent agency of the United States government, established in 1914 by the _____ Act. Its principal mission is the promotion of 'consumer protection' and the elimination and prevention of what regulators perceive to be harmfully 'anti-competitive' business practices, such as coercive monopoly.

The _____ Act was one of President Wilson's major acts against trusts.

- a. 100-year flood
- c. 1921 recession
- b. 130-30 fund
- d. Federal Trade Commission

50. In the theory of artificial neural networks _____ networks are a case of competitive learning in recurrent neural networks. Output nodes in the network inhibit each other and activate themselves through reflexive connections. After some time, only one node in the output layer will be active.

- a. 100-year flood
- c. Winner-take-all
- b. 1921 recession
- d. 130-30 fund

51. An _____ is a person who has possession of an enterprise and assumes significant accountability for the inherent risks and the outcome. It is an ambitious leader who combines land, labor, and capital to create and market new goods or services. The term is a loanword from French and was first defined by the Irish economist Richard Cantillon.

- a. Entrepreneur
- c. ACEA agreement
- b. Expansionary policies
- d. ACCRA Cost of Living Index

52. A _____ is a person or investment firm that makes venture investments, and these _____s are expected to bring managerial and technical expertise as well as capital to their investments. A venture capital fund refers to a pooled investment vehicle that primarily invests the financial capital of third-party investors in enterprises that are too risky for the standard capital markets or bank loans.

Venture capital is also associated with job creation, the knowledge economy and used as a proxy measure of innovation within an economic sector or geography.

- a. Divisional buyout
- c. Club deal
- b. Startup company
- d. Venture capitalist

53. _____ is an agreement between business competitors to sell the same product or service at the same price. In general, it is an agreement intended to ultimately push the price of a product as high as possible, leading to profits for all the sellers. Price-fixing can also involve any agreement to fix, peg, discount or stabilize prices.

- a. Cut-throat competition
- c. Non-price competition
- b. Moral victory
- d. Price fixing

54. _____ exists when sales of identical goods or services are transacted at different prices from the same provider. In a theoretical market with perfect information, no transaction costs or prohibition on secondary exchange (or re-selling) to prevent arbitrage, _____ can only be a feature of monopoly and oligopoly markets, where market power can be exercised. Otherwise, the moment the seller tries to sell the same good at different prices, the buyer at the lower price can arbitrage by selling to the consumer buying at the higher price but with a tiny discount.

- a. Loss leader
- c. Transfer pricing
- b. Lerner Index
- d. Price discrimination

Chapter 13. Game Theory and Competitive Strategy

1. _____ is a branch of applied mathematics that is used in the social sciences (most notably economics), biology, engineering, political science, international relations, computer science, and philosophy. _____ attempts to mathematically capture behavior in strategic situations, in which an individual's success in making choices depends on the choices of others. While initially developed to analyze competitions in which one individual does better at another's expense (zero sum games), it has been expanded to treat a wide class of interactions, which are classified according to several criteria.
   a. Dollar auction
   b. Proper equilibrium
   c. Discriminatory price auction
   d. Game theory

2. The phrase _____ refers to the aspect of corporate strategy, corporate finance and management dealing with the buying, selling and combining of different companies that can aid, finance, or help a growing company in a given industry grow rapidly without having to create another business entity.

   An acquisition, also known as a takeover or a buyout, is the buying of one company (the 'target') by another. An acquisition may be friendly or hostile.

   a. Political economy
   b. Peace dividend
   c. Mergers and acquisitions
   d. Productive and unproductive labour

3. In economics and especially in the theory of competition, _____ are obstacles in the path of a firm that make it difficult to enter a given market.

   _____ are the source of a firm's pricing power - the ability of a firm to raise prices without losing all its customers.

   The term refers to hindrances that an individual may face while trying to gain entrance into a profession or trade.

   a. Limit price
   b. Group boycott
   c. Social dumping
   d. Barriers to entry

4. A _____ is a set of exclusive rights granted by a state to an inventor or his assignee for a limited period of time in exchange for a disclosure of an invention.

   The procedure for granting _____s, the requirements placed on the _____ee and the extent of the exclusive rights vary widely between countries according to national laws and international agreements. Typically, however, a _____ application must include one or more claims defining the invention which must be new, inventive, and useful or industrially applicable.

   a. Bank regulation
   b. Bona fide occupational qualification
   c. Long service leave
   d. Patent

5. _____ in economics and business is the result of an exchange and from that trade we assign a numerical monetary value to a good, service or asset. If Alice trades Bob 4 apples for an orange, the _____ of an orange is 4 apples. Inversely, the _____ of an apple is 1/4 oranges.
   a. Price war
   b. Premium pricing
   c. Price book
   d. Price

Chapter 13. Game Theory and Competitive Strategy

6. A _____ is:

   - Rewrite _____, in generative grammar and computer science
   - Standardization, a formal and widely-accepted statement, fact, definition, or qualification
   - Operation, a determinate _____ for performing a mathematical operation and obtaining a certain result (Mathematics, Logic)
     - Unary operation
     - Binary operation
   - _____ of inference, a function from sets of formulae to formulae (Mathematics, Logic)
   - _____ of thumb, principle with broad application that is not intended to be strictly accurate or reliable for every situation. Also often simply referred to as a _____
   - Moral, an atomic element of a moral code for guiding choices in human behavior
   - Heuristic, a quantized '_____' which shows a tendency or probability for successful function
   - A regulation, as in sports
   - A Production _____, as in computer science
   - Procedural law, a _____ set governing the application of laws to cases
     - A law, which may informally be called a '_____'
     - A court ruling, a decision by a court
   - In the U.S. Government, a regulation mandated by Congress, but written or expanded upon by the Executive Branch.
   - Norm (sociology), an informal but widely accepted _____, concept, truth, definition, or qualification (social norms, legal norms, coding norms)
   - Norm (philosophy), a kind of sentence or a reason to act, feel or believe
   - 'Rulership' is the concept of governance by a government:
     - Military _____, governance by a military body
     - Monastic _____, a collection of precepts that guides the life of monks or nuns in a religious order where the superior holds the place of Christ
   - Slide _____

   - '_____,' a song by Ayumi Hamasaki
   - '_____,' a song by rapper Nas
   - '_____s,' an album by the band The Whitest Boy Alive
   - _____s: Pyaar Ka Superhit Formula, a 2003 Bollywood film
   - ruler, an instrument for measuring lengths
   - _____, a component of an astrolabe, circumferator or similar instrument
   - The _____s, a bestselling self-help book
   - _____ Project (Run Up-to-date Linux Everywhere), a project that aims to use up-to-date Linux software on old PCs
   - _____ engine, a software system that helps managing business _____s
   - Ja _____, a hip hop artist
     - R.U.L.E., a 2005 greatest hits album by rapper Ja _____
   - '_____s,' a KMFDM song

a. Technocracy
c. Procter ' Gamble
b. Demand
d. Rule

7. A _____ is a counterfeit agreement among industries. It is an informal organization of producers that agree to coordinate prices and production. _____s usually occur in an oligopolistic industry, where there is a small number of sellers and usually involve homogeneous products.
   a. Shill
   b. Shanzhai
   c. 100-year flood
   d. Cartel

8. _____ is the transition of a national economy from monopoly control by groups of large businesses to a free market economy. This change rarely arises naturally, and is generally the result of regulation by a governing body.

   A modern example of _____ is the economic restructuring of Germany after the fall of the Third Reich in 1945.

   a. Decartelization
   b. Complementary monopoly
   c. Monopolization
   d. Market power

9. _____ is exchange of capital, goods, and services across international borders or territories. In most countries, it represents a significant share of gross domestic product (GDP.) While _____ has been present throughout much of history , its economic, social, and political importance has been on the rise in recent centuries.
   a. Import license
   b. Incoterms
   c. Intra-industry trade
   d. International trade

10. A _____ or labor union is an organization of workers who have banded together to achieve common goals in key areas and working conditions. The _____, through its leadership, bargains with the employer on behalf of union members (rank and file members) and negotiates labor contracts (Collective bargaining) with employers. This may include the negotiation of wages, work rules, complaint procedures, rules governing hiring, firing and promotion of workers, benefits, workplace safety and policies.
    a. Consumer goods
    b. Trade union
    c. Case-Shiller Home Price Indices
    d. Guaranteed investment contracts

11. The concept was first developed in game theory and consequently zero-sum situations are often called _____s though this does not imply that the concept applies only to what are commonly referred to as games.

    For 2-player finite _____s, the different game theoretic Solution concepts of Nash equilibrium, minimax, and maximin all give the same solution. In the solution, players play a mixed strategy.

    a. Cash or share options
    b. Gordon growth model
    c. General purpose technologies
    d. Zero-sum game

12. In neoclassical economics and microeconomics, _____ describes the perfect being a market in which there are many small firms, all producing homogeneous goods. In the short term, such markets are productively inefficient as output will not occur where mc is equal to ac, but allocatively efficient, as output under _____ will always occur where mc is equal to mr, and therefore where mc equals ar. However, in the long term, such markets are both allocatively and productively efficient.
    a. Perfect competition
    b. Law of supply
    c. General equilibrium
    d. Co-operative economics

Chapter 13. Game Theory and Competitive Strategy

13. _____ is a term used in game theory. A game is said to have _____ if all players know all moves that have taken place.

Chess is an example of a game with _____ as each player can see all of the pieces on the board at all times.

   a. Perfect rationality
   b. Parity game
   c. Game theory
   d. Perfect information

14. _____, in strategic management and marketing is, according to Carlton O'Neal, the percentage or proportion of the total available market or market segment that is being serviced by a company. It can be expressed as a company's sales revenue (from that market) divided by the total sales revenue available in that market. It can also be expressed as a company's unit sales volume (in a market) divided by the total volume of units sold in that market.
   a. Product differentiation
   b. Customer to customer
   c. Pricing science
   d. Market share

15. In game theory, _____ is a solution concept of a game involving two or more players, in which each player is assumed to know the equilibrium strategies of the other players, and no player has anything to gain by changing only his or her own strategy unilaterally. If each player has chosen a strategy and no player can benefit by changing his or her strategy while the other players keep theirs unchanged, then the current set of strategy choices and the corresponding payoffs constitute a _____.

Stated simply, Amy and Bill are in _____ if Amy is making the best decision she can, taking into account Bill's decision, and Bill is making the best decision he can, taking into account Amy's decision.

   a. Linear production game
   b. Proper equilibrium
   c. Lump of labour
   d. Nash equilibrium

16. _____ is the a method of technical and economic research of the systems for purpose to optimize a parity between system's consumer functions or properties and expenses to achieve those functions or properties.

This methodology for continuous perfection of production, industrial technologies, organizational structures was developed by Juryj Sobolev in 1948 at the 'Perm telephone factory'

- 1948 Juryj Sobolev - the first success in application of a method analysis at the 'Perm telephone factory'.
- 1949 - the first application for the invention as result of use of the new method.

Today in economically developed countries practically each enterprise or the company use methodology of the kind of functional-cost analysis as a practice of the quality management, most full satisfying to principles of standards of series ISO 9000.

- Interest of consumer not in products itself, but the advantage which it will receive from its usage.
- The consumer aspires to reduce his expenses
- Functions needed by consumer can be executed in the various ways, and, hence, with various efficiency and expenses. Among possible alternatives of realization of functions exist such in which the parity of quality and the price is the optimal for the consumer.

The goal of _____ is achievement of the highest consumer satisfaction of production at simultaneous decrease in all kinds of industrial expenses Classical _____ has three English synonyms - Value Engineering, Value Management, Value Analysis.

a. Staple financing
b. Willingness to pay
c. Monopoly wage
d. Function cost analysis

17. _____ is an offer (often competitive) of setting a price one is willing to pay for something. A price offer is called a bid. The term may be used in context of auctions, stock exchange, card games, or real estate transactions.
a. Bord halfpenny
b. Central limit order book
c. Bidding
d. Normal good

18. _____ is the acquisition of goods and/or services at the best possible total cost of ownership, in the right quantity and quality, at the right time, in the right place and from the right source for the direct benefit or use of corporations or individuals, generally via a contract. Simple _____ may involve nothing more than repeat purchasing. Complex _____ could involve finding long term partners - or even 'co-destiny' suppliers that might fundamentally commit one organization to another.
a. Sole proprietorship
b. Pre-emerging markets
c. Golden umbrella
d. Procurement

19. _____ is a term used in business to indicate a state of intense competitive rivalry accompanied by a multi-lateral series of price reduction. One competitor will lower its price, then others will lower their prices to match. If one of them reduces their price again, a new round of reductions starts.
a. Price war
b. Transactional Net Margin Method
c. Discounts and allowances
d. Big ticket item

20. _____ is the combined income earned by an entire group of persons. '_____' in economics is a broad conceptual term. It may express the proceeds from total output in the economy for producers of that output.
a. Average propensity to save
b. Unearned income
c. Independent income
d. Aggregate income

21. The _____ consists of a number of economic theories which describe the nature of the firm, company including its existence, its behaviour, and its relationship with the market.

Chapter 13. Game Theory and Competitive Strategy

In simplified terms, the _____ aims to answer these questions:

1. Existence - why do firms emerge, why are not all transactions in the economy mediated over the market?
2. Boundaries - why the boundary between firms and the market is located exactly there? Which transactions are performed internally and which are negotiated on the market?
3. Organization - why are firms structured in such specific way? What is the interplay of formal and informal relationships?

Despite looking simple, these questions are not answered by the established economic theory, which usually views firms as given, and treats them as black boxes without any internal structure.

The First World War period saw a change of emphasis in economic theory away from industry-level analysis which mainly included analysing markets to analysis at the level of the firm, as it became increasingly clear that perfect competition was no longer an adequate model of how firms behaved. Economic theory till then had focussed on trying to understand markets alone and there had been little study on understanding why firms or organisations exist.

- a. Technology gap
- b. Policy Ineffectiveness Proposition
- c. Theory of the firm
- d. Khazzoom-Brookes postulate

22. A _____ is an entity formed between two or more parties to undertake economic activity together. The parties agree to create a new entity by both contributing equity, and they then share in the revenues, expenses, and control of the enterprise. The venture can be for one specific project only, or a continuing business relationship such as the Fuji Xerox _____.
- a. Nexus of contracts
- b. Joint venture
- c. Property right
- d. Business valuation

23. A _____ strategy is the planned method of delivering goods or services to a target market and distributing them there. When importing or exporting services, it refers to establishing and managing contracts in a foreign country.

Many companies successfully operate in a niche market without ever expanding into new markets.

- a. Deep discount broker
- b. Forfaiting
- c. Customer centricity
- d. Market entry

24. An _____ is a person who has possession of an enterprise and assumes significant accountability for the inherent risks and the outcome. It is an ambitious leader who combines land, labor, and capital to create and market new goods or services. The term is a loanword from French and was first defined by the Irish economist Richard Cantillon.
- a. ACEA agreement
- b. Entrepreneur
- c. Expansionary policies
- d. ACCRA Cost of Living Index

25. _____ is the advantage gained by the initial occupant of a market segment. This advantage may stem from the fact that the first entrant can gain control of resources that followers may not be able to match. Sometimes the first mover is not able to capitalise on its advantage, leaving the opportunity for another firm to gain second-mover advantage.

a. Cross-docking
b. Business engineering
c. First-mover advantage
d. Continuous Improvement Process

26. In combinatorial game theory, a _____ is a directed graph whose nodes are positions in a game and whose edges are moves. The complete _____ for a game is the _____ starting at the initial position and containing all possible moves from each position. The first two ply of the _____ for tic-tac-toe.

The diagram shows the first two levels, or ply, in the _____ for tic-tac-toe.

a. Fuzzy game
b. Game complexity
c. Map-coloring games
d. Game tree

27. In game theory, a _____ is a game where one player chooses his action before the others choose theirs. Importantly, the later players must have some information of the first's choice, otherwise the difference in time would have no strategic effect. Extensive form representations are usually used for _____s, since they explicitly illustrate the sequential aspects of a game.

a. Sequential game
b. Conglomerate merger
c. Comparative economic systems
d. Normative economics

28. A true _____ is a specific type of oligopoly where only two producers exist in one market. In reality, this definition is generally used where only two firms have dominant control over a market. In the field of industrial organization, it is the most commonly studied form of oligopoly due to its simplicity.

a. 100-year flood
b. 130-30 fund
c. Megacorpstate
d. Duopoly

29. A limit price is the price set by a monopolist to discourage economic entry into a market, and is illegal in many countries. The limit price is the price that the entrant would face upon entering as long as the incumbent firm did not decrease output. The limit price is often lower than the average cost of production or just low enough to make entering not profitable. The quantity produced by the incumbent firm to act as a deterrent to entry is usually larger than would be optimal for a monopolist, but might still produce higher economic profits than would be earned under perfect competition. The problem with _____ as strategic behavior is that once the entrant has entered the market, the quantity used as a threat to deter entry is no longer the incumbent firm's best response.

a. Conscious parallelism
b. Limit pricing
c. Predatory pricing
d. Third line forcing

30. _____ is one of the four Ps of the marketing mix. The other three aspects are product, promotion, and place. It is also a key variable in microeconomic price allocation theory.

a. Pricing
b. Point of total assumption
c. Guaranteed Maximum Price
d. Premium pricing

31. _____ is the process of reasoning backwards in time, from the end of a problem or situation, to determine a sequence of optimal actions. It proceeds by first considering the last time a decision might be made and choosing what to do in any situation at that time. Using this information, one can then determine what to do at the second-to-last time of decision.

Chapter 13. Game Theory and Competitive Strategy

a. 1921 recession
b. 100-year flood
c. Backward induction
d. 130-30 fund

32. Discounting is a financial mechanism in which a debtor obtains the right to delay payments to a creditor, for a defined period of time, in exchange for a charge or fee. Essentially, the party that owes money in the present purchases the right to delay the payment until some future date. The _____, or charge, is simply the difference between the original amount owed in the present and the amount that has to be paid in the future to settle the debt.
  a. Reliability theory
  b. Discount
  c. Certified Risk Manager
  d. Reinsurance

33. _____ is a financial mechanism in which a debtor obtains the right to delay payments to a creditor, for a defined period of time, in exchange for a charge or fee. Essentially, the party that owes money in the present purchases the right to delay the payment until some future date. The discount, or charge, is simply the difference between the original amount owed in the present and the amount that has to be paid in the future to settle the debt.
  a. Certified Risk Manager
  b. Generalized linear model
  c. Maximum life span
  d. Discounting

34. _____ is an agreement, usually secretive, which occurs between two or more persons to deceive, mislead or to obtain an objective forbidden by law typically involving fraud or gaining an unfair advantage. It is an agreement among firms to divide the market, set prices kickbacks, or misrepresenting the independence of the relationship between the colluding parties.' All acts effected by _____ are considered void.
  a. Bid rigging
  b. Net Book Agreement
  c. Collusion
  d. Dividing territories

35. _____s is the social science that studies the production, distribution, and consumption of goods and services. The term _____s comes from the Ancient Greek oá¼°κονομῖα from oá¼¶κος (oikos, 'house') + vÏŒμος (nomos, 'custom' or 'law'), hence 'rules of the house(hold)'. Current _____ models developed out of the broader field of political economy in the late 19th century, owing to a desire to use an empirical approach more akin to the physical sciences.
  a. Inflation
  b. Economic
  c. Energy economics
  d. Opportunity cost

36. _____ is the process where heritable traits that make it more likely for an organism to survive and successfully reproduce become more common over successive generations of a population. It is a key mechanism of evolution.

The natural genetic variation within a population of organisms means that some individuals will survive and reproduce more successfully than others in their current environment.

  a. 1921 recession
  b. 130-30 fund
  c. 100-year flood
  d. Natural selection

37. _____ is a concept with somewhat disparate meanings in several fields. It also has a common meaning which has a loose connection with some of those more definite meanings.

Casually, it is typically used to denote a lack of order, or purpose, or cause.

a. Randomness
b. 1921 recession
c. 100-year flood
d. 130-30 fund

Chapter 14. Regulation, Public Goods, and Benefit—Cost Analysis

1. _____ is a broad label that refers to any individuals or households that use goods and services generated within the economy. The concept of a _____ is used in different contexts, so that the usage and significance of the term may vary.

Typically when business people and economists talk of _____s they are talking about person as _____, an aggregated commodity item with little individuality other than that expressed in the buy/not-buy decision.

- a. 1921 recession
- b. Consumer
- c. 100-year flood
- d. 130-30 fund

2. A _____ provision refers to any program which seeks to provide a minimum level of income, service or other support for many marginalized groups such as the poor, elderly, and disabled people. _____ programs are undertaken by governments as well as non-governmental organizations (NGOs.) _____ payments and services are typically provided at the expense of taxpayers generally, funded by benefactors, or by compulsory enrollment of the poor themselves.

- a. 130-30 fund
- b. 1921 recession
- c. 100-year flood
- d. Social welfare

3. _____s is the social science that studies the production, distribution, and consumption of goods and services. The term _____s comes from the Ancient Greek oá¼°κovoμῖα from oá¼¶κoς (oikos, 'house') + vῖŒμoς (nomos, 'custom' or 'law'), hence 'rules of the house(hold)'. Current _____ models developed out of the broader field of political economy in the late 19th century, owing to a desire to use an empirical approach more akin to the physical sciences.

- a. Inflation
- b. Opportunity cost
- c. Energy economics
- d. Economic

4. _____ is the increase in the amount of the goods and services produced by an economy over time. It is conventionally measured as the percent rate of increase in real gross domestic product, or real GDP. Growth is usually calculated in real terms, i.e. inflation-adjusted terms, in order to net out the effect of inflation on the price of the goods and services produced.

- a. AD-IA Model
- b. ACEA agreement
- c. ACCRA Cost of Living Index
- d. Economic growth

5. In economics, an _____ is a way of representing various distributions of resources. Edgeworth made his presentation in his famous book, Mathematical Psychics: An essay on the application of mathematics to the moral sciences, 1881. Edgeworth's original two axis depiction was developed into the now familiar box diagram by Pareto in 1906 and was popularized in a later exposition by Bowley.

- a. Equivalent variation
- b. International Social Security Association
- c. ACCRA Cost of Living Index
- d. Edgeworth box

6. In economics, _____ is a rise in the general level of prices of goods and services in an economy over a period of time. When the general price level rises, each unit of currency buys fewer goods and services; consequently, _____ is also a decline in the real value of money--a loss of purchasing power in the medium of exchange which is also the monetary unit of account in the economy. A chief measure of general price-level _____ is the general _____ rate, which is the percentage change in a general price index (normally the Consumer Price Index) over time.

- a. Energy economics
- b. Opportunity cost
- c. Economic
- d. Inflation

Chapter 14. Regulation, Public Goods, and Benefit—Cost Analysis

7. _____ is a branch of economics that deals with the performance, structure, and behavior of a national or regional economy as a whole. Along with microeconomics, _____ is one of the two most general fields in economics. It is the study of the behavior and decision-making of entire economies.

   a. Nominal value
   b. New Trade Theory
   c. Tobit model
   d. Macroeconomics

8. _____ is a branch of economics that studies how individuals, households and firms and some states make decisions to allocate limited resources, typically in markets where goods or services are being bought and sold. _____ examines how these decisions and behaviours affect the supply and demand for goods and services, which determines prices; and how prices, in turn, determine the supply and demand of goods and services.

Whereas macroeconomics involves the 'sum total of economic activity, dealing with the issues of growth, inflation and unemployment, and with national economic policies relating to these issues' and the effects of government actions on them.

   a. Recession
   b. New Keynesian economics
   c. Countercyclical
   d. Microeconomics

9. A _____ is an economic system that incorporates a mixture of private and government ownership or control, or a mixture of capitalism and socialism.

There is not one single definition for a _____, but relevant aspects include: a degree of private economic freedom (including privately owned industry) intermingled with centralized economic planning and government regulation (which may include regulation of the market for environmental concerns and social welfare, or state ownership and management of some of the means of production for national or social objectives.)

For some states, there is not a consensus on whether they are capitalist, socialist, or mixed economies.

   a. Dual economy
   b. Planned liberalism
   c. Hunter-gatherer
   d. Mixed economy

10. In economics, a _____ is a general slowdown in economic activity over a sustained period of time, or a business cycle contraction. During _____s, many macroeconomic indicators vary in a similar way. Production as measured by Gross Domestic Product (GDP), employment, investment spending, capacity utilization, household incomes and business profits all fall during _____s.

   a. Treasury View
   b. Leading indicators
   c. Recession
   d. Monetary economics

11. _____ is generally measured by standards such as real (i.e. inflation adjusted) income per person and poverty rate. Other measures such as access and quality of health care, income growth inequality and educational standards are also used. Examples are access to certain goods (such as number of refrigerators per 1000 people), or measures of health such as life expectancy.

   a. 100-year flood
   b. 130-30 fund
   c. Standard of living
   d. Remuneration

12. To _____ is to impose a financial charge or other levy upon a taxpayer by a state or the functional equivalent of a state.

_____es are also imposed by many subnational entities. _____es consist of direct _____ or indirect _____, and may be paid in money or as its labour equivalent (often but not always unpaid.)

- a. 100-year flood
- b. Tax
- c. 1921 recession
- d. 130-30 fund

13. To tax is to impose a financial charge or other levy upon a taxpayer by a state or the functional equivalent of a state.

_____ are also imposed by many subnational entities. _____ consist of direct tax or indirect tax, and may be paid in money or as its labour equivalent (often but not always unpaid.)

- a. 1921 recession
- b. 100-year flood
- c. 130-30 fund
- d. Taxes

14. In economics, the _____ is the term economists use to describe the self-regulating nature of the marketplace. The _____ is a metaphor coined by the economist Adam Smith in The Wealth of Nations.

Adam Smith mentions the metaphor in Book IV of The Wealth of Nations, arguing that people in any society will certainly employ their capital in foreign trading only if the profits available by that method far exceed those available locally, and that in such a case it is better for society as a whole if they so did.

- a. ACEA agreement
- b. ACCRA Cost of Living Index
- c. Invisible hand
- d. AD-IA Model

15. In economics, a _____ exists when the production or use of goods and services by the market is not efficient. That is, there exists another outcome where all involved can be made better off. _____s can be viewed as scenarios where individuals' pursuit of pure self-interest leads to results that are not efficient - that can be improved upon from the societal point-of-view.

- a. Fixed exchange rate
- b. Financial economics
- c. General equilibrium
- d. Market failure

16. In neoclassical economics and microeconomics, _____ describes the perfect being a market in which there are many small firms, all producing homogeneous goods. In the short term, such markets are productively inefficient as output will not occur where mc is equal to ac, but allocatively efficient, as output under _____ will always occur where mc is equal to mr, and therefore where mc equals ar. However, in the long term, such markets are both allocatively and productively efficient.

- a. General equilibrium
- b. Law of supply
- c. Co-operative economics
- d. Perfect competition

Chapter 14. Regulation, Public Goods, and Benefit—Cost Analysis

17. A _____ is the exclusive authority to determine how a resource is used, whether that resource is owned by government or by individuals. All economic goods have a _____s attribute. This attribute has three broad components

1. The right to use the good
2. The right to earn income from the good
3. The right to transfer the good to others

The concept of _____s as used by economists and legal scholars are related but distinct. The distinction is largely seen in the economists' focus on the ability of an individual or collective to control the use of the good.

a. Post-sale restraint
b. Holder in due course
c. High-reeve
d. Property right

18. In economics, the _____ of an industry is used as an indicator of the relative size of firms in relation to the industry as a whole. It is calculated as the sum of the percent market share of the top n industries. This may also assist in determining the market structure of the industry.

a. Quasi-rent
b. Pacman conjecture
c. Monopolization
d. Concentration ratio

19. In economics, a _____ is a loss of economic efficiency that can occur when equilibrium for a good or service is not Pareto optimal. In other words, either people who would have more marginal benefit than marginal cost are not buying the good or service, or people who would have more marginal cost than marginal benefit are buying the product.

Causes of _____ can include monopoly pricing, externalities, taxes or subsidies, and binding price ceilings or floors.

a. Leapfrogging
b. Contract curve
c. Distributive efficiency
d. Deadweight loss

20. In economics, _____ is the difference between a company's total revenue and its opportunity costs. It is the increase in wealth that an investor has from making an investment, taking into consideration all costs associated with that investment including the opportunity cost of capital.

Profit is the factor income of the entrepreneur.

a. Economic profit
b. ACCRA Cost of Living Index
c. Accounting profit
d. Operating profit

21. The _____ or gross domestic income (GDI), a basic measure of an economy's economic performance, is the market value of all final goods and services produced within the borders of a nation in a year. _____ can be defined in three ways, all of which are conceptually identical. First, it is equal to the total expenditures for all final goods and services produced within the country in a stipulated period of time (usually a 365-day year.)

a. Countercyclical
b. Monopolistic competition
c. Gross domestic product
d. Market structure

Chapter 14. Regulation, Public Goods, and Benefit—Cost Analysis

22. _____ is a common market structure where many competing producers sell products that are differentiated from one another (ie. the products are substitutes, but are not exactly alike.) Many markets are monopolistically competitive, common examples include the markets for restaurants, cereal, clothing, shoes and service industries in large cities.
   a. Perfect competition
   b. Mathematical economics
   c. Monopolistic competition
   d. Financial crisis

23. In economics, a _____ exists when a specific individual or enterprise has sufficient control over a particular product or service to determine significantly the terms on which other individuals shall have access to it. Monopolies are thus characterized by a lack of economic competition for the good or service that they provide and a lack of viable substitute goods. The verb 'monopolize' refers to the process by which a firm gains persistently greater market share than what is expected under perfect competition.
   a. Monopoly
   b. 130-30 fund
   c. 100-year flood
   d. 1921 recession

24. In economics, a _____ occurs when, due to the economies of scale of a particular industry, the maximum efficiency of production and distribution is realized through a single supplier.

   Natural monopolies arise where the largest supplier in an industry, often the first supplier in a market, has an overwhelming cost advantage over other actual or potential competitors. This tends to be the case in industries where capital costs predominate, creating economies of scale which are large in relation to the size of the market, and hence high barriers to entry; examples include water services and electricity.

   a. Common-pool resource
   b. Natural monopoly
   c. Collective goods
   d. Privatizing profits and socializing losses

25. An _____ is a market form in which a market or industry is dominated by a small number of sellers (oligopolists.) Because there are few participants in this type of market, each oligopolist is aware of the actions of the others. The decisions of one firm influence, and are influenced by, the decisions of other firms.
   a. ACEA agreement
   b. Oligopsony
   c. Oligopoly
   d. ACCRA Cost of Living Index

26. Economic _____ is defined as an excess distribution to any factor in a production process above that which is required to induce the factor into the process or any excess above that which is necessary to keep the factor in its current use..

   Classical Factor _____ is primarily concerned with the fee paid for the use of fixed (e.g. natural) resources. The classical definition is expressed as any excess payment above that required to induce or provide for production.

   a. 1921 recession
   b. 100-year flood
   c. Rent
   d. 130-30 fund

27. In economics, _____ occurs when an individual, organization or firm seeks to make money through economic rent.

_____ generally implies the extraction of uncompensated value from others without making any contribution to productivity, such as by gaining control of land and other pre-existing natural resources, or by imposing burdensome regulations or other government decisions that may affect consumers or businesses. While there may be few people in modern industrialized countries who do not gain something, directly or indirectly, through some form or another of _____, Rent seeking in the aggregate imposes substantial losses on society.

a. Good governance
b. 100-year flood
c. 130-30 fund
d. Rent seeking

28. A _____ is an expression that compares quantities relative to each other. The most common examples involve two quantities, but any number of quantities can be compared. _____s are represented mathematically by separating each quantity with a colon, for example the _____ 2:3, which is read as the _____ 'two to three'.

a. 130-30 fund
b. Ratio
c. Y-intercept
d. 100-year flood

29. Competition law, known in the United States as _____ law, has three main elements:

- prohibiting agreements or practices that restrict free trading and competition between business entities. This includes in particular the repression of cartels.
- banning abusive behaviour by a firm dominating a market, or anti-competitive practices that tend to lead to such a dominant position. Practices controlled in this way may include predatory pricing, tying, price gouging, refusal to deal, and many others.
- supervising the mergers and acquisitions of large corporations, including some joint ventures. Transactions that are considered to threaten the competitive process can be prohibited altogether, or approved subject to 'remedies' such as an obligation to divest part of the merged business or to offer licences or access to facilities to enable other businesses to continue competing.

The substance and practice of competition law varies from jurisdiction to jurisdiction. Protecting the interests of consumers (consumer welfare) and ensuring that entrepreneurs have an opportunity to compete in the market economy are often treated as important objectives. Competition law is closely connected with law on deregulation of access to markets, state aids and subsidies, the privatisation of state owned assets and the establishment of independent sector regulators. In recent decades, competition law has been viewed as a way to provide better public services.

a. United Kingdom competition law
b. Intellectual property law
c. Anti-Inflation Act
d. Antitrust

Chapter 14. Regulation, Public Goods, and Benefit—Cost Analysis

30. _____, known in the United States as antitrust law, has three main elements:

- prohibiting agreements or practices that restrict free trading and competition between business entities. This includes in particular the repression of cartels.
- banning abusive behaviour by a firm dominating a market, or anti-competitive practices that tend to lead to such a dominant position. Practices controlled in this way may include predatory pricing, tying, price gouging, refusal to deal, and many others.
- supervising the mergers and acquisitions of large corporations, including some joint ventures. Transactions that are considered to threaten the competitive process can be prohibited altogether, or approved subject to 'remedies' such as an obligation to divest part of the merged business or to offer licences or access to facilities to enable other businesses to continue competing.

The substance and practice of _____ varies from jurisdiction to jurisdiction. Protecting the interests of consumers (consumer welfare) and ensuring that entrepreneurs have an opportunity to compete in the market economy are often treated as important objectives. _____ is closely connected with law on deregulation of access to markets, state aids and subsidies, the privatisation of state owned assets and the establishment of independent sector regulators. In recent decades, _____ has been viewed as a way to provide better public services.

a. Hostile work environment
b. Fee simple
c. Due diligence
d. Competition law

31. The _____ is an independent agency of the United States government, established in 1914 by the _____ Act. Its principal mission is the promotion of 'consumer protection' and the elimination and prevention of what regulators perceive to be harmfully 'anti-competitive' business practices, such as coercive monopoly.

The _____ Act was one of President Wilson's major acts against trusts.

a. 1921 recession
b. 130-30 fund
c. 100-year flood
d. Federal Trade Commission

32. _____ in economics and business is the result of an exchange and from that trade we assign a numerical monetary value to a good, service or asset. If Alice trades Bob 4 apples for an orange, the _____ of an orange is 4 apples. Inversely, the _____ of an apple is 1/4 oranges.

a. Price war
b. Price book
c. Premium pricing
d. Price

33. _____ exists when sales of identical goods or services are transacted at different prices from the same provider. In a theoretical market with perfect information, no transaction costs or prohibition on secondary exchange (or re-selling) to prevent arbitrage, _____ can only be a feature of monopoly and oligopoly markets, where market power can be exercised. Otherwise, the moment the seller tries to sell the same good at different prices, the buyer at the lower price can arbitrage by selling to the consumer buying at the higher price but with a tiny discount.

a. Loss leader
b. Transfer pricing
c. Lerner Index
d. Price discrimination

34. The _____ consists of a number of economic theories which describe the nature of the firm, company including its existence, its behaviour, and its relationship with the market.

In simplified terms, the _____ aims to answer these questions:

1. Existence - why do firms emerge, why are not all transactions in the economy mediated over the market?
2. Boundaries - why the boundary between firms and the market is located exactly there? Which transactions are performed internally and which are negotiated on the market?
3. Organization - why are firms structured in such specific way? What is the interplay of formal and informal relationships?

Despite looking simple, these questions are not answered by the established economic theory, which usually views firms as given, and treats them as black boxes without any internal structure.

The First World War period saw a change of emphasis in economic theory away from industry-level analysis which mainly included analysing markets to analysis at the level of the firm, as it became increasingly clear that perfect competition was no longer an adequate model of how firms behaved. Economic theory till then had focussed on trying to understand markets alone and there had been little study on understanding why firms or organisations exist.

 a. Policy Ineffectiveness Proposition
 b. Khazzoom-Brookes postulate
 c. Technology gap
 d. Theory of the firm

35. _____ is the practice of selling a product or service at a very low price, intending to drive competitors out of the market, or create barriers to entry for potential new competitors. If competitors or potential competitors cannot sustain equal or lower prices without losing money, they go out of business or choose not to enter the business. The predatory merchant then has fewer competitors or is even a de facto monopoly, and can then raise prices above what the market would otherwise bear.
 a. Group boycott
 b. Predatory pricing
 c. Third line forcing
 d. Restraint of trade

36. _____ was a predominant American integrated oil producing, transporting, refining, and marketing company. Established in 1870 as an Ohio Corporation, it was the largest oil refiner in the world and operated as a major company trust and was one of the world's first and largest multinational corporations until it was broken up by the United States Supreme Court in 1911. John D. Rockefeller was a founder, chairman and major shareholder, and the company made him a billionaire and eventually the richest man in history.
 a. 130-30 fund
 b. 1921 recession
 c. 100-year flood
 d. Standard Oil

37. _____ is one of the four Ps of the marketing mix. The other three aspects are product, promotion, and place. It is also a key variable in microeconomic price allocation theory.
 a. Guaranteed Maximum Price
 b. Point of total assumption
 c. Premium pricing
 d. Pricing

Chapter 14. Regulation, Public Goods, and Benefit—Cost Analysis

38. A _____ is:

   - Rewrite _____, in generative grammar and computer science
   - Standardization, a formal and widely-accepted statement, fact, definition, or qualification
   - Operation, a determinate _____ for performing a mathematical operation and obtaining a certain result (Mathematics, Logic)
     - Unary operation
     - Binary operation
   - _____ of inference, a function from sets of formulae to formulae (Mathematics, Logic)
   - _____ of thumb, principle with broad application that is not intended to be strictly accurate or reliable for every situation. Also often simply referred to as a _____
   - Moral, an atomic element of a moral code for guiding choices in human behavior
   - Heuristic, a quantized '_____' which shows a tendency or probability for successful function
   - A regulation, as in sports
   - A Production _____, as in computer science
   - Procedural law, a _____ set governing the application of laws to cases
     - A law, which may informally be called a '_____'
     - A court ruling, a decision by a court
   - In the U.S. Government, a regulation mandated by Congress, but written or expanded upon by the Executive Branch.
   - Norm (sociology), an informal but widely accepted _____, concept, truth, definition, or qualification (social norms, legal norms, coding norms)
   - Norm (philosophy), a kind of sentence or a reason to act, feel or believe
   - 'Rulership' is the concept of governance by a government:
     - Military _____, governance by a military body
     - Monastic _____, a collection of precepts that guides the life of monks or nuns in a religious order where the superior holds the place of Christ
   - Slide _____

   - '_____,' a song by Ayumi Hamasaki
   - '_____,' a song by rapper Nas
   - '_____s,' an album by the band The Whitest Boy Alive
   - _____s: Pyaar Ka Superhit Formula, a 2003 Bollywood film
   - ruler, an instrument for measuring lengths
   - _____, a component of an astrolabe, circumferator or similar instrument
   - The _____s, a bestselling self-help book
   - _____ Project (Run Up-to-date Linux Everywhere), a project that aims to use up-to-date Linux software on old PCs
   - _____ engine, a software system that helps managing business _____s
   - Ja _____, a hip hop artist
     - R.U.L.E., a 2005 greatest hits album by rapper Ja _____
   - '_____s,' a KMFDM song

a. Technocracy
c. Demand

b. Procter ' Gamble
d. Rule

39. The phrase _____ refers to the aspect of corporate strategy, corporate finance and management dealing with the buying, selling and combining of different companies that can aid, finance, or help a growing company in a given industry grow rapidly without having to create another business entity.

An acquisition, also known as a takeover or a buyout, is the buying of one company (the 'target') by another. An acquisition may be friendly or hostile.

- a. Political economy
- b. Productive and unproductive labour
- c. Peace dividend
- d. Mergers and acquisitions

40. A _____ is a counterfeit agreement among industries. It is an informal organization of producers that agree to coordinate prices and production. _____s usually occur in an oligopolistic industry, where there is a small number of sellers and usually involve homogeneous products.
- a. Shanzhai
- b. 100-year flood
- c. Cartel
- d. Shill

41. _____ is the transition of a national economy from monopoly control by groups of large businesses to a free market economy. This change rarely arises naturally, and is generally the result of regulation by a governing body.

A modern example of _____ is the economic restructuring of Germany after the fall of the Third Reich in 1945.

- a. Complementary monopoly
- b. Monopolization
- c. Decartelization
- d. Market power

42. _____ is an agreement, usually secretive, which occurs between two or more persons to deceive, mislead or to obtain an objective forbidden by law typically involving fraud or gaining an unfair advantage. It is an agreement among firms to divide the market, set prices kickbacks, or misrepresenting the independence of the relationship between the colluding parties.' All acts effected by _____ are considered void.
- a. Net Book Agreement
- b. Bid rigging
- c. Dividing territories
- d. Collusion

43. _____ is a term used in competition law to describe price-fixing between competitors in an oligopoly that occurs without an actual spoken agreement between the parties. Instead, one competitor will take the lead in raising prices. The others will then follow suit, raising their prices by the same amount, with the unspoken mutual understanding that all will reap greater profits from the higher prices so long as none attempts to undercut the others.
- a. Social dumping
- b. Net Book Agreement
- c. Group boycott
- d. Conscious parallelism

44. _____ is an agreement between business competitors to sell the same product or service at the same price. In general, it is an agreement intended to ultimately push the price of a product as high as possible, leading to profits for all the sellers. Price-fixing can also involve any agreement to fix, peg, discount or stabilize prices.
- a. Non-price competition
- b. Moral victory
- c. Cut-throat competition
- d. Price fixing

Chapter 14. Regulation, Public Goods, and Benefit—Cost Analysis

45. In economics, _____ is the process by which a firm determines the price and output level that returns the greatest profit. There are several approaches to this problem. The total revenue--total cost method relies on the fact that profit equals revenue minus cost, and the marginal revenue--marginal cost method is based on the fact that total profit in a perfectly competitive market reaches its maximum point where marginal revenue equals marginal cost.
   a. Profit margin
   b. 100-year flood
   c. Normal profit
   d. Profit maximization

46. _____ is a term used in game theory. A game is said to have _____ if all players know all moves that have taken place.

Chess is an example of a game with _____ as each player can see all of the pieces on the board at all times.

   a. Perfect information
   b. Perfect rationality
   c. Game theory
   d. Parity game

47. _____ is a practice of protecting the environment, on individual, organisational or governmental level, for the benefit of the natural environment and (or) humans.

Due to the pressures of population and technology the biophysical environment is being degraded, sometimes permanently. This has been recognised and governments began placing restraints on activities that caused environmental degradation.

   a. AD-IA Model
   b. ACEA agreement
   c. ACCRA Cost of Living Index
   d. Environmental Protection

48. In law and economics, the _____, describes the economic efficiency of an economic allocation or outcome in the presence of externalities. The theorem states that when trade in an externality is possible and there are no transaction costs, bargaining will lead to an efficient outcome regardless of the initial allocation of property rights. In practice, obstacles to bargaining or poorly defined property rights can prevent Coasian bargaining.
   a. Means test
   b. Prior appropriation water rights
   c. General Mining Act of 1872
   d. Coase theorem

49. The _____ is an economic and political union of 27 member states, located primarily in Europe. It was established by the Treaty of Maastricht on 1 November 1993, upon the foundations of the pre-existing European Economic Community. With a population of almost 500 million, the _____ generates an estimated 30% share (US$18.4 trillion in 2008) of the nominal gross world product.
   a. ACEA agreement
   b. European Court of Justice
   c. ACCRA Cost of Living Index
   d. European Union

50. A _____ is the transfer of wealth from one party (such as a person or company) to another. A _____ is usually made in exchange for the provision of goods, services or both, or to fulfill a legal obligation.

The simplest and oldest form of _____ is barter, the exchange of one good or service for another.

a. Going concern
b. Social gravity
c. Payment
d. Soft count

51. _____ is the increase in the average temperature of the Earth's near-surface air and oceans since the mid-twentieth century and its projected continuation. Global surface temperature increased 0.74 ± 0.18 °C (1.33 ± 0.32 °F) during the last century. The Intergovernmental Panel on Climate Change (IPCC) concludes that anthropogenic greenhouse gases are responsible for most of the observed temperature increase since the middle of the twentieth century, and that natural phenomena such as solar variation and volcanoes probably had a small warming effect from pre-industrial times to 1950 and a small cooling effect afterward.
a. Consumer goods
b. Global warming
c. Dividend unit
d. Controlled Foreign Corporations

52. _____ are gases in an atmosphere that absorb and emit radiation within the thermal infrared range. This process is the fundamental cause of the greenhouse effect. Common _____ in the Earth's atmosphere include water vapor, carbon dioxide, methane, nitrous oxide, ozone, and chlorofluorocarbons.
a. Carbon emissions trading
b. Post-Kyoto negotiations
c. G8 Climate Change Roundtable
d. Greenhouse gases

53. A _____ is a set of exclusive rights granted by a state to an inventor or his assignee for a limited period of time in exchange for a disclosure of an invention.

The procedure for granting _____s, the requirements placed on the _____ee and the extent of the exclusive rights vary widely between countries according to national laws and international agreements. Typically, however, a _____ application must include one or more claims defining the invention which must be new, inventive, and useful or industrially applicable.

a. Patent
b. Bona fide occupational qualification
c. Bank regulation
d. Long service leave

54. In economics, an _____ or spillover of an economic transaction is an impact on a party that is not directly involved in the transaction. In such a case, prices do not reflect the full costs or benefits in production or consumption of a product or service. A positive impact is called an external benefit, while a negative impact is called an external cost.
a. Environmental impact assessment
b. Existence value
c. Environmental tariff
d. Externality

55. A _____ is a situation that involves losing one quality or aspect of something in return for gaining another quality or aspect. It implies a decision to be made with full comprehension of both the upside and downside of a particular choice.

In economics the term is expressed as opportunity cost, referring the most preferred alternative given up.

a. Whitemail
b. Friedman-Savage utility function
c. Nonmarket
d. Trade-off

56. In economics and especially in the theory of competition, _____ are obstacles in the path of a firm that make it difficult to enter a given market.

Chapter 14. Regulation, Public Goods, and Benefit—Cost Analysis

_____ are the source of a firm's pricing power - the ability of a firm to raise prices without losing all its customers.

The term refers to hindrances that an individual may face while trying to gain entrance into a profession or trade.

a. Group boycott
b. Limit price
c. Social dumping
d. Barriers to entry

57. A _____ describes one of a number of pieces of legislation relating to the reduction of smog and air pollution in general. The use by governments to enforce clean air standards has contributed to an improvement in human health and longer life spans. Critics argue it has also sapped corporate profits and contributed to outsourcing, while defenders counter that improved environmental air quality has generated more jobs than it has eliminated.

a. Clean Air Act
b. Smog
c. 130-30 fund
d. 100-year flood

58. _____ is the removal or simplification of government rules and regulations that constrain the operation of market forces. _____ does not mean elimination of laws against fraud, but eliminating or reducing government control of how business is done, thereby moving toward a more free market.

The stated rationale for '_____' is often that fewer and simpler regulations will lead to a raised level of competitiveness, therefore higher productivity, more efficiency and lower prices overall.

a. Macroeconomic policy instruments
b. Deregulation
c. Fundamental psychological law
d. Secular basis

59. _____ is a cross-disciplinary area concerned with protecting the safety, health and welfare of people engaged in work or employment. As a secondary effect, it may also protect co-workers, family members, employers, customers, suppliers, nearby communities, and other members of the public who are impacted by the workplace environment. It may involve interactions among many subject areas, including occupational medicine, occupational (or industrial) hygiene, public health, safety engineering, chemistry, health physics, ergonomics, toxicology, epidemiology, environmental health, industrial relations, public policy, sociology, and occupational health psychology.

a. ACEA agreement
b. ACCRA Cost of Living Index
c. AD-IA Model
d. Occupational Safety and Health

60. The _____ is the primary federal law which governs occupational health and safety in the private sector and federal government in the United States. It was enacted by Congress in 1970 and was signed by President Richard Nixon on December 29, 1970. Its main goal is to ensure that employers provide employees with an environment free from recognized hazards, such as exposure to toxic chemicals, excessive noise levels, mechanical dangers, heat or cold stress, or unsanitary conditions.

a. Irish competition law
b. Electronic Commerce Protection Act
c. Escalator clause
d. Occupational Safety and Health Act

61. The phrase _____ and acquisitions refers to the aspect of corporate strategy, corporate finance and management dealing with the buying, selling and combining of different companies that can aid, finance, or help a growing company in a given industry grow rapidly without having to create another business entity.

146 Chapter 14. Regulation, Public Goods, and Benefit—Cost Analysis

An acquisition, also known as a takeover or a buyout, is the buying of one company (the 'target') by another. An acquisition may be friendly or hostile.

a. Differential accumulation
b. Peace dividend
c. Political economy
d. Mergers

62. Although information has been bought and sold since ancient times, the idea of an information marketplace is relatively recent. The nature of such markets is still evolving, which complicates development of sustainable business models. However, certain attributes of _____ are beginning to be understood, such as diminished participation costs, opportunities for customization, shifting customer relations, and a need for order.

a. Underground economy
b. Intention economy
c. Open economy
d. Information markets

63. A _____ is defined in economics as a good that exhibits these properties:

- Excludable - it is reasonably possible to prevent a class of consumers (e.g. those who have not paid for it) from consuming the good.
- Rivalrous - consumptions by one consumer prevents simultaneous consumption by other consumers. _____ s satisfies an individual want while public good satisfies a collective want of the society.

A _____ is the opposite of a public good, as they are almost exclusively made for profit.

An example of the _____ is bread: bread eaten by a given person cannot be consumed by another (rivalry), and it is easy for a baker to refuse to trade a loaf (excludable

a. Pie method
b. Positional goods
c. Demerit good
d. Private good

64. A _____ is an object whose consumption increases the utility of the consumer, for which the quantity demanded exceeds the quantity supplied at zero price. _____ s are usually modeled as having diminishing marginal utility. The first individual purchase has high utility; the second has less.

a. Good
b. Merit good
c. Composite good
d. Pie method

65. In economics, a _____ is a good that is non-rivaled and non-excludable. This means, respectively, that consumption of the good by one individual does not reduce availability of the good for consumption by others; and that no one can be effectively excluded from using the good. In the real world, there may be no such thing as an absolutely non-rivaled and non-excludable good; but economists think that some goods approximate the concept closely enough for the analysis to be economically useful.

a. Neoclassical synthesis
b. Happiness economics
c. Demand-pull theory
d. Public good

66. Economics:

- _____ ,the desire to own something and the ability to pay for it
- _____ curve,a graphic representation of a _____ schedule
- _____ deposit, the money in checking accounts
- _____ pull theory,the theory that inflation occurs when _____ for goods and services exceeds existing supplies
- _____ schedule,a table that lists the quantity of a good a person will buy it each different price
- _____ side economics,the school of economics at believes government spending and tax cuts open economy by raising _____

a. McKesson ' Robbins scandal
b. Variability
c. Production
d. Demand

67. In economics, the _____ can be defined as the graph depicting the relationship between the price of a certain commodity, and the amount of it that consumers are willing and able to purchase at that given price. It is a graphic representation of a demand schedule. The _____ for all consumers together follows from the _____ of every individual consumer: the individual demands at each price are added together.

a. Demand curve
b. Cost curve
c. Wage curve
d. Kuznets curve

68. _____ or government expenditure is classified by economists into three main types. Government purchases of goods and services for current use are classed as government consumption. Government purchases of goods and services intended to create future benefits, such as infrastructure investment or research spending, are classed as government investment.

a. 100-year flood
b. Government spending
c. 1921 recession
d. 130-30 fund

69. The term _____ refers to economy-wide fluctuations in production or economic activity over several months or years. These fluctuations occur around a long-term growth trend, and typically involve shifts over time between periods of relatively rapid economic growth (expansion or boom), and periods of relative stagnation or decline (contraction or recession.)

These fluctuations are often measured using the growth rate of real gross domestic product.

a. Consumer theory
b. Tobit model
c. Nominal value
d. Business cycle

70. _____ is a common concept in economics, and gives rise to derived concepts such as consumer debt. Generally _____ is defined by opposition to production. But the precise definition can vary because different schools of economists define production quite differently.

a. Foreclosure data providers
b. Consumption
c. Federal Reserve Bank Notes
d. Cash or share options

Chapter 14. Regulation, Public Goods, and Benefit—Cost Analysis

71. _____ is the a method of technical and economic research of the systems for purpose to optimize a parity between system's consumer functions or properties and expenses to achieve those functions or properties.

This methodology for continuous perfection of production, industrial technologies, organizational structures was developed by Juryj Sobolev in 1948 at the 'Perm telephone factory'

- 1948 Juryj Sobolev - the first success in application of a method analysis at the 'Perm telephone factory'.
- 1949 - the first application for the invention as result of use of the new method.

Today in economically developed countries practically each enterprise or the company use methodology of the kind of functional-cost analysis as a practice of the quality management, most full satisfying to principles of standards of series ISO 9000.

- Interest of consumer not in products itself, but the advantage which it will receive from its usage.
- The consumer aspires to reduce his expenses
- Functions needed by consumer can be executed in the various ways, and, hence, with various efficiency and expenses. Among possible alternatives of realization of functions exist such in which the parity of quality and the price is the optimal for the consumer.

The goal of _____ is achievement of the highest consumer satisfaction of production at simultaneous decrease in all kinds of industrial expenses Classical _____ has three English synonyms - Value Engineering, Value Management, Value Analysis.

a. Function cost analysis
b. Staple financing
c. Monopoly wage
d. Willingness to pay

72. _____ is an offer (often competitive) of setting a price one is willing to pay for something. A price offer is called a bid. The term may be used in context of auctions, stock exchange, card games, or real estate transactions.

a. Central limit order book
b. Bidding
c. Bord halfpenny
d. Normal good

73. _____ is the acquisition of goods and/or services at the best possible total cost of ownership, in the right quantity and quality, at the right time, in the right place and from the right source for the direct benefit or use of corporations or individuals, generally via a contract. Simple _____ may involve nothing more than repeat purchasing. Complex _____ could involve finding long term partners - or even 'co-destiny' suppliers that might fundamentally commit one organization to another.

a. Sole proprietorship
b. Pre-emerging markets
c. Golden umbrella
d. Procurement

74. _____ is the concept or idea of fairness in economics, particularly as to taxation or welfare economics.

In welfare economics, _____ may be distinguished from economic efficiency in overall evaluation of social welfare. Although '_____' has broader uses, it may be posed as a counterpart to economic inequality in yielding a 'good' distribution of welfare.

Chapter 14. Regulation, Public Goods, and Benefit—Cost Analysis   149

a. AD-IA Model
b. ACEA agreement
c. ACCRA Cost of Living Index
d. Equity

75. In economics, a _____ is a redistribution of income in the market system. These payments are considered to be nonexhaustive because they do not directly absorb resources or create output. Examples of certain _____s include welfare (financial aid), social security, and government subsidies for certain businesses (firms.)
a. 130-30 fund
b. Transfer payment
c. 100-year flood
d. 1921 recession

76. A _____ or labor union is an organization of workers who have banded together to achieve common goals in key areas and working conditions. The _____, through its leadership, bargains with the employer on behalf of union members (rank and file members) and negotiates labor contracts (Collective bargaining) with employers. This may include the negotiation of wages, work rules, complaint procedures, rules governing hiring, firing and promotion of workers, benefits, workplace safety and policies.
a. Trade union
b. Guaranteed investment contracts
c. Consumer goods
d. Case-Shiller Home Price Indices

77. In economics, _____ refers to the ability of a person or a country to produce a particular good at a lower marginal cost and opportunity cost than another person or country. It is the ability to produce a product most efficiently given all the other products that could be produced. It can be contrasted with absolute advantage which refers to the ability of a person or a country to produce a particular good at a lower absolute cost than another.
a. Hot money
b. Triffin dilemma
c. Gravity model of trade
d. Comparative advantage

78. _____, compulsory purchase (United Kingdom, New Zealand, Ireland), resumption/compulsory acquisition (Australia) or expropriation (South Africa and Canada) or land acqusition (India) in common law legal systems is the inherent power of the state to seize a citizen's private property, expropriate property but without the owner's consent. The property is taken either for government use or by delegation to third parties who will devote it to public or civic use or, in some cases, economic development. The most common uses of property taken by _____ are for public utilities, highways, and railroads.
a. ACCRA Cost of Living Index
b. AD-IA Model
c. Eminent domain
d. ACEA agreement

79. _____ refers to the movement of cash into or out of a business or financial product. It is usually measured during a specified, finite period of time. Measurement of _____ can be used

- to determine a project's rate of return or value. The time of _____s into and out of projects are used as inputs in financial models such as internal rate of return, and net present value.
- to determine problems with a business's liquidity. Being profitable does not necessarily mean being liquid. A company can fail because of a shortage of cash, even while profitable.
- as an alternate measure of a business's profits when it is believed that accrual accounting concepts do not represent economic realities. For example, a company may be notionally profitable but generating little operational cash (as may be the case for a company that barters its products rather than selling for cash.) In such a case, the company may be deriving additional operating cash by issuing shares evaluating default risk, re-investment requirements, etc.

_____ is a generic term used differently depending on the context. It may be defined by users for their own purposes.

a. Strip financing
b. Second lien loan
c. Restricted stock
d. Cash flow

80. _____ is a term which is used in economics to refer to the rule or sovereignty of purchasers in markets as to production of goods. It is the power of consumers to decide what gets produced. People use the this term to describe the consumer as the 'king,' or ruler, of the market, the one who determines what products will be produced.

a. Schedule delay
b. Microeconomic reform
c. Reservation price
d. Consumer sovereignty

81. The term surplus is used in economics for several related quantities. The _____ is the amount that consumers benefit by being able to purchase a product for a price that is less than they would be willing to pay. The producer surplus is the amount that producers benefit by selling at a market price mechanism that is higher than they would be willing to sell for.

a. Necessity good
b. Consumer surplus
c. Microeconomic reform
d. Marginal rate of technical substitution

82. _____ is the price at which an asset would trade in a competitive Walrasian auction setting. _____ is often used interchangeably with open _____, fair value or fair _____, although these terms have distinct definitions in different standards, and may differ in some circumstances.

International Valuation Standards defines _____ as 'the estimated amount for which a property should exchange on the date of valuation between a willing buyer and a willing seller in an arm's-length transaction after proper marketing wherein the parties had each acted knowledgeably, prudently, and without compulsion.'

_____ is a concept distinct from market price, which is 'the price at which one can transact', while _____ is 'the true underlying value' according to theoretical standards.

a. Market value
b. Netting
c. Secured loan
d. Personal financial management

83. _____ is exchange of capital, goods, and services across international borders or territories. In most countries, it represents a significant share of gross domestic product (GDP.) While _____ has been present throughout much of history, its economic, social, and political importance has been on the rise in recent centuries.

a. Import license
b. International trade
c. Intra-industry trade
d. Incoterms

84. A _____ represents the combinations of goods and services that a consumer can purchase given current prices and his income. Consumer theory uses the concepts of a _____ and a preference map to analyze consumer choices. Both concepts have a ready graphical representation in the two-good case.

a. Budget constraint
b. Quality bias
c. Revealed preference
d. Joint demand

Chapter 14. Regulation, Public Goods, and Benefit—Cost Analysis

85. _____ is a term used to described a tendency or preference towards a particular perspective, ideology or result, especially when the tendency interferes with the ability to be impartial, unprejudiced, or objective. The term _____ed is used to describe an action, judgment, or other outcome influenced by a prejudged perspective. It is also used to refer to a person or body of people whose actions or judgments exhibit _____.

a. 130-30 fund
b. 1921 recession
c. 100-year flood
d. Bias

86. The phrase _____, according to the Organization for Economic Co-operation and Development, refers to 'creative work undertaken on a systematic basis in order to increase the stock of knowledge, including knowledge of man, culture and society, and the use of this stock of knowledge to devise new applications [sic]'

New product design and development is more than often a crucial factor in the survival of a company. In an industry that is fast changing, firms must continually revise their design and range of products. This is necessary due to continuous technology change and development as well as other competitors and the changing preference of customers.

a. Research and development
b. 100-year flood
c. 130-30 fund
d. 1921 recession

87. _____ is a branch of applied mathematics that is used in the social sciences (most notably economics), biology, engineering, political science, international relations, computer science, and philosophy. _____ attempts to mathematically capture behavior in strategic situations, in which an individual's success in making choices depends on the choices of others. While initially developed to analyze competitions in which one individual does better at another's expense (zero sum games), it has been expanded to treat a wide class of interactions, which are classified according to several criteria.

a. Proper equilibrium
b. Discriminatory price auction
c. Game theory
d. Dollar auction

88. _____ is the process of estimation in unknown situations. Prediction is a similar, but more general term. Both can refer to estimation of time series, cross-sectional or longitudinal data.

a. 130-30 fund
b. Forecasting
c. 1921 recession
d. 100-year flood

89. _____ is the planning process used to determine whether a firm's long term investments such as new machinery, replacement machinery, new plants, new products, and research development projects are worth pursuing. It is budget for major capital, or investment, expenditures.

Many formal methods are used in _____, including the techniques such as

- Net present value
- Profitability index
- Internal rate of return
- Modified Internal Rate of Return
- Equivalent annuity

These methods use the incremental cash flows from each potential investment, or project. Techniques based on accounting earnings and accounting rules are sometimes used - though economists consider this to be improper - such as the accounting rate of return, and 'return on investment.' Simplified and hybrid methods are used as well, such as payback period and discounted payback period.

a. Capital budgeting
c. Preferred stock

b. Voting interest
d. Participating preferred stock

Chapter 15. Asymmetric Information and Organizational Design

1. In economics and sociology, an _____ is any factor (financial or non-financial) that enables or motivates a particular course of action, or counts as a reason for preferring one choice to the alternatives. It is an expectation that encourages people to behave in a certain way. Since human beings are purposeful creatures, the study of _____ structures is central to the study of all economic activity (both in terms of individual decision-making and in terms of co-operation and competition within a larger institutional structure.)

   a. Incentive
   b. Economic reform
   c. Epstein-Zin preferences
   d. Isocost

2. _____, anti-selection insurance, statistics, and risk management. It refers to a market process in which 'bad' results occur when buyers and sellers have asymmetric information (i.e. access to different information): the 'bad' products or customers are more likely to be selected. A bank that sets one price for all its checking account customers runs the risk of being adversely selected against by its low-balance, high-activity (and hence least profitable) customers.

   a. Adverse selection
   b. ACCRA Cost of Living Index
   c. AD-IA Model
   d. ACEA agreement

3. The _____ is a United States government corporation created by the Glass-Steagall Act of 1933. It provides deposit insurance, which guarantees the safety of deposits in member banks, currently up to $250,000 per depositor per bank. Funds in non-interest bearing transaction accounts are fully insured, with no limit, under the temporary Transaction Account Guarantee Program.

   a. Great Leap Forward
   b. Foreign direct investment
   c. Federal Deposit Insurance Corporation
   d. Luxembourg Income Study

4. _____ is the prospect that a party insulated from risk may behave differently from the way it would behave if it were fully exposed to the risk. In insurance, _____ that occurs without conscious or malicious action is called morale hazard.

   _____ is related to information asymmetry, a situation in which one party in a transaction has more information than another.

   a. 1921 recession
   b. 130-30 fund
   c. 100-year flood
   d. Moral hazard

5. _____ is a way of expressing knowledge or belief that an event will occur or has occurred. In mathematics the concept has been given an exact meaning in _____ theory, that is used extensively in such areas of study as mathematics, statistics, finance, gambling, science, and philosophy to draw conclusions about the likelihood of potential events and the underlying mechanics of complex systems.

   The word _____ does not have a consistent direct definition.

   a. 100-year flood
   b. 130-30 fund
   c. 1921 recession
   d. Probability

6. _____, in law and economics, is a form of risk management primarily used to hedge against the risk of a contingent loss. _____ is defined as the equitable transfer of the risk of a loss, from one entity to another, in exchange for a premium, and can be thought of as a guaranteed small loss to prevent a large, possibly devastating loss. An insurer is a company selling the _____; an insured or policyholder is the person or entity buying the _____.

Chapter 15. Asymmetric Information and Organizational Design

    a. AD-IA Model
    b. Insurance
    c. ACEA agreement
    d. ACCRA Cost of Living Index

7. A _____ refers to any type debt instrument, such as a loan, bond, mortgage that does not have a fixed rate of interest over the life of the instrument. Such debt typically uses an index or other base rate for establishing the interest rate for each relevant period. One of the most common rates to use as the basis for applying interest rates is the London Inter-bank Offered Rate, or LIBOR
    a. Money market
    b. Moneylender
    c. Disposal tax effect
    d. Floating interest rate

8. _____ is a fee paid on borrowed assets. It is the price paid for the use of borrowed money, or, money earned by deposited funds. Assets that are sometimes lent with _____ include money, shares, consumer goods through hire purchase, major assets such as aircraft, and even entire factories in finance lease arrangements.
    a. Insolvency
    b. Internal debt
    c. Asset protection
    d. Interest

9. An _____ is the price a borrower pays for the use of money they do not own, for instance a small company might borrow from a bank to kick start their business, and the return a lender receives for deferring the use of funds, by lending it to the borrower. _____s are normally expressed as a percentage rate over the period of one year.

_____s targets are also a vital tool of monetary policy and are used to control variables like investment, inflation, and unemployment.

    a. Enterprise value
    b. Arrow-Debreu model
    c. ACCRA Cost of Living Index
    d. Interest rate

10. The term _____ refers to economy-wide fluctuations in production or economic activity over several months or years. These fluctuations occur around a long-term growth trend, and typically involve shifts over time between periods of relatively rapid economic growth (expansion or boom), and periods of relative stagnation or decline (contraction or recession.)

These fluctuations are often measured using the growth rate of real gross domestic product.

    a. Tobit model
    b. Business cycle
    c. Consumer theory
    d. Nominal value

11. In economics, economic equilibrium is simply a state of the world where economic forces are balanced and in the absence of external influences the (equilibrium) values of economic variables will not change. It is the point at which quantity demanded and quantity supplied are equal. _____, for example, refers to a condition where a market price is established through competition such that the amount of goods or services sought by buyers is equal to the amount of goods or services produced by sellers.
    a. Product-Market Growth Matrix
    b. Regulated market
    c. Marketization
    d. Market Equilibrium

12. _____ in economics and business is the result of an exchange and from that trade we assign a numerical monetary value to a good, service or asset. If Alice trades Bob 4 apples for an orange, the _____ of an orange is 4 apples. Inversely, the _____ of an apple is 1/4 oranges.
   a. Price book
   b. Premium pricing
   c. Price
   d. Price war

13. An _____ is quite usually a standard guarantee from the seller of a product that specifies the extent to which the quality or performance of the product is assured and states the conditions under which the product can be returned, replaced, or repaired. It is often given in the form of a specific, written 'Warranty' document. However, a warranty may also arise by operation of law based upon the seller's description of the goods, and perhaps their source and quality, and any material deviation from that specification would violate the guarantee.
   a. AD-IA Model
   b. ACEA agreement
   c. ACCRA Cost of Living Index
   d. Express warranty

14. In economics, an _____ is a way of representing various distributions of resources. Edgeworth made his presentation in his famous book, Mathematical Psychics: An essay on the application of mathematics to the moral sciences, 1881. Edgeworth's original two axis depiction was developed into the now familiar box diagram by Pareto in 1906 and was popularized in a later exposition by Bowley.
   a. Edgeworth box
   b. International Social Security Association
   c. Equivalent variation
   d. ACCRA Cost of Living Index

15. The _____ consists of a number of economic theories which describe the nature of the firm, company including its existence, its behaviour, and its relationship with the market.

In simplified terms, the _____ aims to answer these questions:

   1. Existence - why do firms emerge, why are not all transactions in the economy mediated over the market?
   2. Boundaries - why the boundary between firms and the market is located exactly there? Which transactions are performed internally and which are negotiated on the market?
   3. Organization - why are firms structured in such specific way? What is the interplay of formal and informal relationships?

Despite looking simple, these questions are not answered by the established economic theory, which usually views firms as given, and treats them as black boxes without any internal structure.

The First World War period saw a change of emphasis in economic theory away from industry-level analysis which mainly included analysing markets to analysis at the level of the firm, as it became increasingly clear that perfect competition was no longer an adequate model of how firms behaved. Economic theory till then had focussed on trying to understand markets alone and there had been little study on understanding why firms or organisations exist.

   a. Policy Ineffectiveness Proposition
   b. Khazzoom-Brookes postulate
   c. Theory of the firm
   d. Technology gap

Chapter 15. Asymmetric Information and Organizational Design

16. A _____ occurs when a bank is unable to meet its obligations to its depositors or other creditors. More specifically, a bank fails economically when the market value of its assets declines to a value that is less than the market value of its liabilities. As such, the bank is unable to fulfill the demands of all of its depositors on time.

   a. Transactional account
   b. Bank failure
   c. Concentration account
   d. Lombard Club

17. The _____ was an institution that administered deposit insurance for savings and loan institutions in the United States. It was abolished in 1989 by the Financial Institutions Reform, Recovery and Enforcement Act, which passed responsibility for savings and loan deposit insurance to the Federal Deposit Insurance Corporation (FDIC.)

   The FSLIC was created as part of the National Housing Act of 1934 in order to insure deposits in savings and loans, a year after the FDIC was created to insure deposits in commercial banks.

   a. Federal Financial Institutions Examination Council
   b. Covered security
   c. Net capital rule
   d. Federal Savings and Loan Insurance Corporation

18. A _____ association is a financial institution that specializes in accepting savings deposits and making mortgage and other loans. The S'L or thrift term is mainly used in the United States; similar institutions in the United Kingdom, Ireland and some Commonwealth countries include building societies and trustee savings banks.

   They are often mutually held, meaning that the depositors and borrowers are members with voting rights, and have the ability to direct the financial and managerial goals of the organization, similar to the policyholders of a mutual insurance company.

   a. Collective investment scheme
   b. Fonds commun de placement
   c. Participating policy
   d. Savings and Loan

19. An _____ is an economic concept that relates to the cost incurred by an entity (such as organizations) associated with problems such as divergent management-shareholder objectives and information asymmetry. The costs consist of two main sources:

   1. The costs inherently associated with using an agent (e.g., the risk that agents will use organizational resource for their own benefit) and
   2. The costs of techniques used to mitigate the problems associated with using an agent (e.g., the costs of producing financial statements or the use of stock options to align executive interests to shareholder interests.)

   Though effects of _____ are present in any agency relationship, the term is most used in business contexts.

   The information asymmetry that exists between shareholders and the Chief Executive Officer is generally considered to be a classic example of a principal-agent problem. The agent (the manager) is working on behalf of the principal (the shareholders), who does not observe the actions of the agent.

   a. AD-IA Model
   b. Agency cost
   c. ACCRA Cost of Living Index
   d. ACEA agreement

Chapter 15. Asymmetric Information and Organizational Design 157

20. A _____, or simply proprietorship is a type of business entity which legally has no separate existence from its owner. Hence, the limitations of liability enjoyed by a corporation and limited liability partnerships do not apply to sole proprietors. All debts of the business are debts of the owner.

   a. Corporate tax
   b. Golden hello
   c. Golden parachute
   d. Sole proprietorship

21. In economics and related disciplines, a _____ is a cost incurred in making an economic exchange. For example, most people, when buying or selling a stock, must pay a commission to their broker; that commission is a _____ of doing the stock deal. Or consider buying a banana from a store; to purchase the banana, your costs will be not only the price of the banana itself, but also the energy and effort it requires to find out which of the various banana products you prefer, where to get them and at what price, the cost of traveling from your house to the store and back, the time waiting in line, and the effort of the paying itself; the costs above and beyond the cost of the banana are the _____s.

   a. Transaction cost
   b. Cost allocation
   c. Sliding scale fees
   d. Cost of poor quality

22. _____ is the production of large amounts of standardized products, including and especially on assembly lines. The concepts of _____ are applied to various kinds of products, from fluids and particulates handled in bulk to discrete solid parts to assemblies of such parts

   _____ of assemblies typically uses electric-motor-powered moving tracks or conveyor belts to move partially complete products to workers, who perform simple repetitive tasks.

   a. 130-30 fund
   b. 1921 recession
   c. Mass production
   d. 100-year flood

23. _____s is the social science that studies the production, distribution, and consumption of goods and services. The term _____s comes from the Ancient Greek oá¼°κονομῖα from oá¼¶κος (oikos, 'house') + vĺŒμος (nomos, 'custom' or 'law'), hence 'rules of the house(hold)'. Current _____ models developed out of the broader field of political economy in the late 19th century, owing to a desire to use an empirical approach more akin to the physical sciences.

   a. Opportunity cost
   b. Energy economics
   c. Inflation
   d. Economic

24. In microeconomics, _____ is quite simply the conversion of inputs into outputs. It is an economic process that uses resources to create a good or service that is suitable for exchange. This can include manufacturing, storing, shipping, and packaging.

   a. Production
   b. MET
   c. Solved
   d. Red Guards

25. _____ is subcontracting a process, such as product design or manufacturing, to a third-party company. The decision to outsource is often made in the interest of lowering cost or making better use of time and energy costs, redirecting or conserving energy directed at the competencies of a particular business, or to make more efficient use of land, labor, capital, (information) technology and resources. _____ became part of the business lexicon during the 1980s.

   a. Additional Funds Needed
   b. Electronic business
   c. Averch-Johnson effect
   d. Outsourcing

Chapter 15. Asymmetric Information and Organizational Design

26. A _____ or labor union is an organization of workers who have banded together to achieve common goals in key areas and working conditions. The _____, through its leadership, bargains with the employer on behalf of union members (rank and file members) and negotiates labor contracts (Collective bargaining) with employers. This may include the negotiation of wages, work rules, complaint procedures, rules governing hiring, firing and promotion of workers, benefits, workplace safety and policies.
   - a. Consumer goods
   - b. Guaranteed investment contracts
   - c. Trade union
   - d. Case-Shiller Home Price Indices

27. In economics, _____ refers to the ability of a person or a country to produce a particular good at a lower marginal cost and opportunity cost than another person or country. It is the ability to produce a product most efficiently given all the other products that could be produced. It can be contrasted with absolute advantage which refers to the ability of a person or a country to produce a particular good at a lower absolute cost than another.
   - a. Gravity model of trade
   - b. Triffin dilemma
   - c. Hot money
   - d. Comparative advantage

28. _____ is a branch of applied mathematics that is used in the social sciences (most notably economics), biology, engineering, political science, international relations, computer science, and philosophy. _____ attempts to mathematically capture behavior in strategic situations, in which an individual's success in making choices depends on the choices of others. While initially developed to analyze competitions in which one individual does better at another's expense (zero sum games), it has been expanded to treat a wide class of interactions, which are classified according to several criteria.
   - a. Proper equilibrium
   - b. Dollar auction
   - c. Discriminatory price auction
   - d. Game theory

29. _____ refers to the pricing of contributions (assets, tangible and intangible, services, and funds) transferred within an organization. For example, goods from the production division may be sold to the marketing division, or goods from a parent company may be sold to a foreign subsidiary. Since the prices are set within an organization (i.e. controlled), the typical market mechanisms that establish prices for such transactions between third parties may not apply.
   - a. Transfer pricing
   - b. Rational pricing
   - c. Two-part tariff
   - d. San Francisco congestion pricing

30. _____ is one of the four Ps of the marketing mix. The other three aspects are product, promotion, and place. It is also a key variable in microeconomic price allocation theory.
   - a. Point of total assumption
   - b. Premium pricing
   - c. Guaranteed Maximum Price
   - d. Pricing

31. _____ exists when sales of identical goods or services are transacted at different prices from the same provider. In a theoretical market with perfect information, no transaction costs or prohibition on secondary exchange (or re-selling) to prevent arbitrage, _____ can only be a feature of monopoly and oligopoly markets, where market power can be exercised. Otherwise, the moment the seller tries to sell the same good at different prices, the buyer at the lower price can arbitrage by selling to the consumer buying at the higher price but with a tiny discount.
   - a. Transfer pricing
   - b. Loss leader
   - c. Lerner Index
   - d. Price discrimination

Chapter 15. Asymmetric Information and Organizational Design

32. _____ is the term denoting either an entrance or changes which are inserted into a system and which activate/modify a process. It is an abstract concept, used in the modeling, system(s) design and system(s) exploitation. It is usually connected with other terms, e.g., _____ field, _____ variable, _____ parameter, _____ value, _____ signal, _____ device and _____ file.

a. AD-IA Model
b. ACCRA Cost of Living Index
c. ACEA agreement
d. Input

33. _____, when used as a special term, refers to various incentive plans introduced by businesses that provide direct or indirect payments to employees that depend on company's profitability in addition to employees' regular salary and bonuses. In publicly traded companies these plans typically amount to allocation of shares to employees.

The _____ plans are based on predetermined economic sharing rules that define the split of gains between the company as a principal and the employee as an agent.

a. Living wage
b. Pension insurance contract
c. Spiff
d. Profit sharing

34. A _____ is a situation that involves losing one quality or aspect of something in return for gaining another quality or aspect. It implies a decision to be made with full comprehension of both the upside and downside of a particular choice.

In economics the term is expressed as opportunity cost, referring the most preferred alternative given up.

a. Friedman-Savage utility function
b. Whitemail
c. Trade-off
d. Nonmarket

35. _____ , as defined by the _____ Association of America (Information technologyAA), is 'the study, design, development, implementation, support or management of computer-based information systems, particularly software applications and computer hardware.' _____ deals with the use of electronic computers and computer software to convert, store, protect, process, transmit, and securely retrieve information.

Today, the term _____ has ballooned to encompass many aspects of computing and technology, and the term has become very recognizable. The _____ umbrella can be quite large, covering many fields.

a. AD-IA Model
b. ACEA agreement
c. ACCRA Cost of Living Index
d. Information technology

36. A _____ is a professionally managed type of collective investment scheme that pools money from many investors and invests it in stocks, bonds, short-term money market instruments, and/or other securities. The _____ will have a fund manager that trades the pooled money on a regular basis. As of early 2008, the worldwide value of all _____s totals more than $26 trillion.

a. Participating policy
b. Mutual fund
c. Self-invested personal pension
d. Dark pools of liquidity

Chapter 15. Asymmetric Information and Organizational Design

37. _____ is the revenue to a brokerage firm when commissioned securities and insurance salespeople sell a product, whether it is an investment like stocks, bonds or insurance like life insurance or long term care insurance. The commission that the agent receives is usually a percentage of this figure, although some firms like Merrill Lynch use figures called Production Credits, usually smaller than _____, to determine payouts and retain more revenue.

For example, a mutual fund with a 5.75% sales charge is sold to someone who invests $10,000.

- a. Number of Shares
- b. Discretionary policy
- c. Monopoly price
- d. Gross Dealer Concession

38. A mutual _____ or stockholder is an individual or company (including a corporation) that legally owns one or more shares of stock in a joint stock company. A company's _____s collectively own that company. Thus, the typical goal of such companies is to enhance _____ value.
- a. Relative valuation
- b. Profit warning
- c. Prime Standard
- d. Shareholder

39. _____ was a survey conducted by the U.S. Department of Justice to gauge the prevalence of alcohol and illegal drug use among prior arrestees. It was a reformulation of the prior Drug Use Forecasting (DUF) program, focused on five drugs in particular: cocaine, marijuana, methamphetamine, opiates, and PCP.

Participants were randomly selected from arrest records in major metropolitan areas; because no personally identifying information is taken from each record chosen, the resulting data can be correlated to arrest rates, but not to the total population of persons charged.

- a. ACEA agreement
- b. ACCRA Cost of Living Index
- c. AD-IA Model
- d. Arrestee Drug Abuse Monitoring

40. _____ was a Scottish moral philosopher and a pioneer of political economy. One of the key figures of the Scottish Enlightenment, Smith is the author of The Theory of Moral Sentiments and An Inquiry into the Nature and Causes of the Wealth of Nations. The latter, usually abbreviated as The Wealth of Nations, is considered his magnum opus and the first modern work of economics.
- a. Alan Greenspan
- b. Adolf Hitler
- c. Adolph Fischer
- d. Adam Smith

41. _____ relates to decisions that define expectations, grant power, or verify performance. It consists either of a separate process or of a specific part of management or leadership processes. Sometimes people set up a government to administer these processes and systems.
- a. 1921 recession
- b. 130-30 fund
- c. 100-year flood
- d. Governance

Chapter 15. Asymmetric Information and Organizational Design 161

42. A _____ is:

- Rewrite _____, in generative grammar and computer science
- Standardization, a formal and widely-accepted statement, fact, definition, or qualification
- Operation, a determinate _____ for performing a mathematical operation and obtaining a certain result (Mathematics, Logic)
    - Unary operation
    - Binary operation
- _____ of inference, a function from sets of formulae to formulae (Mathematics, Logic)
- _____ of thumb, principle with broad application that is not intended to be strictly accurate or reliable for every situation. Also often simply referred to as a _____
- Moral, an atomic element of a moral code for guiding choices in human behavior
- Heuristic, a quantized '_____' which shows a tendency or probability for successful function
- A regulation, as in sports
- A Production _____, as in computer science
- Procedural law, a _____ set governing the application of laws to cases
    - A law, which may informally be called a '_____'
    - A court ruling, a decision by a court
- In the U.S. Government, a regulation mandated by Congress, but written or expanded upon by the Executive Branch.
- Norm (sociology), an informal but widely accepted _____, concept, truth, definition, or qualification (social norms, legal norms, coding norms)
- Norm (philosophy), a kind of sentence or a reason to act, feel or believe
- 'Rulership' is the concept of governance by a government:
    - Military _____, governance by a military body
    - Monastic _____, a collection of precepts that guides the life of monks or nuns in a religious order where the superior holds the place of Christ
- Slide _____

- '_____,' a song by Ayumi Hamasaki
- '_____,' a song by rapper Nas
- '_____s,' an album by the band The Whitest Boy Alive
- _____s: Pyaar Ka Superhit Formula, a 2003 Bollywood film
- ruler, an instrument for measuring lengths
- _____, a component of an astrolabe, circumferator or similar instrument
- The _____s, a bestselling self-help book
- _____ Project (Run Up-to-date Linux Everywhere), a project that aims to use up-to-date Linux software on old PCs
- _____ engine, a software system that helps managing business _____s
- Ja _____, a hip hop artist
    - R.U.L.E., a 2005 greatest hits album by rapper Ja _____
- '_____s,' a KMFDM song

a. Procter ' Gamble
c. Rule
b. Demand
d. Technocracy

43. The _____ is a statistical test used in inference, in which a given statistical hypothesis will be rejected when the value of the statistic is either sufficiently small or sufficiently large. The test is named after the 'tail' of data under the far left and far right of a bell-shaped normal data distribution, or bell curve. However, the terminology is extended to tests relating to distributions other than normal.
   a. Posterior probability
   b. Secular variation
   c. Semiparametric regression
   d. Two-tailed test

44. Procter is a surname, and may also refer to:

   - Bryan Waller Procter (pseud. Barry Cornwall), English poet
   - Goodwin Procter, American law firm
   - _____, consumer products multinational

   a. Drawdown
   b. Procter ' Gamble
   c. Tightness
   d. Bucket shop

45. In economics, _____ behavior is in between risk aversion and risk seeking. If offered either â,¬50 or a 50% chance of â,¬100, a risk averse person will take the â,¬50, a risk seeking person will take the 50% chance of â,¬100, and a _____ person would have no preference between the two options.

   In finance, when pricing an asset, a common technique is to figure out the probability of a future cash flow, then to discount that cash flow at the risk free rate.

   a. Currency risk
   b. Transaction risk
   c. Risk neutral
   d. Taleb distribution

46. In economics, _____ is a measure of the relative satisfaction from consumption of various goods and services. Given this measure, one may speak meaningfully of increasing or decreasing _____, and thereby explain economic behavior in terms of attempts to increase one's _____. For illustrative purposes, changes in _____ are sometimes expressed in units called utils.
   a. Utility
   b. Ordinal utility
   c. Utility function
   d. Expected utility hypothesis

47. A _____ is the minimum difference a person requires to be willing to take an uncertain bet, between the expected value of the bet and the certain value that he is indifferent to.

   The certainty equivalent is the guaranteed payoff at which a person is 'indifferent' between accepting the guaranteed payoff and a higher but uncertain payoff. (It is the amount of the higher payout minus the _____.)

   a. Linear model
   b. Ruin theory
   c. Risk premium
   d. Workers compensation

1. In a _____ there is both a monopoly (a single seller) and monopsony (a single buyer) in the same market.

In such market price and output will be determined by the non economic forces like bargaining power of both buyer and seller. A _____ model is often used in situations where the switching costs of both sides are prohibitively high.

- a. Bilateral monopoly
- b. Market concentration
- c. Revenue-cap regulation
- d. Price takers

2. In economics, a _____ exists when a specific individual or enterprise has sufficient control over a particular product or service to determine significantly the terms on which other individuals shall have access to it. Monopolies are thus characterized by a lack of economic competition for the good or service that they provide and a lack of viable substitute goods. The verb 'monopolize' refers to the process by which a firm gains persistently greater market share than what is expected under perfect competition.

- a. 1921 recession
- b. 100-year flood
- c. 130-30 fund
- d. Monopoly

3. _____ is an offer (often competitive) of setting a price one is willing to pay for something. A price offer is called a bid. The term may be used in context of auctions, stock exchange, card games, or real estate transactions.

- a. Central limit order book
- b. Bidding
- c. Normal good
- d. Bord halfpenny

4. In microeconomics, the reservation (or reserve) price is the maximum price a buyer is willing to pay for a good or service; or, conversely, the minimum price at which a seller is willing to sell a good or service. _____s are commonly used in auctions.

_____s vary for the buyer according to their disposable income, their desire for the good, and the prices of, and their information about substitute goods.

- a. Reservation price
- b. Mohring effect
- c. Returns to scale
- d. Producer surplus

5. _____s is the social science that studies the production, distribution, and consumption of goods and services. The term _____s comes from the Ancient Greek οἰκονομῖα from οἶκος (oikos, 'house') + νόμος (nomos, 'custom' or 'law'), hence 'rules of the house(hold)'. Current _____ models developed out of the broader field of political economy in the late 19th century, owing to a desire to use an empirical approach more akin to the physical sciences.

- a. Inflation
- b. Opportunity cost
- c. Energy economics
- d. Economic

6. _____ in economics and business is the result of an exchange and from that trade we assign a numerical monetary value to a good, service or asset. If Alice trades Bob 4 apples for an orange, the _____ of an orange is 4 apples. Inversely, the _____ of an apple is 1/4 oranges.

- a. Premium pricing
- b. Price
- c. Price war
- d. Price book

7. A _____ is a set of exclusive rights granted by a state to an inventor or his assignee for a limited period of time in exchange for a disclosure of an invention.

Chapter 16. Baraainina and Neaotiation

The procedure for granting _____s, the requirements placed on the _____ee and the extent of the exclusive rights vary widely between countries according to national laws and international agreements. Typically, however, a _____ application must include one or more claims defining the invention which must be new, inventive, and useful or industrially applicable.

a. Bank regulation
c. Long service leave
b. Bona fide occupational qualification
d. Patent

8. _____ is a way of expressing knowledge or belief that an event will occur or has occurred. In mathematics the concept has been given an exact meaning in _____ theory, that is used extensively in such areas of study as mathematics, statistics, finance, gambling, science, and philosophy to draw conclusions about the likelihood of potential events and the underlying mechanics of complex systems.

The word _____ does not have a consistent direct definition.

a. 1921 recession
c. Probability
b. 130-30 fund
d. 100-year flood

9. _____ is the a method of technical and economic research of the systems for purpose to optimize a parity between system's consumer functions or properties and expenses to achieve those functions or properties.

This methodology for continuous perfection of production, industrial technologies, organizational structures was developed by Juryj Sobolev in 1948 at the 'Perm telephone factory'

- 1948 Juryj Sobolev - the first success in application of a method analysis at the 'Perm telephone factory' .
- 1949 - the first application for the invention as result of use of the new method.

Today in economically developed countries practically each enterprise or the company use methodology of the kind of functional-cost analysis as a practice of the quality management, most full satisfying to principles of standards of series ISO 9000.

- Interest of consumer not in products itself, but the advantage which it will receive from its usage.
- The consumer aspires to reduce his expenses
- Functions needed by consumer can be executed in the various ways, and, hence, with various efficiency and expenses. Among possible alternatives of realization of functions exist such in which the parity of quality and the price is the optimal for the consumer.

The goal of _____ is achievement of the highest consumer satisfaction of production at simultaneous decrease in all kinds of industrial expenses Classical _____ has three English synonyms - Value Engineering, Value Management, Value Analysis.

a. Monopoly wage
c. Willingness to pay
b. Function cost analysis
d. Staple financing

10. _____ is the acquisition of goods and/or services at the best possible total cost of ownership, in the right quantity and quality, at the right time, in the right place and from the right source for the direct benefit or use of corporations or individuals, generally via a contract. Simple _____ may involve nothing more than repeat purchasing. Complex _____ could involve finding long term partners - or even 'co-destiny' suppliers that might fundamentally commit one organization to another.
   a. Golden umbrella
   b. Procurement
   c. Pre-emerging markets
   d. Sole proprietorship

11. _____ is a concept in economics, finance, and psychology related to the behaviour of consumers and investors under uncertainty. _____ is the reluctance of a person to accept a bargain with an uncertain payoff rather than another bargain with a more certain, but possibly lower, expected payoff. For example, a risk-averse investor might choose to put his or her money into a bank account with a low but guaranteed interest rate, rather than into a stock that is likely to have high returns, but also has a chance of becoming worthless.
   a. Risk theory
   b. Reinsurance
   c. Compound annual growth rate
   d. Risk aversion

12. The phrase _____ refers to the aspect of corporate strategy, corporate finance and management dealing with the buying, selling and combining of different companies that can aid, finance, or help a growing company in a given industry grow rapidly without having to create another business entity.

    An acquisition, also known as a takeover or a buyout, is the buying of one company (the 'target') by another. An acquisition may be friendly or hostile.

   a. Peace dividend
   b. Political economy
   c. Productive and unproductive labour
   d. Mergers and acquisitions

13. In economics and sociology, an _____ is any factor (financial or non-financial) that enables or motivates a particular course of action, or counts as a reason for preferring one choice to the alternatives. It is an expectation that encourages people to behave in a certain way. Since human beings are purposeful creatures, the study of _____ structures is central to the study of all economic activity (both in terms of individual decision-making and in terms of co-operation and competition within a larger institutional structure.)
   a. Isocost
   b. Economic reform
   c. Epstein-Zin preferences
   d. Incentive

14. _____ is one of the four Ps of the marketing mix. The other three aspects are product, promotion, and place. It is also a key variable in microeconomic price allocation theory.
   a. Premium pricing
   b. Point of total assumption
   c. Guaranteed Maximum Price
   d. Pricing

15. _____ is a term used in game theory. A game is said to have _____ if all players know all moves that have taken place.

    Chess is an example of a game with _____ as each player can see all of the pieces on the board at all times.

a. Game theory
b. Perfect rationality
c. Parity game
d. Perfect information

16. A _____ or labor union is an organization of workers who have banded together to achieve common goals in key areas and working conditions. The _____, through its leadership, bargains with the employer on behalf of union members (rank and file members) and negotiates labor contracts (Collective bargaining) with employers. This may include the negotiation of wages, work rules, complaint procedures, rules governing hiring, firing and promotion of workers, benefits, workplace safety and policies.
   a. Trade union
   b. Consumer goods
   c. Guaranteed investment contracts
   d. Case-Shiller Home Price Indices

17. In economics, _____ refers to the ability of a person or a country to produce a particular good at a lower marginal cost and opportunity cost than another person or country. It is the ability to produce a product most efficiently given all the other products that could be produced. It can be contrasted with absolute advantage which refers to the ability of a person or a country to produce a particular good at a lower absolute cost than another.
   a. Gravity model of trade
   b. Hot money
   c. Triffin dilemma
   d. Comparative advantage

18. _____ is the concept or idea of fairness in economics, particularly as to taxation or welfare economics.

In welfare economics, _____ may be distinguished from economic efficiency in overall evaluation of social welfare. Although '_____' has broader uses, it may be posed as a counterpart to economic inequality in yielding a 'good' distribution of welfare.

   a. ACEA agreement
   b. AD-IA Model
   c. ACCRA Cost of Living Index
   d. Equity

19. A _____ is a counterfeit agreement among industries. It is an informal organization of producers that agree to coordinate prices and production. _____s usually occur in an oligopolistic industry, where there is a small number of sellers and usually involve homogeneous products.
   a. Shanzhai
   b. Shill
   c. 100-year flood
   d. Cartel

20. _____ is the transition of a national economy from monopoly control by groups of large businesses to a free market economy. This change rarely arises naturally, and is generally the result of regulation by a governing body.

A modern example of _____ is the economic restructuring of Germany after the fall of the Third Reich in 1945.

   a. Market power
   b. Monopolization
   c. Complementary monopoly
   d. Decartelization

21. _____, in law and economics, is a form of risk management primarily used to hedge against the risk of a contingent loss. _____ is defined as the equitable transfer of the risk of a loss, from one entity to another, in exchange for a premium, and can be thought of as a guaranteed small loss to prevent a large, possibly devastating loss. An insurer is a company selling the _____; an insured or policyholder is the person or entity buying the _____.

Chapter 16. Bargaining and Negotiation

a. AD-IA Model
b. ACEA agreement
c. Insurance
d. ACCRA Cost of Living Index

22. The _____ is an economic law stated as: 'In an efficient market all identical goods must have only one price.' The _____ relates to the outcome of free trade and globalization. It is the theory that some day all areas of the world will make the same amount of money as every other part of the world for equal work/product quality.

The intuition for this law is that all sellers will flock to the highest prevailing price, and all buyers to the lowest current market price.

a. Precaria
b. Leave of absence
c. Loss of use
d. Law of one price

23. A _____ is a process of buying and selling goods when potential buyers submit their bids and potential sellers simultaneously submit their ask prices to an auctioneer, and then an auctioneer chooses some price p that clears the market: all the sellers who asked less than p sell and all buyers who bid more than p buy at this price p.

A _____ can be analyzed as a game. Players are buyers and sellers.

a. Graph continuous
b. Double Auction
c. Repeated game
d. Complete information

Chapter 17. Auctions and Competitive Bidding

1. _____ is the acquisition of goods and/or services at the best possible total cost of ownership, in the right quantity and quality, at the right time, in the right place and from the right source for the direct benefit or use of corporations or individuals, generally via a contract. Simple _____ may involve nothing more than repeat purchasing. Complex _____ could involve finding long term partners - or even 'co-destiny' suppliers that might fundamentally commit one organization to another.
   - a. Sole proprietorship
   - b. Golden umbrella
   - c. Pre-emerging markets
   - d. Procurement

2. _____ is an offer (often competitive) of setting a price one is willing to pay for something. A price offer is called a bid. The term may be used in context of auctions, stock exchange, card games, or real estate transactions.
   - a. Central limit order book
   - b. Bord halfpenny
   - c. Normal good
   - d. Bidding

3. An _____ is a type of auction, whose most typical form is the 'open outcry' auction. The auctioneer opens the auction by announcing a Suggested Opening Bid, a starting price or reserve for the item on sale and then accepts increasingly higher bids from the floor consisting of buyers with a possible interest in the item. Unlike sealed bid auctions, 'open outcry' auctions are 'open' or fully transparent as the identity of all bidders is disclosed to each other bidder during the auction.
   - a. Online auction business model
   - b. English auction
   - c. Auction school
   - d. Auction sniping

4. A _____ is a type of auction where the auctioneer begins with a high asking price which is lowered until some participant is willing to accept the auctioneer's price, or a predetermined reserve price (the seller's minimum acceptable price) is reached. The winning participant pays the last announced price. This is also known as a 'clock auction' or an open-outcry descending-price auction.
   - a. Box social
   - b. French auction
   - c. Vickrey auction
   - d. Dutch auction

5. In probability theory and statistics, the _____ (or expectation value or mean and for continuous random variables with a density function it is the probability density -weighted integral of the possible values.

   The term '_____' can be misleading.
   - a. AD-IA Model
   - b. ACEA agreement
   - c. ACCRA Cost of Living Index
   - d. Expected value

6. _____ is the a method of technical and economic research of the systems for purpose to optimize a parity between system's consumer functions or properties and expenses to achieve those functions or properties.

   This methodology for continuous perfection of production, industrial technologies, organizational structures was developed by Juryj Sobolev in 1948 at the 'Perm telephone factory'

   - 1948 Juryj Sobolev - the first success in application of a method analysis at the 'Perm telephone factory'.
   - 1949 - the first application for the invention as result of use of the new method.

Chapter 17. Auctions and Competitive Bidding

Today in economically developed countries practically each enterprise or the company use methodology of the kind of functional-cost analysis as a practice of the quality management, most full satisfying to principles of standards of series ISO 9000.

- Interest of consumer not in products itself, but the advantage which it will receive from its usage.
- The consumer aspires to reduce his expenses
- Functions needed by consumer can be executed in the various ways, and, hence, with various efficiency and expenses. Among possible alternatives of realization of functions exist such in which the parity of quality and the price is the optimal for the consumer.

The goal of _____ is achievement of the highest consumer satisfaction of production at simultaneous decrease in all kinds of industrial expenses Classical _____ has three English synonyms - Value Engineering, Value Management, Value Analysis.

a. Willingness to pay
c. Staple financing
b. Function cost analysis
d. Monopoly wage

7. In a _____ there is both a monopoly (a single seller) and monopsony (a single buyer) in the same market.

In such market price and output will be determined by the non economic forces like bargaining power of both buyer and seller. A _____ model is often used in situations where the switching costs of both sides are prohibitively high.

a. Market concentration
c. Price takers
b. Revenue-cap regulation
d. Bilateral monopoly

8. _____ is a term used in game theory. A game is said to have _____ if all players know all moves that have taken place.

Chess is an example of a game with _____ as each player can see all of the pieces on the board at all times.

a. Perfect rationality
c. Perfect information
b. Parity game
d. Game theory

9. A mutual _____ or stockholder is an individual or company (including a corporation) that legally owns one or more shares of stock in a joint stock company. A company's _____s collectively own that company. Thus, the typical goal of such companies is to enhance _____ value.

a. Prime Standard
c. Profit warning
b. Shareholder
d. Relative valuation

10. In economics, a _____ exists when a specific individual or enterprise has sufficient control over a particular product or service to determine significantly the terms on which other individuals shall have access to it. Monopolies are thus characterized by a lack of economic competition for the good or service that they provide and a lack of viable substitute goods. The verb 'monopolize' refers to the process by which a firm gains persistently greater market share than what is expected under perfect competition.
   a. Monopoly
   b. 1921 recession
   c. 100-year flood
   d. 130-30 fund

11. _____ is a branch of applied mathematics that is used in the social sciences (most notably economics), biology, engineering, political science, international relations, computer science, and philosophy. _____ attempts to mathematically capture behavior in strategic situations, in which an individual's success in making choices depends on the choices of others. While initially developed to analyze competitions in which one individual does better at another's expense (zero sum games), it has been expanded to treat a wide class of interactions, which are classified according to several criteria.
   a. Proper equilibrium
   b. Discriminatory price auction
   c. Game theory
   d. Dollar auction

12. A _____ is a type of sealed-bid auction, where bidders submit written bids without knowing the bid of the other people in the auction. The highest bidder wins, but the price paid is the second-highest bid. The auction was created by William Vickrey.
   a. Box social
   b. Mystery auction
   c. Vickrey auction
   d. Forward auction

13. _____ is a way of expressing knowledge or belief that an event will occur or has occurred. In mathematics the concept has been given an exact meaning in _____ theory, that is used extensively in such areas of study as mathematics, statistics, finance, gambling, science, and philosophy to draw conclusions about the likelihood of potential events and the underlying mechanics of complex systems.

The word _____ does not have a consistent direct definition.

   a. Probability
   b. 100-year flood
   c. 1921 recession
   d. 130-30 fund

14. In microeconomics, the reservation (or reserve) price is the maximum price a buyer is willing to pay for a good or service; or, conversely, the minimum price at which a seller is willing to sell a good or service. _____s are commonly used in auctions.

_____s vary for the buyer according to their disposable income, their desire for the good, and the prices of, and their information about substitute goods.

   a. Producer surplus
   b. Reservation price
   c. Returns to scale
   d. Mohring effect

15. _____ in economics and business is the result of an exchange and from that trade we assign a numerical monetary value to a good, service or asset. If Alice trades Bob 4 apples for an orange, the _____ of an orange is 4 apples. Inversely, the _____ of an apple is 1/4 oranges.

Chapter 17. Auctions and Competitive Bidding

a. Price book
b. Price war
c. Premium pricing
d. Price

16. An _____ is a market form in which a market or industry is dominated by a small number of sellers (oligopolists.) Because there are few participants in this type of market, each oligopolist is aware of the actions of the others. The decisions of one firm influence, and are influenced by, the decisions of other firms.
    a. ACEA agreement
    b. ACCRA Cost of Living Index
    c. Oligopsony
    d. Oligopoly

17. _____ is a measure of the strength of a brand, product, service relative to competitive offerings. There is often a geographic element to the competitive landscape. In defining _____, you must see to what extent a product, brand, or firm controls a product category in a given geographic area.
    a. Price elasticity of supply
    b. Demand shaping
    c. Market dominance
    d. Horizontal territorial allocation

18. In economics, _____ behavior is in between risk aversion and risk seeking. If offered either â¬50 or a 50% chance of â¬100, a risk averse person will take the â¬50, a risk seeking person will take the 50% chance of â¬100, and a _____ person would have no preference between the two options.

    In finance, when pricing an asset, a common technique is to figure out the probability of a future cash flow, then to discount that cash flow at the risk free rate.

    a. Risk neutral
    b. Taleb distribution
    c. Currency risk
    d. Transaction risk

19. Discounting is a financial mechanism in which a debtor obtains the right to delay payments to a creditor, for a defined period of time, in exchange for a charge or fee. Essentially, the party that owes money in the present purchases the right to delay the payment until some future date. The _____, or charge, is simply the difference between the original amount owed in the present and the amount that has to be paid in the future to settle the debt.
    a. Discount
    b. Reliability theory
    c. Certified Risk Manager
    d. Reinsurance

20. The _____ is an interest rate a central bank charges depository institutions that borrow reserves from it.

    The term _____ has two meanings:

    - the same as interest rate; the term 'discount' does not refer to the meaning of the word, but to the purpose of using the quantity, such as computations of present value, e.g. net present value or discounted cash flow

    - the annual effective _____, which is the annual interest divided by the capital including that interest; this rate is lower than the interest rate; it corresponds to using the value after a year as the nominal value, and seeing the initial value as the nominal value minus a discount; it is used for Treasury Bills and similar financial instruments

The annual effective _____ is the annual interest divided by the capital including that interest, which is the interest rate divided by 100% plus the interest rate. It is the annual discount factor to be applied to the future cash flow, to find the discount, subtracted from a future value to find the value one year earlier.

For example, suppose there is a government bond that sells for $95 and pays $100 in a year's time.

- a. Stochastic volatility
- b. Perpetuity
- c. Johansen test
- d. Discount rate

21. _____ is the planning process used to determine whether a firm's long term investments such as new machinery, replacement machinery, new plants, new products, and research development projects are worth pursuing. It is budget for major capital, or investment, expenditures.

Many formal methods are used in _____, including the techniques such as

- Net present value
- Profitability index
- Internal rate of return
- Modified Internal Rate of Return
- Equivalent annuity

These methods use the incremental cash flows from each potential investment, or project. Techniques based on accounting earnings and accounting rules are sometimes used - though economists consider this to be improper - such as the accounting rate of return, and 'return on investment.' Simplified and hybrid methods are used as well, such as payback period and discounted payback period.

- a. Capital budgeting
- b. Participating preferred stock
- c. Voting interest
- d. Preferred stock

22. _____ is a concept in economics, finance, and psychology related to the behaviour of consumers and investors under uncertainty. _____ is the reluctance of a person to accept a bargain with an uncertain payoff rather than another bargain with a more certain, but possibly lower, expected payoff. For example, a risk-averse investor might choose to put his or her money into a bank account with a low but guaranteed interest rate, rather than into a stock that is likely to have high returns, but also has a chance of becoming worthless.
- a. Compound annual growth rate
- b. Risk aversion
- c. Reinsurance
- d. Risk theory

23. _____s is the social science that studies the production, distribution, and consumption of goods and services. The term _____s comes from the Ancient Greek οἰκονομῐ́α from οἶκος (oikos, 'house') + νόμος (nomos, 'custom' or 'law'), hence 'rules of the house(hold)'. Current _____ models developed out of the broader field of political economy in the late 19th century, owing to a desire to use an empirical approach more akin to the physical sciences.
- a. Energy economics
- b. Opportunity cost
- c. Inflation
- d. Economic

Chapter 17. Auctions and Competitive Bidding

24. In economics and sociology, an _____ is any factor (financial or non-financial) that enables or motivates a particular course of action, or counts as a reason for preferring one choice to the alternatives. It is an expectation that encourages people to behave in a certain way. Since human beings are purposeful creatures, the study of _____ structures is central to the study of all economic activity (both in terms of individual decision-making and in terms of co-operation and competition within a larger institutional structure.)

   a. Epstein-Zin preferences
   b. Economic reform
   c. Isocost
   d. Incentive

25. A _____ is a situation that involves losing one quality or aspect of something in return for gaining another quality or aspect. It implies a decision to be made with full comprehension of both the upside and downside of a particular choice.

In economics the term is expressed as opportunity cost, referring the most preferred alternative given up.

   a. Nonmarket
   b. Whitemail
   c. Friedman-Savage utility function
   d. Trade-off

26. A United States Treasury security is a government debt issued by the United States Department of the Treasury through the Bureau of the Public Debt. Treasury securities are the debt financing instruments of the United States Federal government, and they are often referred to simply as Treasuries. There are four types of marketable treasury securities: _____, Treasury notes, Treasury bonds, and Treasury Inflation Protected Securities (TIPS.)

   a. Treasury bills
   b. Labour battalions
   c. Debt to Assets
   d. Lawcards

Chapter 18. Linear Programming

1. _____ is the planning process used to determine whether a firm's long term investments such as new machinery, replacement machinery, new plants, new products, and research development projects are worth pursuing. It is budget for major capital, or investment, expenditures.

Many formal methods are used in _____, including the techniques such as

- Net present value
- Profitability index
- Internal rate of return
- Modified Internal Rate of Return
- Equivalent annuity

These methods use the incremental cash flows from each potential investment, or project. Techniques based on accounting earnings and accounting rules are sometimes used - though economists consider this to be improper - such as the accounting rate of return, and 'return on investment.' Simplified and hybrid methods are used as well, such as payback period and discounted payback period.

a. Capital budgeting
b. Preferred stock
c. Participating preferred stock
d. Voting interest

2. _____ is used to assign the available resources in an economic way. It is part of resource management.

In strategic planning, is a plan for using available resources, for example human resources, especially in the near term, to achieve goals for the future.

a. 130-30 fund
b. 1921 recession
c. 100-year flood
d. Resource allocation

3. _____s (economically referred to as land or raw materials) occur naturally within environments that exist relatively undisturbed by mankind, in a natural form. A _____'s is often characterized by amounts of biodiversity existent in various ecosystems.

Mining, petroleum extraction, fishing, hunting, and forestry are generally considered natural-resource industries.

a. 130-30 fund
b. 100-year flood
c. Natural resource
d. 1921 recession

4. The Organization of the Petroleum Exporting Countries is a cartel of twelve countries made up of Algeria, Angola, Ecuador, Iran, Iraq, Kuwait, Libya, Nigeria, Qatar, Saudi Arabia, the United Arab Emirates, and Venezuela. The cartel has maintained its headquarters in Vienna since 1965, and hosts regular meetings among the oil ministers of its Member Countries. Indonesia withdrew its membership in _____ in 2008 after it became a net importer of oil, but stated it would likely return if it became a net exporter in the world.

a. OPEC
b. AD-IA Model
c. ACEA agreement
d. ACCRA Cost of Living Index

Chapter 18. Linear Programming

5. A _____ is a counterfeit agreement among industries. It is an informal organization of producers that agree to coordinate prices and production. _____s usually occur in an oligopolistic industry, where there is a small number of sellers and usually involve homogeneous products.
   a. Cartel
   b. Shill
   c. 100-year flood
   d. Shanzhai

6. _____ is the transition of a national economy from monopoly control by groups of large businesses to a free market economy. This change rarely arises naturally, and is generally the result of regulation by a governing body.

   A modern example of _____ is the economic restructuring of Germany after the fall of the Third Reich in 1945.

   a. Market power
   b. Monopolization
   c. Complementary monopoly
   d. Decartelization

7. _____s is the social science that studies the production, distribution, and consumption of goods and services. The term _____s comes from the Ancient Greek oá¼°κονομῖα from oá¼¶κος (oikos, 'house') + vÏŒμος (nomos, 'custom' or 'law'), hence 'rules of the house(hold)'. Current _____ models developed out of the broader field of political economy in the late 19th century, owing to a desire to use an empirical approach more akin to the physical sciences.
   a. Economic
   b. Energy economics
   c. Inflation
   d. Opportunity cost

8. The terms 'dependent variable' and '_____' are used in similar but subtly different ways in mathematics and statistics as part of the standard terminology in those subjects. They are used to distinguish between two types of quantities being considered, separating them into those available at the start of a process and those being created by it, where the latter (dependent variables) are dependent on the former (_____s.)

   The _____ is typically the variable being manipulated or changed and the dependent variable is the observed result of the _____ being manipulated.

   a. Independent variable
   b. AD-IA Model
   c. ACCRA Cost of Living Index
   d. ACEA agreement

9. _____ in economics and business is the result of an exchange and from that trade we assign a numerical monetary value to a good, service or asset. If Alice trades Bob 4 apples for an orange, the _____ of an orange is 4 apples. Inversely, the _____ of an apple is 1/4 oranges.
   a. Price book
   b. Price war
   c. Premium pricing
   d. Price

10. Loosely, the _____ is the change in the objective value of the optimal solution of an optimization problem obtained by relaxing the constraint by one unit. In a business application, a _____ is the maximum price that management is willing to pay for an extra unit of a given limited resource. For example, if a production line is already operating at its maximum 40 hour limit, the _____ would be the price of keeping the line operational for an additional hour.

a. 130-30 fund
c. 1921 recession
b. 100-year flood
d. Shadow price

11. A _____ is a situation that involves losing one quality or aspect of something in return for gaining another quality or aspect. It implies a decision to be made with full comprehension of both the upside and downside of a particular choice.

In economics the term is expressed as opportunity cost, referring the most preferred alternative given up.

a. Whitemail
c. Nonmarket
b. Friedman-Savage utility function
d. Trade-off

12. In mathematics, a _____ system is a system which is not linear, that is, a system which does not satisfy the superposition principle, or whose output is not proportional to its input. Less technically, a _____ system is any problem where the variable(s) to be solved for cannot be written as a linear combination of independent components. A nonhomogeneous system, which is linear apart from the presence of a function of the independent variables, is _____ according to a strict definition, but such systems are usually studied alongside linear systems, because they can be transformed to a linear system of multiple variables.

a. 100-year flood
c. Nonlinear
b. 130-30 fund
d. Nonlinear system

13. In economics and finance, _____ is the change in total cost that arises when the quantity produced changes by one unit. It is the cost of producing one more unit of a good. Mathematically, the _____ function is expressed as the first derivative of the total cost (TC) function with respect to quantity (Q.)

a. Marginal cost
c. Quality costs
b. Khozraschyot
d. Variable cost

14. _____ or economic opportunity loss is the value of the next best alternative foregone as the result of making a decision. _____ analysis is an important part of a company's decision-making processes but is not treated as an actual cost in any financial statement. The next best thing that a person can engage in is referred to as the _____ of doing the best thing and ignoring the next best thing to be done.

a. Economic
c. Economic ideology
b. Industrial organization
d. Opportunity cost

15. The terms '_____' and 'independent variable' are used in similar but subtly different ways in mathematics and statistics as part of the standard terminology in those subjects. They are used to distinguish between two types of quantities being considered, separating them into those available at the start of a process and those being created by it, where the latter (_____s) are dependent on the former (independent variables.)

In traditional calculus, a function is defined as a relation between two terms called variables because their values vary.

a. 100-year flood
c. Dependent variable
b. 130-30 fund
d. 1921 recession

Chapter 19. Capital Budgeting

1. _____ is the planning process used to determine whether a firm's long term investments such as new machinery, replacement machinery, new plants, new products, and research development projects are worth pursuing. It is budget for major capital, or investment, expenditures.

Many formal methods are used in _____, including the techniques such as

- Net present value
- Profitability index
- Internal rate of return
- Modified Internal Rate of Return
- Equivalent annuity

These methods use the incremental cash flows from each potential investment, or project. Techniques based on accounting earnings and accounting rules are sometimes used - though economists consider this to be improper - such as the accounting rate of return, and 'return on investment.' Simplified and hybrid methods are used as well, such as payback period and discounted payback period.

a. Preferred stock
c. Voting interest
b. Capital budgeting
d. Participating preferred stock

2. The _____ consists of a number of economic theories which describe the nature of the firm, company including its existence, its behaviour, and its relationship with the market.

In simplified terms, the _____ aims to answer these questions:

1. Existence - why do firms emerge, why are not all transactions in the economy mediated over the market?
2. Boundaries - why the boundary between firms and the market is located exactly there? Which transactions are performed internally and which are negotiated on the market?
3. Organization - why are firms structured in such specific way? What is the interplay of formal and informal relationships?

Despite looking simple, these questions are not answered by the established economic theory, which usually views firms as given, and treats them as black boxes without any internal structure.

The First World War period saw a change of emphasis in economic theory away from industry-level analysis which mainly included analysing markets to analysis at the level of the firm, as it became increasingly clear that perfect competition was no longer an adequate model of how firms behaved. Economic theory till then had focussed on trying to understand markets alone and there had been little study on understanding why firms or organisations exist.

a. Khazzoom-Brookes postulate
c. Policy Ineffectiveness Proposition
b. Technology gap
d. Theory of the firm

3. _____ is the value on a given date of a future payment or series of future payments, discounted to reflect the time value of money and other factors such as investment risk. _____ calculations are widely used in business and economics to provide a means to compare cash flows at different times on a meaningful 'like to like' basis.

Chapter 19. Capital Budgeting

Money value fluctuates over time: $100 today are not worth $100 in five years.

a. Present value
b. Tax shield
c. Present value of costs
d. Future value

4. _____ is the a method of technical and economic research of the systems for purpose to optimize a parity between system's consumer functions or properties and expenses to achieve those functions or properties.

This methodology for continuous perfection of production, industrial technologies, organizational structures was developed by Juryj Sobolev in 1948 at the 'Perm telephone factory'

- 1948 Juryj Sobolev - the first success in application of a method analysis at the 'Perm telephone factory'.
- 1949 - the first application for the invention as result of use of the new method.

Today in economically developed countries practically each enterprise or the company use methodology of the kind of functional-cost analysis as a practice of the quality management, most full satisfying to principles of standards of series ISO 9000.

- Interest of consumer not in products itself, but the advantage which it will receive from its usage.
- The consumer aspires to reduce his expenses
- Functions needed by consumer can be executed in the various ways, and, hence, with various efficiency and expenses. Among possible alternatives of realization of functions exist such in which the parity of quality and the price is the optimal for the consumer.

The goal of _____ is achievement of the highest consumer satisfaction of production at simultaneous decrease in all kinds of industrial expenses Classical _____ has three English synonyms - Value Engineering, Value Management, Value Analysis.

a. Willingness to pay
b. Function cost analysis
c. Staple financing
d. Monopoly wage

5. _____ measures the nominal future sum of money that a given sum of money is 'worth' at a specified time in the future assuming a certain interest rate rate of return; it is the present value multiplied by the accumulation function.

The value does not include corrections for inflation or other factors that affect the true value of money in the future. This is used in time value of money calculations.

a. Negative gearing
b. Future-oriented
c. Present value
d. Future value

6. _____ is a fee paid on borrowed assets. It is the price paid for the use of borrowed money, or, money earned by deposited funds. Assets that are sometimes lent with _____ include money, shares, consumer goods through hire purchase, major assets such as aircraft, and even entire factories in finance lease arrangements.

Chapter 19. Capital Budgeting

a. Internal debt
c. Asset protection

b. Insolvency
d. Interest

7. An _____ is the price a borrower pays for the use of money they do not own, for instance a small company might borrow from a bank to kick start their business, and the return a lender receives for deferring the use of funds, by lending it to the borrower. _____s are normally expressed as a percentage rate over the period of one year.

_____s targets are also a vital tool of monetary policy and are used to control variables like investment, inflation, and unemployment.

a. Interest rate
c. Enterprise value

b. Arrow-Debreu model
d. ACCRA Cost of Living Index

8. The term _____ refers to economy-wide fluctuations in production or economic activity over several months or years. These fluctuations occur around a long-term growth trend, and typically involve shifts over time between periods of relatively rapid economic growth (expansion or boom), and periods of relative stagnation or decline (contraction or recession.)

These fluctuations are often measured using the growth rate of real gross domestic product.

a. Consumer theory
c. Business cycle

b. Nominal value
d. Tobit model

9. _____ refers to the movement of cash into or out of a business or financial product. It is usually measured during a specified, finite period of time. Measurement of _____ can be used

- to determine a project's rate of return or value. The time of _____s into and out of projects are used as inputs in financial models such as internal rate of return, and net present value.
- to determine problems with a business's liquidity. Being profitable does not necessarily mean being liquid. A company can fail because of a shortage of cash, even while profitable.
- as an alternate measure of a business's profits when it is believed that accrual accounting concepts do not represent economic realities. For example, a company may be notionally profitable but generating little operational cash (as may be the case for a company that barters its products rather than selling for cash.) In such a case, the company may be deriving additional operating cash by issuing shares evaluating default risk, re-investment requirements, etc.

_____ is a generic term used differently depending on the context. It may be defined by users for their own purposes.

a. Strip financing
c. Second lien loan

b. Restricted stock
d. Cash flow

10. _____ is the concept of adding accumulated interest back to the principal, so that interest is earned on interest from that moment on. The act of declaring interest to be principal is called compounding (i.e., interest is compounded.) A loan, for example, may have its interest compounded every month: in this case, a loan with $100 principal and 1% interest per month would have a balance of $101 at the end of the first month.

a. Fama-French three factor model
b. General purpose technologies
c. Compound interest
d. Foreclosure data providers

11. _____ is a term used in accounting, economics and finance to spread the cost of an asset over the span of several years.

In simple words we can say that _____ is the reduction in the value of an asset due to usage, passage of time, wear and tear, technological outdating or obsolescence, depletion, inadequacy, rot, rust, decay or other such factors.

In accounting, _____ is a term used to describe any method of attributing the historical or purchase cost of an asset across its useful life, roughly corresponding to normal wear and tear.

a. Historical cost
b. Net income per employee
c. Salvage value
d. Depreciation

12. _____ or net present worth (NPW) is defined as the total present value (PV) of a time series of cash flows. It is a standard method for using the time value of money to appraise long-term projects. Used for capital budgeting, and widely throughout economics, it measures the excess or shortfall of cash flows, in present value terms, once financing charges are met.

a. Net present value
b. Maturity
c. Refinancing risk
d. Future value

13. To _____ is to impose a financial charge or other levy upon a taxpayer by a state or the functional equivalent of a state.

_____es are also imposed by many subnational entities. _____es consist of direct _____ or indirect _____, and may be paid in money or as its labour equivalent (often but not always unpaid.)

a. 1921 recession
b. 130-30 fund
c. 100-year flood
d. Tax

14. To tax is to impose a financial charge or other levy upon a taxpayer by a state or the functional equivalent of a state.

_____ are also imposed by many subnational entities. _____ consist of direct tax or indirect tax, and may be paid in money or as its labour equivalent (often but not always unpaid.)

a. 100-year flood
b. 130-30 fund
c. Taxes
d. 1921 recession

15. Discounting is a financial mechanism in which a debtor obtains the right to delay payments to a creditor, for a defined period of time, in exchange for a charge or fee. Essentially, the party that owes money in the present purchases the right to delay the payment until some future date. The _____, or charge, is simply the difference between the original amount owed in the present and the amount that has to be paid in the future to settle the debt.

Chapter 19. Capital Budgeting

a. Reliability theory
c. Certified Risk Manager
b. Reinsurance
d. Discount

16. The _____ is an interest rate a central bank charges depository institutions that borrow reserves from it.

The term _____ has two meanings:

- the same as interest rate; the term 'discount' does not refer to the meaning of the word, but to the purpose of using the quantity, such as computations of present value, e.g. net present value or discounted cash flow

- the annual effective _____, which is the annual interest divided by the capital including that interest; this rate is lower than the interest rate; it corresponds to using the value after a year as the nominal value, and seeing the initial value as the nominal value minus a discount; it is used for Treasury Bills and similar financial instruments

The annual effective _____ is the annual interest divided by the capital including that interest, which is the interest rate divided by 100% plus the interest rate. It is the annual discount factor to be applied to the future cash flow, to find the discount, subtracted from a future value to find the value one year earlier.

For example, suppose there is a government bond that sells for $95 and pays $100 in a year's time.

a. Discount rate
c. Perpetuity
b. Johansen test
d. Stochastic volatility

17. In economics, _____ is a rise in the general level of prices of goods and services in an economy over a period of time. When the general price level rises, each unit of currency buys fewer goods and services; consequently, _____ is also a decline in the real value of money--a loss of purchasing power in the medium of exchange which is also the monetary unit of account in the economy. A chief measure of general price-level _____ is the general _____ rate, which is the percentage change in a general price index (normally the Consumer Price Index) over time.

a. Opportunity cost
c. Energy economics
b. Inflation
d. Economic

18. _____ is the income of individuals or nations after adjusting for inflation. It is calculated by subtracting inflation from the nominal income. Real variables, such as _____, real GDP, and real interest rate are variables that are measured in physical units, while nominal variables such as nominal income, nominal GDP, and nominal interest rate are measured in monetary units.

a. Net national income
c. Family income
b. Windfall gain
d. Real income

19. The '_____' is approximately the nominal interest rate minus the inflation rate Since the inflation rate over the course of a loan is not known initially, volatility in inflation represents a risk to both the lender and the borrower.

In economics and finance, an individual who lends money for repayment at a later point in time expects to be compensated for the time value of money, or not having the use of that money while it is lent.

Chapter 19. Capital Budgeting

a. Reflation
b. Cost-push inflation
c. Core inflation
d. Real interest rate

20. _____ is a financial mechanism in which a debtor obtains the right to delay payments to a creditor, for a defined period of time, in exchange for a charge or fee. Essentially, the party that owes money in the present purchases the right to delay the payment until some future date. The discount, or charge, is simply the difference between the original amount owed in the present and the amount that has to be paid in the future to settle the debt.

a. Certified Risk Manager
b. Generalized linear model
c. Maximum life span
d. Discounting

21. The term _____ has three unrelated technical definitions, and is also used in a variety of non-technical ways.

- In financial economics, it refers to any asset used to make money, as opposed to assets used for personal enjoyment or consumption. This is an important distinction because two people can disagree sharply about the value of personal assets, one person might think a sports car is more valuable than a pickup truck, another person might have the opposite taste. But if an asset is held for the purpose of making money, taste has nothing to do with it, only differences of opinion about how much money the asset will produce. With the further assumption that people agree on the probability distribution of future cash flows, it is possible to have an objective _____ pricing model. Even without the assumption of agreement, it is possible to set rational limits on _____ value.
- In governmental accounting, it is defined as any asset used in operations with an initial useful life extending beyond one reporting period. Generally, government managers have a 'stewardship' duty to maintain _____s under their control. See International Public Sector Accounting Standards for details.
- In US tax accounting, it is defined as any property other than a list of exceptions. The main exceptions are anything held for sale, and any real estate or depreciable property used in business. Almost everything you own and use for personal purposes, pleasure or investment is a _____. If something is a _____ for tax purposes, gains or losses on sale or disposition are capital gains or capital losses. For individuals, however, capital losses on property held for personal use are generally not deductible. See the IRS publication Tax Facts about Capital Gains and Losses for details.

A well-known financial accounting textbook advises that the term be avoided except in tax accounting because it is used in so many different senses, not all of them well-defined. For example it is often used as a synonym for fixed assets or for investments in securities.

A common non-technical usage occurs when people ask that employees or the environment or something else be treated as a _____.

a. Capital asset
b. Consumption beta
c. Dynamic asset allocation
d. Mid price

22. In finance, the _____ is used to determine a theoretically appropriate required rate of return of an asset, if that asset is to be added to an already well-diversified portfolio, given that asset's non-diversifiable risk. The model takes into account the asset's sensitivity to non-diversifiable risk (also known as systemic risk or market risk), often represented by the quantity beta (β) in the financial industry, as well as the expected return of the market and the expected return of a theoretical risk-free asset.

Chapter 19. Capital Budgeting

The model was introduced by Jack Treynor (1961, 1962), William Sharpe (1964), John Lintner (1965a,b) and Jan Mossin (1966) independently, building on the earlier work of Harry Markowitz on diversification and modern portfolio theory.

a. Fama-MacBeth regression
b. Martingale pricing
c. Ho-Lee model
d. Capital asset pricing model

23. _____s is the social science that studies the production, distribution, and consumption of goods and services. The term _____s comes from the Ancient Greek oἰκονομῖα from oἶκος (oikos, 'house') + νóμος (nomos, 'custom' or 'law'), hence 'rules of the house(hold)'. Current _____ models developed out of the broader field of political economy in the late 19th century, owing to a desire to use an empirical approach more akin to the physical sciences.
a. Opportunity cost
b. Energy economics
c. Inflation
d. Economic

24. In probability theory and statistics, the _____ (or expectation value or mean and for continuous random variables with a density function it is the probability density -weighted integral of the possible values.

The term '_____' can be misleading.

a. ACEA agreement
b. ACCRA Cost of Living Index
c. AD-IA Model
d. Expected value

25. In business and accounting, _____ are everything of value that is owned by a person or company. It is a claim on the property your income of a borrower. The balance sheet of a firm records the monetary value of the _____ owned by the firm.
a. Assets
b. ACCRA Cost of Living Index
c. Amortization schedule
d. ACEA agreement

26. _____ is one of the four Ps of the marketing mix. The other three aspects are product, promotion, and place. It is also a key variable in microeconomic price allocation theory.
a. Premium pricing
b. Guaranteed Maximum Price
c. Point of total assumption
d. Pricing

27. A _____ is a situation that involves losing one quality or aspect of something in return for gaining another quality or aspect. It implies a decision to be made with full comprehension of both the upside and downside of a particular choice.

In economics the term is expressed as opportunity cost, referring the most preferred alternative given up.

a. Whitemail
b. Trade-off
c. Nonmarket
d. Friedman-Savage utility function

28. _____, in law and economics, is a form of risk management primarily used to hedge against the risk of a contingent loss. _____ is defined as the equitable transfer of the risk of a loss, from one entity to another, in exchange for a premium, and can be thought of as a guaranteed small loss to prevent a large, possibly devastating loss. An insurer is a company selling the _____; an insured or policyholder is the person or entity buying the _____.

a. ACCRA Cost of Living Index
b. AD-IA Model
c. Insurance
d. ACEA agreement

29. In finance, _____ rate of profit or sometimes just return, is the ratio of money gained or lost on an investment relative to the amount of money invested. The amount of money gained or lost may be referred to as interest, profit/loss, gain/loss, or net income/loss. The money invested may be referred to as the asset, capital, principal, or the cost basis of the investment.
   a. Sortino ratio
   b. Current ratio
   c. Rate of return
   d. Cost accrual ratio

30. _____ is an online peer-reviewed magazine published by the Agricultural ' Applied Economics Association (AAEA) for readers interested in the policy and management of agriculture, the food industry, natural resources, rural communities, and the environment. _____ is published quarterly and is available free online. It is currently one of three outreach products offered by AAEA, along with the more timely Policy Issues and the forthcoming Shared Materials section of the AAEA Web site.
   a. Choices
   b. 1921 recession
   c. 100-year flood
   d. 130-30 fund

31. _____s (economically referred to as land or raw materials) occur naturally within environments that exist relatively undisturbed by mankind, in a natural form. A _____'s is often characterized by amounts of biodiversity existent in various ecosystems.

Mining, petroleum extraction, fishing, hunting, and forestry are generally considered natural-resource industries.

   a. 130-30 fund
   b. Natural resource
   c. 1921 recession
   d. 100-year flood

32. A _____ is a counterfeit agreement among industries. It is an informal organization of producers that agree to coordinate prices and production. _____s usually occur in an oligopolistic industry, where there is a small number of sellers and usually involve homogeneous products.
   a. Shanzhai
   b. Cartel
   c. 100-year flood
   d. Shill

33. _____ Is the transition of a national economy from monopoly control by groups of large businesses to a free market economy. This change rarely arises naturally, and is generally the result of regulation by a governing body.

A modern example of _____ is the economic restructuring of Germany after the fall of the Third Reich in 1945.

   a. Monopolization
   b. Market power
   c. Complementary monopoly
   d. Decartelization

34. In economics, _____ is equal to total cost divided by the number of goods produced (the output quantity, Q.) It is also equal to the sum of average variable costs (total variable costs divided by Q) plus average fixed costs (total fixed costs divided by Q.) _____s may be dependent on the time period considered (increasing production may be expensive or impossible in the short term, for example.)

Chapter 19. Capital Budgeting

a. Average cost
c. Average fixed cost
b. Average variable cost
d. Explicit cost

35. _____ is the average weighted of cost of equity capital (ke) and cost of debt (kd.)

According to the 'Modigliani-Miller theorem', under certain assumptions a firm's WACC remains constant regardless of changes in its capital structure. These assumptions are outlined below:

1. Assume no individual or corporate taxes
2. Assume that individuals are able to borrow at the same rate as the firm, (known as home-made gearing)
3. Assume that the market is frictionless, that is no there are no transaction costs
4. Assume that the company has a fixed investment policy being implemented in the strategy of the company

Furthermore, M'M theory hypotheses that the cost of equity capital does change as the company increase its gearing level in the same direction of the gearing level. The reason is that as a company increases its leverage, the shareholders require a higher rate of return because the higher fixed interest costs lead to a higher variance in earnings.

a. Seemingly unrelated regression
c. Censored regression models
b. Method of simulated moments
d. Weighted cost of capital

36. The _____ is an expected return that the provider of capital plans to earn on their investment.

Capital (money) used for funding a business should earn returns for the capital providers who risk their capital. For an investment to be worthwhile, the expected return on capital must be greater than the _____.

a. Capital intensive
c. Capital expenditure
b. Cost of capital
d. Modigliani-Miller theorem

37. _____ is the concept or idea of fairness in economics, particularly as to taxation or welfare economics.

In welfare economics, _____ may be distinguished from economic efficiency in overall evaluation of social welfare. Although '_____' has broader uses, it may be posed as a counterpart to economic inequality in yielding a 'good' distribution of welfare.

a. ACCRA Cost of Living Index
c. Equity
b. AD-IA Model
d. ACEA agreement

38. In statistics, _____ refers to techniques for the modeling and analysis of numerical data consisting of values of a dependent variable and of one or more independent variables The dependent variable in the regression equation is modeled as a function of the independent variables, corresponding parameters, and an error term. The error term is treated as a random variable.

a. 130-30 fund
c. 100-year flood
b. 1921 recession
d. Regression analysis

Chapter 19. Capital Budgeting

39. A _____ is the minimum difference a person requires to be willing to take an uncertain bet, between the expected value of the bet and the certain value that he is indifferent to.

The certainty equivalent is the guaranteed payoff at which a person is 'indifferent' between accepting the guaranteed payoff and a higher but uncertain payoff. (It is the amount of the higher payout minus the _____.)

    a. Workers compensation   b. Ruin theory
    c. Linear model   d. Risk premium

40. A _____ is a public market for the trading of company stock and derivatives at an agreed price; these are securities listed on a stock exchange as well as those only traded privately.

The size of the world _____ was estimated at about $36.6 trillion US at the beginning of October 2008 . The total world derivatives market has been estimated at about $791 trillion face or nominal value, 11 times the size of the entire world economy.

    a. Adolf Hitler   b. Adolph Fischer
    c. Adam Smith   d. Stock market

41. In finance, _____, also sometimes called market risk, aggregate risk is the risk associated with aggregate market returns. _____ is a risk of security that cannot be reduced through diversification. It should not be confused with systemic risk, which is the risk that the entire financial system will collapse as a result of some catastrophic event.

    a. Cleanup clause   b. Systematic risk
    c. Global Depository Receipt   d. Concentration risk

42. _____ measures the rate of return on the ownership interest (shareholders' equity) of the common stock owners. It measures a firm's efficiency at generating profits from every dollar of shareholders' equity (also known as net assets or assets minus liabilities.) It shows how well a company uses investment dollars to generate earnings growth.

    a. Rate of return   b. Cash conversion cycle
    c. Return on Equity   d. Like for like

ANSWER KEY

Chapter 1

1. d	2. a	3. a	4. d	5. b	6. a	7. d	8. d	9. d	10. d
11. d	12. d	13. d	14. c	15. b	16. b	17. d	18. b	19. b	20. b
21. b	22. c	23. d	24. d	25. b	26. d	27. c	28. b	29. d	30. b
31. b	32. a	33. c	34. d	35. d	36. b	37. c	38. d	39. d	40. c
41. b	42. b	43. d	44. c	45. d	46. d	47. b	48. a	49. a	50. d
51. b									

Chapter 2

1. b	2. d	3. d	4. d	5. a	6. d	7. b	8. b	9. d	10. a
11. d	12. b	13. d	14. d	15. b	16. c	17. d	18. c	19. b	20. d
21. d	22. a	23. b	24. d	25. c	26. d	27. c	28. d	29. c	30. d
31. c	32. d	33. c							

Chapter 3

1. b	2. a	3. d	4. b	5. b	6. c	7. d	8. b	9. a	10. d
11. a	12. a	13. d	14. d	15. c	16. d	17. d	18. d	19. a	20. d
21. d	22. d	23. d	24. a	25. d	26. b	27. b	28. b	29. d	30. a
31. d	32. c	33. a	34. b	35. d	36. c	37. b	38. b	39. b	40. b
41. d	42. a	43. b	44. a	45. d	46. d	47. c	48. d	49. b	50. d
51. a	52. a	53. d	54. d	55. c	56. d	57. a	58. d	59. a	

Chapter 4

1. a	2. d	3. d	4. c	5. a	6. c	7. d	8. d	9. d	10. a
11. c	12. d	13. a	14. d	15. d	16. d	17. d	18. b	19. a	20. d
21. d	22. c	23. b	24. c	25. a	26. d	27. b	28. c	29. d	30. c
31. d	32. a	33. a	34. d	35. b	36. a	37. d	38. c	39. a	40. c
41. a									

Chapter 5

1. a	2. c	3. d	4. d	5. b	6. d	7. a	8. d	9. a	10. d
11. d	12. c	13. d	14. c	15. b	16. d	17. d	18. b	19. b	20. d
21. d	22. d	23. c	24. d	25. d	26. a	27. d	28. d	29. c	30. d
31. d	32. d	33. d	34. d	35. d	36. c	37. d	38. d	39. d	40. a
41. c	42. c	43. b	44. d	45. d	46. b	47. d	48. b	49. d	50. d
51. d	52. d	53. d	54. d	55. a	56. a	57. d	58. d	59. c	60. d
61. d	62. c								

Chapter 6

1. a	2. d	3. d	4. d	5. d	6. d	7. b	8. d	9. d	10. d
11. c	12. d	13. b	14. d	15. b	16. b	17. d	18. b	19. b	20. b
21. d	22. d	23. d	24. a	25. c	26. d	27. d	28. b	29. d	30. d
31. d	32. d	33. d	34. d	35. c	36. d	37. d	38. d	39. c	40. d

Chapter 7

1. d	2. d	3. a	4. d	5. d	6. c	7. b	8. c	9. c	10. d
11. b	12. a	13. d	14. d	15. a	16. d	17. d	18. d	19. d	20. a
21. d	22. c	23. a	24. a	25. b	26. b	27. d	28. d	29. c	30. d
31. d	32. d	33. a	34. d	35. a	36. d	37. d	38. d	39. d	40. a
41. d	42. d	43. d	44. c	45. b	46. d	47. d	48. c	49. d	50. a
51. c	52. d	53. c	54. a	55. d	56. a	57. b	58. d	59. b	60. c
61. a	62. d								

Chapter 8

1. d	2. b	3. a	4. d	5. a	6. d	7. a	8. d	9. d	10. d
11. a	12. d	13. c	14. b	15. d	16. a	17. d	18. d	19. a	20. d
21. a	22. c	23. d	24. d	25. d	26. d	27. b	28. d	29. a	30. a
31. d	32. c								

Chapter 9

1. d	2. d	3. c	4. c	5. d	6. b	7. a	8. c	9. d	10. c
11. d	12. c	13. b	14. c	15. d	16. d	17. d	18. b	19. c	20. d
21. b	22. d	23. c	24. d	25. d	26. c	27. d	28. d	29. c	30. d
31. c	32. c	33. b	34. d	35. d					

Chapter 10

1. d	2. a	3. b	4. d	5. d	6. b	7. d	8. b	9. d	10. c
11. d	12. a	13. d	14. d	15. d	16. b	17. d	18. a	19. d	20. d
21. d	22. a	23. a	24. d	25. d	26. d	27. c	28. d	29. d	30. d
31. d	32. c	33. d	34. c	35. b	36. d	37. d	38. b	39. d	40. d
41. c	42. d	43. d	44. b	45. d	46. d	47. d	48. a	49. a	50. c
51. d	52. d	53. d	54. c	55. c	56. d	57. a	58. b		

Chapter 11

1. d	2. b	3. d	4. b	5. d	6. d	7. c	8. d	9. d	10. d
11. a	12. c	13. d	14. b	15. b	16. b	17. c	18. c	19. d	20. d
21. b	22. d	23. d	24. d	25. c	26. d	27. d	28. d	29. a	30. a
31. a	32. d	33. d	34. d	35. d	36. d	37. d	38. a	39. a	40. a
41. d	42. d	43. d	44. d						

Chapter 12

1. c	2. a	3. d	4. d	5. d	6. a	7. d	8. d	9. d	10. a
11. d	12. d	13. a	14. a	15. b	16. c	17. d	18. d	19. a	20. c
21. a	22. d	23. d	24. d	25. d	26. b	27. d	28. d	29. b	30. d
31. d	32. d	33. a	34. d	35. b	36. b	37. c	38. d	39. d	40. d
41. d	42. a	43. c	44. d	45. b	46. a	47. b	48. d	49. d	50. c
51. a	52. d	53. d	54. d						

ANSWER KEY

Chapter 13
1. d	2. c	3. d	4. d	5. d	6. d	7. d	8. a	9. d	10. b
11. d	12. a	13. d	14. d	15. d	16. d	17. c	18. d	19. a	20. d
21. c	22. b	23. d	24. b	25. c	26. d	27. a	28. d	29. b	30. a
31. c	32. b	33. d	34. c	35. b	36. d	37. a			

Chapter 14
1. b	2. d	3. d	4. d	5. d	6. d	7. d	8. d	9. d	10. c
11. c	12. b	13. d	14. c	15. d	16. d	17. d	18. d	19. d	20. a
21. c	22. c	23. a	24. b	25. c	26. c	27. d	28. b	29. d	30. d
31. d	32. d	33. d	34. d	35. b	36. d	37. d	38. d	39. d	40. c
41. c	42. d	43. d	44. d	45. d	46. a	47. d	48. d	49. d	50. c
51. b	52. d	53. a	54. d	55. d	56. d	57. a	58. b	59. d	60. d
61. d	62. d	63. d	64. a	65. d	66. d	67. a	68. b	69. d	70. b
71. a	72. b	73. d	74. d	75. b	76. a	77. d	78. c	79. d	80. d
81. b	82. a	83. b	84. a	85. d	86. a	87. c	88. b	89. a	

Chapter 15
1. a	2. a	3. c	4. d	5. d	6. b	7. d	8. d	9. d	10. b
11. d	12. c	13. d	14. a	15. c	16. b	17. d	18. d	19. b	20. d
21. a	22. c	23. d	24. a	25. d	26. c	27. d	28. d	29. a	30. d
31. d	32. d	33. d	34. c	35. d	36. b	37. d	38. d	39. d	40. d
41. d	42. c	43. d	44. b	45. c	46. a	47. c			

Chapter 16
1. a	2. d	3. b	4. a	5. d	6. b	7. d	8. c	9. b	10. b
11. d	12. d	13. d	14. d	15. d	16. a	17. d	18. d	19. d	20. d
21. c	22. d	23. b							

Chapter 17
1. d	2. d	3. b	4. d	5. d	6. b	7. d	8. c	9. b	10. a
11. c	12. c	13. a	14. b	15. d	16. d	17. c	18. a	19. a	20. d
21. a	22. b	23. d	24. d	25. d	26. a				

Chapter 18
1. a	2. d	3. c	4. a	5. a	6. d	7. a	8. a	9. d	10. d
11. d	12. c	13. a	14. d	15. c					

Chapter 19
1. b	2. d	3. a	4. b	5. d	6. d	7. a	8. c	9. d	10. c
11. d	12. a	13. d	14. c	15. d	16. a	17. b	18. d	19. d	20. d
21. a	22. d	23. d	24. d	25. a	26. d	27. b	28. c	29. c	30. a
31. b	32. b	33. d	34. a	35. d	36. b	37. c	38. d	39. d	40. d
41. b	42. c								

www.ingramcontent.com/pod-product-compliance
Lightning Source LLC
Chambersburg PA
CBHW082147230426
43672CB00015B/2863